DATE DUE			

The Black Novelist

A CHARLES E. MERRILL LITERARY TEXT

CHARLES E. MERRILL LITERARY TEXTS

Under the General Editorship of
Matthew J. Bruccoli and Joseph Katz

Anthologies by genre, period, theme, or other significant principle for the study of American literature. Each volume provides reliable texts introduced by a noted authority.

The Black Novelist

Edited by

Robert Hemenway

The University of Wyoming

Charles E. Merrill Publishing Company
A Bell & Howell Company
Columbus, Ohio

ISBN: 0-675-09497-6 Clothbound edition
        0-675-09498-4 Paperbound edition

Library of Congress Catalog Number: 73-120811

1 2 3 4 5 6 7 8 9 10–76 75 74 73 72 71 70

Printed in the United States of America

For 14 Black Men

Preface

THE essays in this book are intended (1) to suggest the historical tradition and esthetic worth of novels written by black Americans*; (2) to indicate the range of critical attitudes toward these novels; and (3) to permit the black American novelist to speak for himself about his craft and his fellow craftsmen. Obviously no collection can cover all the black novelists who deserve inclusion, and there are some notable absences here, a lamentable but necessary fact of editorial life. There was a conscious attempt to choose essays illustrating a wide spectrum of views, and some controversial and perhaps unrepresentative opinions are included. In Part One, "Critical Judgments," both black and white critics are represented, but their race is usually

---

*A word, perhaps, needs to be said about nomenclature. I have used the word "Negro" to refer to writers, critics or others who have indicated no dissatisfaction with the term. I have used the word "black" specifically to refer to writers identified with Black Nationalism or the Black Arts Movement, and generally to refer to contemporary black novelists. However, like my fellow editor for Charles E. Merrill, Darwin T. Turner, I have also used "black" in a general sense to contrast with white, and I have sometimes used "black," "Afro-American" and "Negro" interchangeably.

not editorially indicated; when it is, the purpose is to identify an important Afro-American critic. In Part Two, "The Black Novelist Speaks," all the speakers are black, and with the exception of Eldridge Cleaver, all have written novels (Cleaver has published fiction and is apparently working on an autobiographical novella). The effort to give the book a historical perspective causes some distortion of esthetic judgment, since the novels of early Negro writers are frequently uneven. The value of recognizing a tradition within the Afro-American novel hopefully outweighs any such minor distortion.

The merit of an anthology of this sort will ultimately be determined by its readers, but I should like to make clear what my hopes for the book are and my reasons for compiling it. American literature is too often thought of as a white literature. This is particularly true in the educational institution, that part of our culture which perpetuates and defines literary history. With only a few exceptions, usually in predominantly black colleges, the American student hears little discussion of black writers and learns little about works by black authors. This is a disgrace; it has caused generations of Americans—both black and white—to be deprived of one of the most vital parts of their literary culture. However, a re-assessment of our literary heritage is presently taking place, and for the first time the black writer is being significantly included. *The Black Novelist* is intended to contribute in a small way to this re-evaluation of American literary history, and by extension, in an even smaller way, to a re-evaluation of American life.

R. H.

Contents

Introduction   1

Part One: Critical Judgments

HUGH GLOSTER
Sutton E. Griggs: Novelist of the New Negro   9

RUSSELL AMES
Social Realism in Charles W. Chesnutt   23

DARWIN T. TURNER
Paul Laurence Dunbar: The Rejected Symbol   33

WILLIAM STANLEY BRAITHWAITE
The Novels of Jessie Fauset   46

ROBERT BONE
Zora Neale Hurston   55

DARWIN T. TURNER
Frank Yerby as Debunker   62

NATHAN A. SCOTT, JR.
The Dark and Haunted Tower of Richard Wright   72

RICHARD KOSTELANETZ
The Politics of Ellison's Booker: *Invisible
Man* as Symbolic History   88

ROBERT BONE
The Novels of James Baldwin   111

JAMES T. STEWART
The Development of the Black Revolutionary Artist   134

Part Two: The Black Novelist Speaks

W. E. B. DuBOIS
  Two Novels   145

ARNA BONTEMPS
  The Negro Renaissance: Jean Toomer and the
  Harlem Writers of the 1920's   150

RICHARD WRIGHT
  How "Bigger" Was Born   166

J. SAUNDERS REDDING
  The Negro Writer—Shadow and Substance   191

WILLIAM GARDNER SMITH
  The Negro Writer—Pitfalls and Compensations   197

RALPH ELLISON
  The Art of Fiction: An Interview   205

JAMES BALDWIN
  Everybody's Protest Novel   218

JOHN A. WILLIAMS
  The Literary Ghetto   227

ELDRIDGE CLEAVER
  Notes on a Native Son   231

Selected Bibliography   243

The Black Novelist

Introduction

THE ESSAYS IN THIS BOOK ARE EITHER BY OR ABOUT SIGNIFICANT AMERICAN novelists, writers sharply aware of the anguish in literary creation. As their own words indicate, this particular anguish was often attended by special despair and unique anger, by a complex of racial ambiguities that affected not only their art but also their very existence. Their novels came from the underside of a dominant, racist culture intent on defining black humanity in order to limit its possibilities. They were not simply artists, but also "Negroes"—black Americans.

The situation, as William Gardner Smith remarks in this volume, has its "pitfalls" and its "compensations." It can leave the novelist with a repository of bitterness that results in humorless social tracts, or it can endow his art with emotional depth and social significance. The dilemma of the black novelist traditionally has been the reconciliation of these possibilities, and the tension between craft and condition has produced an important body of fiction. By articulating the black experience the Afro-American novelist has frequently served the highest purpose of art; he has protested, in Ralph Ellison's phrase, "against the limitations of human life." This fact has been too often ignored in

1

the American literary subculture, especially in that part of it which sanctions "high art." The major reason is probably the willful tradition of ignorance about black culture maintained by the proprietors of white institutions; but there are secondary reasons too, and they arise in part from the conception of the artist and his art which is the legacy of the "New Criticism."

There is no other critical habit of mind which has had more influence on the modern literary scene than that complex of attitudes called the New Criticism. It is difficult to define exactly what the New Criticism is, but generally it is the label applied to that entire body of contemporary criticism which examines a work of literature as an object in itself with a special language and process of its own; the New Critics assume that the full significance of the language and the total meaning of the process will only be revealed as a result of close textual analysis. Although it is a methodology which has come under increasing attack, it is probably the dominant critical method presently at use in the American classroom. But Henry Nash Smith has complained that "the effect of the New Criticism in practice has been to establish an apparently impassable chasm between the facts of our existence in comtemporary society and the values of art." Revolting against a critical standard of verisimilitude from the "age of realism" and the political orientation of criticism in the twenties and thirties, the New Critics undoubtedly served a useful function in reminding readers of the inviolable supremacy of the esthetic artifact. But their methods have also caused the biographical and cultural matrix of that artifact to be slighted or ignored. The effect of this in modern appraisals of the black novelist has been to cause his work to be judged by a critical standard which assumes a violent disjuncture between the body and the spirit, reality and fiction. Yet there is no body of American literature that more profoundly examines this very disjuncture than the Afro-American novel: black America has had to reclaim first body and then spirit from the tyranny of American racism, and the art which expresses this reclamation must be understood in the context of American social reality. Operating from a belief that the task of the critic is to evaluate the created reality of the novel almost entirely from within the self-contained fictive world, the New Criticism has frequently condemned novels by black writers as "protest novels." Even a writer of Richard Wright's achievement has suffered from such censure. The argument is that black "protest novelists" permit their novel's reality to correspond almost precisely with the social reality of being black in America, and that they thus fail to create a viable and plausible fictional existence from within. The black novelist has been urged to "forget" race—forget his reality—in order to create "universal" art. The implication is that there are no "universal" values in black experience.

Some black estheticians now argue that the New Critics are simply a representative phenomenon of Western culture; they point out that Western esthetics always assume a separation between social attitudes and the artist's creation, a disconnection between a man's art and his actions, and they conclude that this is a major reason why the black writer is so frequently misunderstood. Such a critical stance, growing out of the cultural nationalism which has become a dominant force in the Black Arts Movement, has a degree of validity. But there is also the testimony of LeRoi Jones, one of the most "militant" and able spokesmen for the contemporary Black Arts revolution, that there is a definite "mediocrity" to most early Afro-American literature, especially fiction written prior to Jean Toomer's *Cane* (1923). Jones attributes this mediocrity to the middle-class bias of most black writers; but whatever the reason his judgment seems sound. The early novels written by black Americans are hardly artistic triumphs; in retrospect it would be remarkable if they were. Before emancipation it was forbidden by statute in some states to teach a Negro to read or write. Although there was a long tradition of oral narrative through folk expression, as well as a history of didactic poetry by both slave and freeman authors, the first Negro novel was not published until mid-nineteenth century. William Wells Brown's *Clotel; or the President's Daughter* (1853) is the first in a series of poorly-written propagandistic novels of the last half of the nineteenth century and the first part of the twentieth, most of them dedicated in one way or another to proving through fiction that Negroes were human and that some of them (particularly mulattoes) could act like white folks. The novelists who stand out in this formative period are Sutton Griggs, Paul Laurence Dunbar, Charles Waddell Chesnutt, W. E. B. DuBois, and James Weldon Johnson. Griggs' novels are sometimes strident, but generally they effectively challenge the entire structure of American racial relations. DuBois' *Quest of the Silver Fleece* (1911) is as much sociology as fiction, but important for its portrayal of the cotton culture of the South. Dunbar and Chesnutt wrote novels conforming to white standards for Negro expression, but both were also artists of uncommon talent. Johnson's *Autobiography of an Ex-Colored Man* (1912) is perhaps the best novel written by a black American before *Cane*.

The real rise of the black American novelist comes during the period of the twenties called "The Harlem Renaissance" (also sometimes labeled "The Negro Renaissance"). A fortuitous set of circumstances combined to make Harlem the cultural capitol of black America, and

in the decade of 1920-1930 the black American novel, chiefly emanating
from New York, proclaimed the coming of age for Afro-American fiction. Swelled by "the great migration," that flood of rural immigrants
from the South, Harlem was the focal point for "The New Negro"
movement symbolizing W. E. B. DuBois' ascendence over Booker T.
Washington in the ideological struggle for the Negro's self-image. At
this time it represented cultural opportunity, racial pride (most loudly
expressed by Marcus Garvey), and economic promise. It welcomed
the "roaring twenties" and contributed its music to the jazz age; it
became a mecca for writers of all kinds and talents, encouraging
interracial friendships which helped the black writer find publishers
for his work; it became also a center for publishing ventures specifically designed to provide an outlet for the black author. Many of the
Negro artists who published novels during the decade become central
figures in Afro-American literary history. Claude McKay published the
controversial *Home To Harlem* (1928) and *Banjo* (1929); Langston
Hughes wrote of his childhood in *Not Without Laughter* (1930);
Jessie Fauset chronicled the Negro middle class in *There Is Confusion*
(1924) and *Plum Bun* (1928); Walter White wrote the anti-lynching
novel, *The Fire in the Flint* (1924); Rudolph Fisher treated Harlem in
The Walls of Jericho (1928); Wallace Thurman dealt with color
consciousness within the black community in *The Blacker the Berry*
(1929); Nella Larsen examined the effects of miscegenation with
Quicksand (1928) and *Passing* (1929). W. E. B. DuBois published
his second novel, *Dark Princess* (1928). The most important book of
the "Renaissance," Jean Toomer's *Cane* (1923), became a symbol for
the quality of writing in Harlem during the decade.

There were also a number of writers who published poetry and short
stories during the Renaissance but did not write novels until the
thirties. The stock market crash of 1929 had dashed the high hopes of
many young black authors, but among those who published their first
novels in the thirties were Zora Neale Hurston (*Their Eyes Were
Watching God*, 1937; *Jonah's Gourd Vine*, 1934); Arna Bontemps (*God
Sends Sunday*, 1931; *Black Thunder*, 1936; *Drums at Dusk*, 1939);
George Schuyler (*Black No More*, 1931); and the poet Countee Cullen
(*One Way to Heaven*, 1932). Fauset, Thurman, and McKay all published novels during the decade too, and new talents were found in
the works of William Attaway, George Henderson, Victor Daly,
O'Wendell Shaw, and Waters Turpin. Nevertheless, the depression era
was largely a time of regrouping and rethinking for black novelists, a
consolidation of the insights and methods that had given such impetus
to Negro authorship during the twenties. As Langston Hughes remi-
nisced, it was also a time to find a job, and had it not been for the

Federal Writers Project of the Works Progress Administration, many black writers would have been hard-pressed to pursue their craft. It was a Chicago and New York Federal Writers Project employee named Richard Wright whose 1940 novel *Native Son* really built on the base of the twenties and thirties to herald the modern era of black American fiction.

Native Son is an angry, uncompromising indictment of racism in American life, perhaps the most powerful protest novel ever written in America. It revealed totally new possibilities for black fiction; it showed how art and protest could coalesce into a powerful esthetic document, and it articulated black psychology which had gone previously undramatized. Another effect of the novel was to produce what one critic has called "the school of Wright": protest novels which exposed and challenged the structure of American society in the Wright manner. The writers most strongly influenced by Wright were Chester Himes (*If He Hollers Let Him Go,* 1945; *Lonely Crusade,* 1947); Willard Savoy (*Alien Land,* 1949); William Gardner Smith (*Last of the Conquerors,* 1948); Alden Bland (*Behold a Cry,* 1947); Ann Petry (*The Street,* 1946); and Willard Motley (*Knock on Any Door,* 1947). There were other black novelists of the decade who cannot really be called a part of any "school" (there are also disputes about who is, or is not, a pupil of Wright's), and they include William Attaway who published his second novel, *Blood on the Forge,* in 1941, and Dorothy West who wrote the satirical *The Living Is Easy* (1948). One Negro novelist who founded his own school (with a rather lucrative tax base) was Frank Yerby, who in 1946 began writing a book a year in the form of the "costume novel."

Since mid-century a growing number of novels by black Americans have generated widespread interest, even though it has been only the writers of really extraordinary talent—Baldwin and Ellison—who have captured nationwide, popular recognition. William Demby, Julian Mayfield, Owen Dodson, Paule Marshall, Gordon Parks, Henry Van Dyke, and Ronald Fair have all written important novels. Chester Himes has continued to publish from his exile in Europe; John O. Killens has written about the curiously similar violence of World War II and the American South; John A. Williams has become a significant best selling novelist; William Melvin Kelley, Kristin Hunter, Jane Phillips, Robert Boles, Rosa Guy, and LeRoi Jones are all becoming known as novelists of talent and insight, writers well worth reading.

In short, some of the most significant writing in America today is being done by Afro-American novelists, many of them angry, some bitter, others funny, and they write out of an Afro-American literary tradition which has existed within, and yet not been a part of, the "mainstream" of American literature. Like many of his predecessors, the modern black novelist affirms the values of survival and triumph found in the black experience and repudiates the inhumanity that so often threatens it. These are universal values that inform all significant literature, some of the "old verities and truths of the heart" that Faulkner talked about in Stockholm.

It has been argued that literary movements grow out of a communal vision. There was a shared conception of the world among the Transcendentalists of nineteenth century New England, the expatriates of the twenties, and white Southern writers of the "Fugitive Group." Today there is a sense of black community that illuminates much of the writing being done by black American artists, and it seems likely that the amount of significant writing which grows out of that communal vision will steadily increase. The Black Revolution of the 1960's and its cultural manifestations in the Black Arts Movement provide a special impetus for today's black novelist. Contemporary black artists emphasize black identity and assert black experience in direct opposition to "white" values, and although it is difficult to predict precisely what this means for the American novel, there is little question that the communal matrix of modern black writing will ultimately cause American literature to be remarkably enriched—perhaps even revitalized. If American literature does nothing else for American society it asserts the possibilities of national life. Contemporary black novelists know very well what these possibilities are—and what they are not. Their knowledge is important and their voices will be heard.

PART ONE

Critical

Judgments

HUGH M. GLOSTER

Sutton E. Griggs:

Novelist

of the

New Negro

THE NOVELS OF SUTTON E. GRIGGS (1872-1930) WERE DESIGNED TO refute racist attitudes, and his compulsion for racial propaganda undoubtedly affected his art. As Hugh Gloster puts it, "weaknesses in plot, characterization and diction loom obtrusively in the novels of Griggs." But Gloster also argues that Griggs is "one of the earliest symbols in American Negro fiction of the spiritual emancipation of his people." In fact, Griggs' concern with the psychological freedom of black Americans is not really so different from the ideas of the revolutionary James T. Stewart in the last essay of this section. Griggs wished to free the Negro masses from constricting white stereotypes; Stewart wants to liberate the contemporary black artist from the confines of white Western culture. Whether Griggs' art is destroyed by a predilection for social protest ultimately becomes a reader's subjective decision, but reading him from within the Stewart perspective suggests a general question about the so-called protest novel. Is such a novel "bad art," or is it usually judged by inappropriate critical standards? And further, may not most novels of "racial protest" in America implicitly ask a cultural, rather than an esthetic question: do values inhere in

9

the very structure of Western, democratic culture which are ultimately responsible for racial prejudice?

Hugh Gloster, a noted critic and teacher of American literature, is President of Morehouse College. He is the author of *Negro Voices in American Fiction* (Chapel Hill, 1939), a pioneering study of the Negro novel.

HUGH M. GLOSTER

Sutton E. Griggs: Novelist of the New Negro

DURING THE PERIOD OF DISFRANCHISEMENT THOMAS NELSON PAGE AND Thomas Dixon, Jr., were outstanding among those Southern writers who abetted anti-Negro legislative action by showing the black man to disadvantage before the American reading public. Page was pre-eminently the perpetuator of the plantation motif which had received emphasis before the Civil War in the works of such writers as John Pendleton Kennedy, W. A. Carruthers, John Eston Cooke, and James W. Hungerford. In the opinion of Page, the ante-bellum South enshrined the "sweetest, purest, and most beautiful civilization" the nation has ever known; and in such works as *In Ole Virginia, or Marse Chan and Other Stories* (1887), *The Old South* (1892), and *Social Life in Old Virginia* (1897) he paints a gorgeous plantation scene peopled by chivalric, benevolent aristocrats and contented, doting slaves. But Page was more than the retrospective romancer of a vanished feudal society: he was also the ardent sponsor of a reconstructed South in which the Negro would be kept in a subordinate position. In this latter capacity he helped to expedite disfranchisement and other legalized handicaps applied to freedmen. His novel *Red Rock* (1898), for example, is chiefly an apotheosis of Southern bluebloods and a disparagement of scalawags, carpetbaggers, Negro politicians and Northern missionaries. A more forthright statement of his racial attitude, however, is given in "The Negro Question," an essay in which he, after marshaling arguments to prove the backwardness and inferiority of the black man, states

> These examples cited, if they establish anything, establish the fact that the Negro race does not possess, in any development which he has yet attained, the elements of character, the essential qualifications to conduct a government, even for himself; and that if the reins of government be intrusted to his unaided hands, he will fling reason to the winds and drive to ruin.[1]

Though demanding Anglo-Saxon supremacy, Page at least approved educated Negroes who "knew their place," and never attempted to exculpate the Ku Klux Klan of all guilt for lawlessness. On the other hand, Dixon voiced the very epitome of Negrophobia in two novels which he describes as follows

---

[1] *The Old South*, p. 324.

Reprinted from *Phylon*, IV (Fourth Quarter 1943), 335-45, by permission of the publisher and the author. Copyright © 1943 by *Phylon*.

. . . .*The Leopard's Spots* was the statement in historical outline of the conditions from the enfranchisement of the Negro to his disfranchisement.

The Clansman develops the true story of the "Ku Klux Klan Conspiracy," which overturned the Reconstruction Regime.[2]

As a matter of fact, neither of the two works is a realistic rendering of history. Betraying its incendiary sensationalism by such chapter titles as "A Thousand-Legged Beast" and "The Black Peril," *The Leopard's Spots: A Romance of the White Man's Burden, 1865-1900* (1902) is mainly concerned with complimenting the slaveholding landlords; attacking the carpetbaggers, scalawags, Freedmen's Bureau, Northern missionaries, and Negro politicians and intellectuals; ridiculing Yankees whose liberal racial theories do not obtain in actual social situations; establishing the Negro as a degenerate, inferior, irresponsible, bestial creature, "transformed by the exigency of war from a chattel to be bought and sold into a possible beast to be feared and guarded";[3] decrying intermarriage because it would destroy through Africanization the racial integrity of the Anglo-Saxon; and extolling the Invisible Empire as the defender of the weak, the expeller of thieves and parasites, the preserver of Aryan culture, and "the old answer of organized manhood to organized crime."[4] The eulogy of the Invisible Empire is continued in *The Clansman: An Historical Romance of the Ku Klux Klan* (1905), dedicated to the author's uncle, a former Grand Titan of the hooded order, and converted in 1916 by D. W. Griffith into *The Birth of a Nation*, one of the most popular and inflammatory box-office attractions in the history of the American motion picture industry.

Aroused by the literary libels of the schools of Page and Dixon as well as by political, social, and economic discrimination and persecution, Negro authors undertook to offset the misrepresentations of Southern propagandists by defending and glorifying the black man. Among the Negro fictionists of the *fin de siecle* and of the first decade of the present century, who participated in this campaign of racial apology and extollment were Frances Ellen Watkins Harper, Charles W. Chesnutt, J. McHenry Jones, Pauline E. Hopkins, Charles Henry Fowler, G. Langhorne Pryor, George Marion McClellan, J. W. Grant, and Sutton E. Griggs. In this group Griggs was outstanding because of his productivity and influence.

The author of five race-motivated novels—*Imperium in Imperio* (1899), *Overshadowed* (1901), *Unfettered* (1902), *The Hindered Hand* (1905), and *Pointing the Way* (1908)—Griggs not only operated

---

[2] *The Clansman*, p. v.
[3] *The Leopard's Spots*, p. 5.
[4] *Ibid.*, pp. 150-151.

his own publishing company but also, during his travels as a prominent minister and orator, promoted an extensive sale of his works among the black masses of the country. Though virtually unknown to white American readers, his novels were probably more popular among the rank and file of Negroes than the fiction of Chesnutt and Dunbar. Militant and assertive, Griggs chronicled the passing of the servile black man and hailed the advent of the intellectually emancipated Negro

> The cringing, fawning, sniffling, cowardly Negro which slavery left, had disappeared, and a new Negro, self-respecting, fearless and determined in the assertion of his rights, was at hand.[5]

In view of Griggs' active literary career and forthright demands for racial justice, it is somewhat surprising that but one historian of twentieth century Negro literature[6] has mentioned his work as a novelist and that no scholar in this field has treated at length the significance of his contribution.

Griggs' first novel, *Imperium in Imperio,* is a fantastic account of a national Negro political organization. The main characters are dark-skinned Belton Piedmont and mulatto Bernard Belgrave, graduates of Stowe (Roger Williams?) and Harvard universities respectively. Invited by Piedmont, Fairfax joins the Imperium in Imperio, an agency secretly formed "to unite all Negroes in a body to do that which the whimpering government childishly but truthfully" said it could not do. Elected president of the Imperium, Fairfax urges the open revolt of the Negro and proposes a demand for the surrender of Texas and Louisiana, the former to be retained and the latter to be ceded to foreign allies in return for aid. Opposing Fairfax, Piedmont advocates that Negroes voluntarily segregate themselves in Texas to work out their destiny. The Imperium adopts Fairfax's plan and offers Piedmont a choice between cooperation and death. At the expiration of his time limit Piedmont offers himself to be shot, and Griggs asks

> When will all races and classes of men learn that men made in the image of God will not be the slaves of another image?[7]

Though weakened by melodramatic situations, idealized characters, and stilted conversation, *Imperium in Imperio* is the first American Negro novel with a strictly political emphasis. Besides exposing miscegenation, oppression, and Jim-Crowism, it attacks the exploitation

---

[5] *Imperium in Imperio,* p. 62.

[6] Sterling Brown in *The Negro in American Fiction* (1937), pp. 100-101. Professor Brown briefly discusses *Unfettered* and *The Hindered Hand,* two of Griggs' five novels.

[7] *Imperium in Imperio,* p. 252.

of the black man in American politics and stresses the need for an agency to protect Negro interests not safeguarded by the government. While extravagant in conception, *Imperium in Imperio* exhibits the racial outlook that produced the National Association for the Advancement of Colored People and other organizations striving for the full participation of the Negro in American democracy.

In *Overshadowed,* his second novel, Griggs surveys the national scene with a feeling of futility. In the preface he foresees a hard road ahead for the Negro, "whose grandfather was a savage and whose father was a slave," in a social order evolved and dominated by the Anglo-Saxon. With Richmond, Virginia, as its main background, *Overshadowed* traces the love of Erma Wysong and Astral Herndon. While Herndon is in college, John Benson Lawson, an ex-governor's son, engages Dolly Smith to procure Erma as a mistress. Unknown to young Lawson is the fact that Dolly is the sister of Erma's mother, the unfortunate victim of an earlier liaison with his father. To obtain revenge, Dolly eventually brings young Lawson to court, where she makes public the illicit affairs of the father and son. As a result of the trial, the ex-governor loses his mind, Dolly is tarred and feathered, and young Lawson receives a jail sentence. Later Herndon and Erma, having married and become the parents of a boy, are surprised one winter night by the coming of Erma's brother John, who had been placed in the chaingang for the murder of a master workman who insisted that labor unions bar Negroes. Soon after his arrival John dies of exposure, and Erma quickly succumbs to shock and grief. A white friend subsequently advises the grieved husband that the adoption of a Booker T. Washington racial philosophy would ease his burden

> Your status here is but due to conditions inherent in the situation. Why not bow to the inevitable, accept conditions as you find them, extract from life as much good as can come from well-directed efforts, and beyond this point have no yearnings? Develop character, earn money, contribute to the industrial development of the country, exercise your wonderful capacity for humility, move continuously in the line of least resistance and, somehow, all will be well.[8]

Rejecting this counsel and later discarding the idea of emigration to Africa because "it, too, is overshadowed," Herndon buries his wife in mid-ocean, where "there abides no social group in which conditions operate toward the overshadowing of such elements as are not deemed assimilable."[9]

---

[8] *Overshadowed,* p. 215.
[9] *Ibid.,* p. 217.

The thesis of *Overshadowed* is that the Negro must face a racial handicap in all parts of the world and particularly in the United States and Africa. Attention is focused, however, upon the American scene, where miscegenation causes the death of Erma and her mother, the suicide of Dolly, the insanity of ex-Governor Lawson, the imprisonment of his son John, and the loss of Herndon's wife and mother. The novel also exposes the instability of Negro employment, the exclusion of the Negro by labor unions, and the maladministration of justice in Southern courts. Especially interesting is the subtle attack upon the racial platform of Booker T. Washington. It is after an optimistic speech by Washington, for example, that Erma persuades her brother to make a confession which eventually results in his miserable death. A further veiled thrust at the Tuskegee educator's program is made when Herndon rejects Washingtonian arguments for remaining in America and severs relations with all lands in which the Negro is oppressed. Generally speaking, *Overshadowed* paints a gloomy picture of Southern racial difficulties and offers slight prospect for adjustment in the immediate future.

"It is the aim of *Unfettered*," states Griggs in an introductory note to his third novel, "to lead the reader into the inner life of the Negro race and lay bare the aspirations that are fructifying there."[10] The action opens with the death of a Tennessee plantation owner who leaves the bulk of his wealth to a nephew, Lemuel Dalton, but at the same time provides liberally for an old Negro nurse and a beautiful mulatto girl named Morlene. After dispossessing the colored beneficiaries of his uncle's will, Lemuel almost provokes a riot by wounding Harry Dalton, a young Negro who had overcome him some years earlier. Concluding that formal training had caused Harry and his sister Beulah to assume social equality and "that the only safe education for the Negro was the education that taught him better to work," angered whites drive the pair out of the community and thereby cause a mass exodus of black folk. Later Beulah, believed to be the inciter of the migration, is killed during an attack by a group of young white men. In order to avoid further bloodshed, the whites draft as a mediator a Negro school teacher, a typical representative of the professional man whom Griggs calls perhaps "the greatest conservator of peace in the South, laboring *for* the Negroes by the *appointment* of the whites, being thus placed in a position where it was to his interest to keep on good terms with both races."[11] After reluctantly marrying Harry, Morlene goes with him to a nearby city, where she meets Dorlan Warthell, a successful Negro politician who is at once attracted by her

---

[10] *Unfettered*, p. 5.
[11] *Ibid.*, p. 56.

unusual beauty. Warthell, who is at odds with the Republican Party, aims to use the Negro vote to force the United States to grant ultimate liberty to the Philippine Islands. Angered by Warthell's intention, a treacherous congressman engaged Harry to take the Negro politician's life; but Morlene overhears the plot, warns the intended victim, and deserts her husband. Left by his wife and repudiated by right-thinking Republicans, Harry sacrifices himself to save the lives of a woman and her children. Thereupon Warthell proposes to Morlene, who promises to consent if he will outline a plan which will unfetter the mind of the Negro and enable the two races to live together in peace and amity. When Warthell submits his project, entitled "Dorlan's Plan," Morlene immediately agrees to become his wife. Meanwhile Lemuel's young Northern bride, who has been taught by her husband to hate and fear the Negro, becomes so hysterically frightened upon seeing a colored boy that she suffers a fatal fall from horseback. Painfully aware of the dire effects of misinstructing his wife, Lemuel realizes that interracial good-will is necessary for the happiness and welfare of both groups in the South.

Like *Overshadowed*, *Unfettered* provides a dismal picture of race relations. The opposition of prejudiced Southern whites to the education of the Negro is set forth, and an analysis is made of the motives underlying intimidation and segregation. Especially interesting are the political views of Warthell, who, though distrustful of the Democrats because their "chief tenets are the white man's supremacy and exclusiveness in government," nevertheless recognizes no unseverable party ties. In his advocacy of the liberation of the Philippines, moreover, Warthell manifests a worldwide as well as a national concern for the advancement of darker races.

As a statement of racial policy, however, the most important section of *Unfettered* is the appended essay called "Dorlan's Plan: Sequel to *Unfettered*: A Dissertation on the Race Problem."[12] This essay, which is a serious approach to the problem of racial adjustment in the United States, points out that the major task is to institute merit and not color as the standard of preferment. Since the oppression of the Negro stems from unfortunate circumstances of the past, the race is urged to "meet and combat the timorous conservatism that has hitherto impeded our progress." The Negro is advised not to rely wholly upon the Republican Party. Listed as necessary in the task of preparing the race for a better future are character development, worthy home life, public school education for the masses, technological institutions for the training of industrial workers, and universities for the development

---

[12] *Ibid.*, pp. 217-276.

of "men capable of interpreting and influencing world movements, men able to adjust the race to any new conditions that may arise." Land ownership and a back-to-the-farm movement are recommended. Good government and simple justice, not race supremacy and partisan patronage, are defined as the desirable goals of Negro political action. The cultivation of the friendship of the white South as well as of the moral support of other sections of the country and of other civilized nations is also emphasized as a *sine qua non* of enlightened racial policy. In the promotion of this program the support of the orator, journalist, literary artist, painter, sculptor, and composer is solicited. As a statement of desirable procedure for the colored people of the United States, "Dorlan's Plan" is a forerunner of James Weldon Johnson's *Negro Americans, What Now?* (1934) and numerous other guides to interracial harmony in the United States.

In his next novel, *The Hindered Hand*, Griggs explores the tragic results of miscegenation in the South and attacks the biased portrayal of the Negro in Dixon's *The Leopard's Spots*. The tragedy sometimes caused by interbreeding is shown in the lives of a mulatto couple's three children—Tiara Merlow, who, because of her dark complexion, is early separated from her family in order to make "passing" easier for her parents and the other two children; the Reverend Percy G. Marshall, who is killed by a Negro when seen holding his sister Tiara in his arms; and Eunice Seabright, who, after being forced into an unhappy marriage with a white man, becomes demented when her racial identity is revealed. Concerning Eunice's insanity a Northern specialist says

> The one specific cause of her breakdown is the Southern situation which has borne tremendously upon her. That whole region of the country is affected by a sort of sociological hysteria, and we physicians are expecting more and more pathological manifestations as a result of the strain upon the people.[13]

The effect of American caste upon the Negro is considered in Tiara's defense of her mother:

> My mother is dead and paid dearly for her unnatural course. But do not judge her too harshly. You people who are white do not know what an awful burden it is to be black in these days of the world. If some break down beneath the awful load of caste which you thrust upon them, mingle pity with your blame.[14]

The maladministration of justice in the South is mirrored in the unwarranted lynching of Foresta Crump and Bud Harper in Mississippi.

---

[13] *The Hindered Hand, or The Reign of the Repressionist*, p. 249.
[14] *Ibid.*, p. 238.

An investigator, upon asking a white native whether mob action against the Negro couple was caused by "the one crime," receives the following explanation

> That's all rot about one crime. We lynch niggers down here for anything. We lynch them for being sassy and sometimes lynch them on general principles. The truth of the matter is the real "one crime" that paves the way for a lynching whenever we have the notion, is the crime of being black.[15]

At a subsequent trial of the lynchers a young prosecuting attorney becomes a political outcast for demanding justice, and the jury sets the mobbers free.

In the first and second editions of *The Hindered Hand,* a review of Dixon's *The Leopard's Spots* appears in the form of a conversation between two of the characters of the novel, but in the third edition this discussion is amplified in a review at the end of the book. Even in the third edition, however, *The Leopard's Spots* is mentioned in the body of the novel when A. Hostility, in a fruitless effort to enlist Negro aid in a Slav movement against the Anglo-Saxon, calls the attention of Tiara's love, Ensal Ellwood, "to the book written for the express purpose of thoroughly discrediting the Negro race in America."[16] Ellwood is disturbed by the literary campaign against the Negro

> Ensal thought of the odds against the Negro in this literary battle: how that Southern white people, being more extensive purchasers of books than Negroes, would have the natural bias of the great publishing agencies on their side; how that Northern white people, resident in the South, for social and business reasons, might hesitate to father books not in keeping with the prevailing sentiment of Southern white people; how that residents of the North, who essayed to write in defense of the Negro, were laughed out of school as mere theorists ignorant of actual conditions; and, finally, how that a lack of leisure and the absence of general culture handicapped the Negro in fighting his own battle in this species of warfare.[17]

In "A Hindering Hand, Supplementary to *The Hindered Hand:* A Review of the Anti-Negro Crusade of Mr. Thomas Dixon, Jr.,"[18] Griggs

---

15 *Ibid.,* p. 136.
16 *Ibid.,* p. 206.
17 *Ibid.,* p. 207.
18 This essay, which follows the novel, appears on pp. 301-333. Griggs states that he does not intend "to deal with Mr. Dixon's second book *[the Clansman]* bearing on the race problem, it being the hope of the writer to give that matter serious and independent attention." *Ibid.,* p. 298. This investigator has found no record of such a study of *The Clansman* by Griggs.

states that Dixon's malice derives from the traditional dislike of the Southern poor white for the Negro and that his purpose is to effect the expulsion of those having African blood from the United States. To accomplish this aim, according to Griggs, Dixon attempts "to thoroughly discredit the Negroes, to stir up the baser passions of men against them, and to send them forth with a load of obloquy and the withering scorn of their fellows the world over, sufficient to appall a nation of angels." Among the propagandistic techniques allegedly used by Dixon are the depiction of the Negro as the lustful despoiler of white womankind, the portrayal of degenerates as representative types of black men, and the attribution of natural inferiority to those of African extraction. In consideration of Dixon's methods and materials, Griggs submits the following epitaph for the author of *The Leopard's Spots*

> This misguided soul ignored all of the good in the aspiring Negro; made every vicious offshoot that he pictured typical of the entire race; presented all mistakes independent of their environments and provocations; ignored or minimized all the evil in the more vicious elements of whites; said and did all things which he deemed necessary to leave behind him the greatest heritage of hatred the world has ever known. Humanity claims him not as one of her children.[19]

Though weak according to artistic standards, *The Hindered Hand* is the most elaborate attack upon Thomas Dixon in American Negro fiction. In addition, the book presents the well-worn themes of miscegenation and racial injustice, and shows the Negro mind weighing open revolt and emigration to Africa[20] against bearing the burdens of an ethnic minority in the United States. The denial of political rights is designated as the chief factor which "causes the Ethiopian in America to feel that his is indeed 'The Hindered Hand.' "[21]

Like *The Hindered Hand*, *Pointing the Way* treats interbreeding and politics in the South, but ends upon a more hopeful note. Letitia

---

[19] *Ibid.*, p. 332.

[20] In appended "Notes to the Serious," Griggs, somewhat anticipating Marcus Garvey, declares that the idea of a Negro exodus to Africa is his own dream and not the wish of most American Negroes:

The overwhelmingly predominant sentiment of the American Negroes is to fight out their battle on these shores. The assigning of the thoughts of the race to the uplift of Africa, as affecting the situation in America, must be taken more as dream of the author than as representing any considerable responsible sentiment within the race, which, as has been stated, seems at present thoroughly and unqualifiedly American, a fact that must never be overlooked by those seeking to deal with this grave question in a practical manner. *Ibid.*, p. 297.

[21] *Ibid.*, p. 292.

Gilbreath, spinster daughter of a white man and his ex-slave mistress, considers it "a shocking crime for two dark persons to marry each other" and therefore undertakes to compel her niece Clotille to become the wife of Baug Peppers, a mulatto lawyer. Clotille, however, loves Conroe Driscoll, her dark-skinned college sweatheart, and, while studying in Boston, invites Eina, a beautiful English-Spanish-Indian girl, to her Southern home in Belrose with the hope that the visitor would marry Peppers and thus leave her free to wed the young man of her choice. After reaching Belrose, Eina becomes seriously interested in Peppers; but Seth Molair, a white attorney who admires the attractive newcomer, warns her that "to work, to eat, to sleep, to die is the utmost programme that organized society in the South offers" the Negro, and informs her that she may not mingle socially with both races

> . . . . In the South social freedom is not permitted, for reasons that I need not discuss here. Whoever affiliates socially with the one race in the South is denied the social life of the other.[22]

After Eina asks whether there is any hope for interracial harmony, Molair replies

> The one thing needed in the South is political cooperation between the better elements of whites and the Negroes, but the manner of the coming of emancipation, enfranchisement, and elevation to high public station seems to have riveted the Negro into one party, while the terror of being ruled by an alien and backward race has chained the real strength of the white race into an opposing party. . . . As long as there is a bitter political war between the Negroes and the whites of the South, how can conditions change?[23]

Resolving to bring about better race relations in Belrose and definitely aligning herself with the Negro group, Eina persuades Peppers to ask Molair to run for mayor on a platform pledging justice to all citizens. Moved by the ruthless murder of a colored youth by a white chaingang guard, Molair enters the race and wins the election. His impartial and progressive administration, during which Driscoll becomes a captain in the municipal fire department, not only draws national attention and presidential commendation, but also elicits the enthusiastic interest and financial support of a millionaire ex-Southerner who opposes the steady northward migration of Negroes and resolves to improve the status of the blacks and poor whites of the South. Successful in her campaign for better race relations in Belrose, Eina induces Peppers to test Southern disfranchising legislation before the Supreme Court.

---

[22] *Pointing the Way*, p. 26.
[23] *Ibid.*, p. 41.

Assisted by a bequest from Letitia, who earlier died in a fire in which Driscoll made a fatal effort to save her life, Peppers carries a test case to the highest tribunal in the land and makes an eloquent plea for the enfranchisement of his people. The novel closes with praise of the Belrose experiment and with the marriage of Peppers and Eina.

Pointing the Way emphasizes the tragic consequences of intraracial prejudice by showing how the happiness of lovers is thwarted through the efforts of a color-conscious old maid to force her niece to marry a mulatto. The novel also seeks to show that the political cooperation of the races in the South not only contributes to the solution of the problems of that section but also to the general improvement of conditions throughout the country. While deficient according to standards of art, *Pointing the Way* adds to Griggs' reputation as a political propagandist in fiction.

At this place it might be well to draw a few comparisons between Griggs and his well-known contemporary, Charles W. Chesnutt. To begin, both employ the conventional subject-matter of miscegenation, color prejudice, and racial oppression. Unlike Chesnutt, however, Griggs recommends a way to a better life for his people. Rejecting open revolt, exodus to Africa, and the program of Booker T. Washington, he offers the solution of political cooperation with the white South and alignment with whatever party offers the Negro the fullest participation in government. Unlike Chesnutt again, Griggs tends to glorify black pigmentation, as the following description of Warthell, the hero of *Unfettered*, indicates: "As to color he was black, but even those prejudiced to color forgot that prejudice when they gazed upon this ebony-like Apollo."[24] While ridiculing the color line within the race in several of his works, Chesnutt nevertheless shows a predilection for mulattoes and occasionally uses certain black stereotypes which most of his Negro contemporaries disdained. As an artist, however, Chesnutt is the superior in every way, for weaknesses in plot, characterization, and diction loom obstrusively in the novels of Griggs.

But regardless of his failings as an artist, Griggs is a significant pioneer in the history of American Negro fiction. Like Oscar Michaux and J. A. Rogers today, he personally distributed his books among the masses of his people. In his novels he shows the advantages of racial organization as a technique for gaining the full benefits of American democracy, answers the writers who belittled and vilified the Negro before the national reading public, points unerringly to the distorting influence of prejudice and discrimination upon members of both races, and manifests a deep humanitarian interest in the welfare of oppressed

---

[24] *Unfettered, op. cit.,* p. 71.

peoples in other parts of the world. Most important of all, he is one of the earliest symbols in American Negro fiction of the spiritual emancipation of his people and the first important author of the political novel among his race in this country.

RUSSELL AMES

Social

Realism

in

Charles W. Chesnutt

BEST KNOWN AS A SHORT STORY WRITER, CHARLES WADDELL CHESNUTT (1858-1932) was one of the best of the early black writers of fiction in America, but his achievement always seemed to fall short of his talents. Born in Cleveland and reared in North Carolina, Chesnutt was largely self-educated. He taught school in the South and eventually moved North to work as a court stenographer, later to practice law. Although he lived until 1932, Chesnutt wrote little after 1905; thus, most of his fiction was created during a period of literary history labeled the "age of realism." A protégé of William Dean Howells, Chesnutt was conscious of the realistic movement and dealt with a more realistic subject matter than previous black novelists. In his short stories he subtly tried to remake the "plantation tradition"; in two of his novels, *The Marrow of Tradition* and *The Colonel's Dream*, he concerned himself with the ugliness of violent racial prejudice and its dehumanizing effects for both black and white. In a third novel, *The House Behind The Cedars*, he wrote of the complex psychological issues in "mixed blood." But Chesnutt could never break through to a realistic style appropriate to his material and as a consequence his novels appear frequently overwritten and are often disappointing.

His subject matter, however, raises a question of esthetic balance that has long perplexed critics of Afro-American writing. Russell Ames clearly feels that "social realism" is the hallmark of successful fiction, so much so that he argues Chesnutt's portrayal of Southern life superior to Faulkner's. Whether one agrees with Ames or not, his essay illustrates that strain of modern American criticism that has rated the Negro novelist according to the verisimilitude of his novel, an understandable if perhaps overly excessive reaction to the esthetic criteria of the New Criticism. Yet if a critic were to accept Ames's argument that "there are no people in the books of Hemingway, Dos Passos, Faulkner, Joyce, and . . . Steinbeck" he would also deny a significant body of literature of quality written in the twentieth century.

RUSSELL AMES

Social Realism in Charles W. Chesnutt

HELEN CHESNUTT'S STORY OF HER FATHER'S LIFE[1] TELLS A GREAT DEAL about what it meant to be a Negro intellectual in the late nineteenth and early twentieth centuries. It is a straightforward, human account of the efforts, success in business, and "failure" in literature of a fine but little-known American writer. Reasonably enough, Miss Chesnutt does not attempt a full evaluation of his short stories and novels, for this would require discussion of the substantial erasure of Negro writers from the history of literature in the United States, and would bring into question the standards of criticism prevailing today. Some consideration of these matters, however, is necessary to an appreciation of this unusual biography and this unusual writer. Chesnutt was the first distinguished American Negro author of short stories and novels. He remains in certain respects the best. Neglect of his life and work represents, therefore, a general neglect of Negro literature.

Both *The Cambridge History of American Literature* and Parrington's *Main Currents in American Thought* ignore Chesnutt altogether, and hardly mention any Negro authors. The recent *Literary History of the United States* (edited by Spiller, Canby, and others, 1948) "discusses" Chesnutt in a fourteen-line paragraph given mainly to Paul Lawrence [sic] Dunbar. Both are restricted to the status of dialect writers, "followers in the wake of Harris." The paragraph makes the trivial or inaccurate points that Chesnutt was an Ohioan, that his "legal training involved a number of years in North Carolina" (in fact he got his legal training in Ohio; North Carolina was the place where he grew up, taught school, and the scene of most of his fiction). It is stated that he and Dunbar enriched "that branch of nineteenth century literature which relates to the oldtime Southern Negro," and this is a reference to his first and least important book. His major work is passed over with the remark that "his career included also three novels which expose the consequences of racial prejudice." (Vol. 11, p. 854 f.)

The best of these novels, *The Marrow of Tradition* (1901), was based on first-hand investigation of the Wilmington, North Carolina, riots of 1898, and it describes a conspiracy to rob Negroes of the vote that ends in a tragic drama of mass lynching and courageous resistance. It is this novel that is summed up as being "about the struggles of Negro and white half-sisters" in a concisely inaccurate article on Ches-

---

[1] *Charles Waddell Chesnutt: Pioneer of the Color Line,* by Helen M. Chesnutt. University of North Carolina Press. Chapel Hill, 1952. $5.00. Pp. viii, 324.

Reprinted from *Phylon,* XIV (Second Quarter 1953), 199-206, by permission of the publisher. Copyright © 1953 by *Phylon.*

nutt in *The Oxford Companion to American Literature* (1948). Among the rare studies by white scholars that give some attention to writing by Negroes, John H. Nelson's *Negro Character in American Literature* (University of Kansas *Humanistic Studies*, 1932, Vol. IV, No. 1) is typical:

> Only one negro, in fact—Charles W. Chesnutt—can seriously lay claim to the title of novelist, and for the most part, Chesnutt was more propagandist than literary artist. He dissipated his energies in working for the social betterment of his people. . . . *The Marrow of Tradition* . . . is unfair in tone, crudely partisan in design, inflammatory in suggestion, and worthless except as a polemical tract. Southern whites, so the novelist contends, not only engage in mob riots, but enjoy them. . . . (p. 135).

One might ask, in passing, if Mr. Nelson believes that it is artistically sound to portray lynchings as long as the lynchers do not enjoy themselves? In any case, it is interesting to note that the well-known Negro critic Alain Locke, as we shall see below, considers Chesnutt's work to be objective, balanced, and accurate, though Locke is sternly opposed to polemics and propaganda in fiction. One is tempted to say that propaganda is what we dislike, and objectivity is what we agree with.

Mr. Nelson concludes his "objective" study by saying that

> The pure black has been, at best, only wistful or mildly pathetic; usually he has appeared amusing even in his ambitions and strivings; nearly always he provokes a laugh or at least a smile. Thousands of readers of American literature have been entertained by his drollery, his incongruous display of civilization and savagery, his poetical outlook on the world. Without exemplifying exalted qualities or filling the position of epic hero, he has proved a great comic type, and for many decades has lent to much of American fiction a raciness, an enlivening element, a savor of the natural and primitive which could ill be spared. (p. 137).

Nelson is right in one thing at least: it is true that the Negro has been restricted in the arts to the roles of clown, child, and primitive. Very rarely indeed has he been allowed the "exalted qualities" of an "epic hero," even though an American writer could best turn to Negro history, to such figures as Nat Turner, Harriet Tubman, and Frederick Douglass for the exalted heroes of epic stories.

For a Negro hero of full stature, I believe, we must go back to Frederick Douglass's little-known "The Heroic Slave" (published in *Autographs for Freedom*, 1853; reprinted in part in *The Negro Caravan*, 1941)—a long story about Madison Washington and his leadership of a successful uprising on the slave-ship *Creole* in 1841. When, after fifty years in which there was not much fiction written by Negroes, we come to Chesnutt's stories and novels, the heroes and the heroines are less exalted and more frustrated. They are not typical of the Negro people: half or more than half white in color of skin and, in one major work, *The Colonel's Dream*, not Negro at all; chiefly from the middle or upper classes. They indicate the possibilities of achievement and progress, but their role is defensive and half-defeated. In the period when U.S. capital first took part in the drama of world empire and shared the control of new millions of colored peoples, the Negroes in ·the South were re-subjugated by a parallel process. Speaking ironically to the people of the Philippine Islands, Finley Peter Dunne's Mister Dooley said: " 'We can't give ye anny votes, because we haven't more thin enough to go round now; but we'll threat ye th' way a father shud threat his childher if we have to break ivry bone in ye'er bodies. So come to our ar-arms,' says we." At the same time and with the operation of similar ideas, Negroes in the South were losing the vote, political office and jobs, through laws, terror, and lynchings. This process Chesnutt described. His main theme could not be liberation but had to be resistance and retreat. His protagonists could not be very large, victorious, or forward-moving.

Nevertheless, Chesnutt's Negroes are larger and more admirable than most of their successors in fiction written by Negroes—though it should be noted that this fiction, in the twentieth century, has in general showed people working and striving in a way that fiction by non-Negro writers has not. Chesnutt expresses some of the hidden heroic history of his people, for example, in minor characters in *The Marrow of Tradition*—through mention of an editor who risks lynching to write against lynching, and through the fuller portrait of Josh Green, the stevedore who would "rather be a dead nigger any day dan a live dog."

Chesnutt believed, however, that it was necessary to make concessions to the prejudices of the well-to-do white book-buyers. Among his characters there was more than a "fair" share of well-meaning and liberal white Southerners, of disreputable Negroes. His method was first to disarm his readers with conventional scenes and seeming stereotypes—for example, with idyllic relations between servants and aristocrats—and then in lightning flashes to reveal the underlying facts of injustice and rebellion. Chesnutt had long pondered his purpose, audience, and method as letters and diaries quoted by his daughter show. As early as 1880, when he was twenty-one, he wrote in his journal:

> I think I must write a book. . . .
> The object of my writings would be not so much the elevation of the colored people as the elevation of the whites. . . . Not a fierce indiscriminate onset, not an appeal to force, for this is some-

thing that force can but slightly affect, but a moral revolution which must be brought about in a different manner. The subtle almost indefinable feeling of repulsion toward the Negro, which is common to most Americans—cannot be stormed and taken by assault; the garrison will not capitulate, so their position must be mined, and we will find ourselves in their midst before they think it.

No doubt it was with this indirect, persuasive method in mind that Chesnutt began, about 1884 in Cleveland, to write stories for newspapers and magazines including, within a few years, the Olympian *Atlantic Monthly.* His tales of Negro life during slavery, Reconstruction, and the "Counter-Revolution," were written with such restraint and with such a skillful blending of melodrama and realism that finally two volumes of them were published in 1899 by Houghton Mifflin and Company, and William Dean Howells said, in *The Atlantic* (May, 1900), that

> for the far greatest part Mr. Chesnutt seems to know quite as well what he wants to do in a given case as Maupassant, or Tourguenief, or Mr. James, or Miss Jewett, or Miss Wilkins . . . . and if he has it in him to go forward on the way which he has traced for himself, to be true to life as he has known it, to deny himself the glories of the cheap success which awaits the charlatan in fiction, one of the places at the top is open to him.

Chesnutt did have it in him to go forward on the way of truth, but his country did not have it in the civilization to value his work adequately. He gave up a lucrative business as lawyer, court reporter, and stenographer to devote himself to a high purpose in literature. He went on to write, with ever-increasing scope and depth, realistic novels about the South. But the "passionless handling," "the delicate skill," and the "quiet self-restraint" that Howells had praised were not enough to overcome the revulsion of many critics and the indifference of most book-buyers when *The House Behind the Cedars* was published in 1900, *The Marrow of Tradition* in 1901, and *The Colonel's Dream* in 1905. Even those who have read these novels seem, often, unable to understand what is written. For example, *The House Behind the Cedars* is described in *The Oxford Companion to American Literature* as "concerned with a light-complexioned Negress who is undecided whether to enjoy comfort as a white man's mistress or the sincere love of a Negro"; but the fact is that she does not at any time even remotely consider becoming the white man's mistress. It seems that a mind warped by prejudice automatically turns a high-principled Negro woman into a woman of loose morals. *The Marrow of Tradition* compelled admiration from William Dean Howells, but he found it too bitter for his taste. Paul Elmer More complained that in it Chesnutt had tried "to humiliate the whites" and that the last chapter was "utterly revolting." It is remarkable that so many critics, over the years, suddenly develop a sense of "fair play" when white people are "maltreated" by Chesnutt; and it is equally remarkable that no critic appears to protest when he shows Negroes in an unfavorable light. "The American Mind" has never welcomed such unpleasant truths as those told by Chesnutt, and racist attitudes were at a peak when his books were published. The muckrake of the reformers did not reach to the worst-smelling muck. This was a major period in American fiction in which substantial social novels, comparable to Chesnutt's were directed against monopoly—Norris's *The Octopus,* Dreiser's *Sister Carrie,* London's *The Iron Heel,* Sinclair's *The Jungle.* These novels did not, however, comprehend the relation of monopoly to imperialism or the use of racism to both. At a time when "the blessings of civilization," ironically praised by Mark Twain, were being extended to colored people in China, Cuba, the Philippines, and the United States, the best-sellers on the Negro question were racist novels like those of the Reverend Thomas Dixon—*The Leopard's Spots* and *The Clansman,* from which the motion picture *The Birth of a Nation* was made.

This particular motion picture, it so happens, brings up very sharply certain central questions and paradoxes concerning art that deals with Negroes or is created by Negroes. There is much "objective" art criticism that pleads a case for Griffith's "masterpiece" although it is admittedly propaganda for slavery and the Ku Klux Klan. Here, as in the British cinema's *David Copperfield* and the verse of Eliot and Pound, where anti-Semitism flourishes, "Art" triumphs over propaganda. Why is it, then, that the same or similar critics mechanically discover that pro-Negro, progressive, and radical propaganda unfailingly and fatally destroys "Art"? Here we have a strange formula: Art is impervious to reactionary propaganda; Art is blighted by radical propaganda.

Chesnutt's books have received just appraisal only from Negro scholars like Hugh Gloster, in *Negro Voices in American Fiction,* or the editors of *The Negro Caravan.* But even such critics have accepted the current preference for "Art." The decline of the Negro "purpose" novel, with its "crude propaganda," "racial hypersensitivity," and "race-conscious idealization of Negroes" has been welcomed. In a recent symposium on "The Negro in Literature: The Current Scene" (*Phylon,* Winter, 1950), most, though by no means all, of the leading Negro writers involved condemned racial "propaganda" and favored "objectivity," "universality," and "artistry."

Chesnutt's "objectivity"—which is apparent to Negro observers but not to whites—is praised by the Dean of American Negro literary critics, Alain Locke, in "The Negro in American Literature," (*New World Writing*, 1952). Locke, however, considers Chesnutt an imitative, old-fashioned writer of very limited artistry: he "quite successfully modeled his short-story style on Bret Harte, his novel technique on Cable's, but with decidedly less success." It was not till the Twenties that Negro writers outgrew "the handicap of allowing didactic emphasis and propagandistic motives to choke their sense of artistry." Locke thinks that Richard Wright "climaxed the development" and, with others, "brought Negro writing abreast of contemporary American realism and within hailing distance of cultural maturity." It is suggested that full cultural maturity inhabits William Faulkner with his "brave introspection," "his unexcelled, intensive portrayal of Southern life," and his "honest liberalism."

If literary history in the United States is looked at in this way—if we have been advancing toward Faulkner instead of decaying toward Faulkner, if Negro writing has always lagged behind that of whites and is yet to grow up—then a writer like Chesnutt is a worthy but clumsy ancient whose work is merely of historical interest, for it was crippled by problems and purposes. If, on the other hand, one considers most fiction today, and typically the fiction of Faulkner, to be decadent, both in what it says and in the garbled way in which it is said, then the social realism of Chesnutt represents a peak from which our fiction has declined. It can certainly be argued that Chesnutt's portrayal of Southern life is far more inclusive, truthful, complex, interesting, and artistic than Faulkner's. But this argument can carry weight only if we abandon the pervasive "modern" belief that artistry consists in obscurity, the torturing of language, impressionism, the avoidance of story-telling, and concentration on madness, lust, and despair.

Faulkner portrays, if we have the patience to puzzle him out, the symbolic decay of aristocracy (Compsons, Sartorises) and rise of commerce (Snopses) while strange Negroes are a tragic chorus and a symbol of the white Southerner's guilt. Chesnutt showed us far more of the South and its history—the web of its economy, its semi-colonial relation to the North, its mills and farms and stores, its politics and courts, its peonage and forced labor camps—in short, the relations between its rulers and its workers—with a broad gallery of living, typical characters.

Decadent fiction is propaganda for the view that life is a bad dream in which the trapped human animal is a victim of his own "instincts" and of history's bad jokes. It is a poor, narrow form of naturalism. It is thin, disorderly, and unreal compared to the naturalism of Norris and

Dreiser or the realism of Chesnutt and London. The writing of Chesnutt is propaganda for reason, for the understanding of society, for the development of human beings. It is artistic in the large, sound meanings of the term. He did not have the modern, artistic gift for scattering impressions—leaving the organization of fragments to the initiated reader who has the Freudian and symbolic tools needed to do the job. He told stories, traced the connections between people and events.

Chesnutt is a man very much worth knowing, through his books and through the record of his life which his daughter has made with careful and loving labor. Her biography will be an important experience for any American, Negro or white, who reads it. From it we can learn much about how to work, how to think, how to be a human being; and from it we can learn a great deal of informal social history of the United States. Chesnutt, unable to go to college, became at twenty-two the principal of the State Normal School at Fayetteville, North Carolina, taught Latin, singing, and the organ to young colored people, studied Greek, Latin, French, German, stenography, and music in addition to history, economics, and French and English literature. By comparison Jack London's and his Martin Eden's heroic efforts to master culture seem ordinary. And yet he found time to be such a husband that his wife wrote him, when he was seeking work, and a home for her, in the North:

> You were a companion, and you knew me better than even my father or mother, or at least you were more in sympathy with me than anybody else, and my failings were overlooked. No one can tell, my dearest husband, how I miss that companionship.

He was a man who wrote, in language like that of Mark Twain, to George Washington Cable, advocating federal enforcement of the Negro's right to vote:

> It is easy to temporize with the bull when you are on the other side of the fence, but when you are in the pasture with him, as the colored people of the South are, the case is different. . . . The ever-lengthening record of Southern wrongs and insults, both lawless and under the form of law, calls for whatever there is of patriotism, of justice, of fair play in the American people, to cry "hands off" and give the Negro a show, not five years hence, or a generation hence, but now, while he is alive, and can appreciate it; posthumous fame is a glorious thing, even if it is only posthumous; posthumous liberty is not, in the homely language of the rural Southerner "wu'th shucks." . . .

And Chesnutt, though "white" in appearance himself, wrote that

> Judge Tourgee's cultivated white Negroes are always bewailing
> their fate and cursing the drop of black blood which "taints"—I hate
> the word, it implies corruption—their otherwise pure race.

We may learn something about the obstacles faced by Negroes and
women as writers when we read: "Self-confidence I believe as essential
to success in literature as in acrobatics." We may better understand
that truth exists in motion and develops out of conflict when we read
Chesnutt's remark to Booker T. Washington: "Let the white man dwell
upon the weakness of the Negro race; it is a matter which neither you
nor I need to emphasize."

Chesnutt's work was the forerunner of a substantial body of fiction
written by Negroes which has maintained an unusual level of social
realism. A broad sampling of Negro fiction in this century indicates
that it has been less escapist, more concerned with world history and
culture, with working people and women, with courage and hope,
than comparable fiction written by non-Negro authors.

A further, somewhat subjective point should be made. Character has
almost disappeared from contemporary literature. Everyone knows
that the characters of Shakespeare can be discussed as if they are real
people whom we know, whose actions we can judge, whose decisions
we can reconsider, whose individuality we retain. And we all know
that this is also true of the people in what are universally recognized as
the great novels. But in this sense there are no people in the books of
Hemingway, Dos Passos, Faulkner, Joyce, and most of Steinbeck. It is
the chief value of the writing of Thomas Wolfe that he creates living
characters when he can get away from himself. A remarkable quality
of Chesnutt's novels—and a quality we have got out of the habit of
looking for—is clarity and liveliness of characterization. Not only his
major characters but nearly all of his minor ones are distinct, memorable, and individual. They are not the author and they are not
ourselves. They are not universal in the empty modern sense of the
term. They are real social beings tied to a particular social fabric.

DARWIN T. TURNER

Paul Laurence Dunbar:

The

Rejected

Symbol

PAUL LAURENCE DUNBAR (1872-1906) IS POPULARLY KNOWN FOR HIS poetry, some of which (but by no means all) became a dialectal account of the semi-slaves of the Southern "plantation tradition." Because of this he is frequently condemned for helping to perpetuate a racist stereotype that had doubtful basis in fact and did incalculable harm to American racial attitudes. Yet, as Darwin Turner proves, Dunbar could mount an effective protest against the intolerance of white society, and he often chose to do so through the medium of fiction—particularly so in his novel *The Sport of the Gods*.

The interesting thing about Dunbar's use of the plantation stereotype—the grinning, black child of Nature, ignorant but quaint, sub-human but happy—is the way in which it coalesced with the agrarian mythology which dominated American thought during the nineteenth century. The image of the individual American as a new Adam living a pastoral idyll in the garden of the new world maintained a remarkable hold on the national imagination during a century of urbanization and industrialization in American life. In a sense, of course, Dunbar's interest in rural Negroes was appropriate—most black Americans still lived in the rural South. They were not, however, living a particularly idyllic life and even though some tried to convince themselves that the "American Dream" applied to them too, there was little reason for blacks to think of themselves as American Adamic figures; they could hardly feel that America (for all its natural grandeur) represented Edenic possibilities. Dunbar knew all of this, just as he knew that the plantation image was essentially fraudulent, but his interest in the pastoral idyll (and its antithesis, an evil, threatening city) suggests that he was as much a victim of popular American mythology as his white countrymen. As a result, his fiction becomes a curious blend of white myths and black stereotypes, muted black protest and indirect white injustice, perhaps explaining why Dunbar's novels are considered primarily of historical importance.

Darwin T. Turner has written extensively about black American novelists; his essay on Frank Yerby also appears in this collection. Presently the Dean of the Graduate School at North Carolina A & T University, he is the editor of three companion volumes in the Charles E. Merrill Literary Texts Series: *Black American Literature: Essays*, *Black American Literature: Fiction*, and *Black American Literature: Poetry*.

DARWIN T. TURNER

Paul Laurence Dunbar: The Rejected Symbol

AT TWENTY-FOUR, PAUL LAURENCE DUNBAR BECAME A SYMBOL OF THE creative and intellectual potential of the American Negro. He was envisaged thus by his earliest patrons, who hoped that his literary talent and his black skin would encourage the doubtful to contribute financially to the humanistic education of Negroes. He was envisaged thus by William Dean Howells, one of America's most respected literary critics, who praised *Majors and Minors,* Dunbar's second book, as "the first instance of an American Negro writer who evinced innate distinction in literature."[1] Because he was one of America's most popular poets at the beginning of the twentieth century, he was acclaimed as a symbol by many early critics, who praised him excessively.

More recently, however, his image has been defaced by scholars who have censured him for tarnishing the symbol by perpetuating the derogatory caricatures of the minstrel show and the plantation tales. His reputation has suffered from such a scholar as Robert Bone, author of *The Negro Novel in America* who, from a study of Dunbar's novels, alleged that whenever he "had something to say which transcended the boundaries of the plantation tradition . . . he resorted to the subterfuge of employing white characters, rather than attempting a serious literary portrait of the Negro.[2] His reputation has suffered also from those readers who, seeking to compress his thought into pithy phrases, have failed to reveal the significant changes in his subject-matter and attitudes. His reputation has suffered from those who have been blinded by a single work or who have failed to discern his attempts at ironic protest. The result has been the currently popular images of Dunbar as a disenchanted angel fluttering his wings against publishers' restrictions or as a money-hungry Esau willing to betray his birthright for a mess of popularity. Careful examination of Dunbar and of his works explains the reasons for his inability to write the kind of protest which some of his critics wish. Simultaneously, such scrutiny reveals Dunbar to be far more bitter and scathing, much more a part of the protest tradition than his reputation suggests.

Paul Laurence Dunbar's experiences, his political and economic philosophies, and his artistic ideals prevented his writing the acerbate criticism of the South which some readers desire. Paul Laurence Dun-

---

[1] "Introduction," *Lyrics of Lowly Life* (New York, 1896).
[2] Robert Bone, *The Negro Novel in America* (New Haven, 1958).

Reprinted from *The Journal of Negro History,* LII (January 1967), 1-13, by permission of the publisher and the author. Copyright © 1967 by *The Association for the Study of Negro Life and History, Inc.*

bar's cardinal sin is that he violated the unwritten commandment which American Society has handed down to the Negro: "Thou shalt not laugh at thy black brother" (Especially thou shalt not laugh at thy black brother who spoke dialect and was a slave). But Paul Laurence Dunbar could not identify himself with the slave or freedman about whom he wrote. Born free in Dayton, Ohio, elected president of the high school literary club and editor of the school newspaper by his white classmates, published and praised in America and in England, Dunbar judged the color of his skin to be a very thin bond linking him to the half-Christian, half-pagan slaves a mere two-hundred years removed from savagery, in his opinion. That bond of color was insufficiently tight to gag his chuckles about some of their ridiculous antics which his mother, an ex-slave, had narrated.

Even if Dunbar had been completely free to write scathing protest about the South, he could not have written it, or would have written it ineptly. His experiences and those of his family had not compelled him to hate white people as a group or the South as a region. After Dunbar was twenty, every major job he secured, every publication, and all national recognition resulted directly from the assistance of white benefactors. It is not remarkable that Dunbar assumed that successful Negroes need such help or that, knowing the actuality of Northern benefactors, he believed in the existence of their Southern counterparts. Dunbar was not a unique disciple of such a creed. In *The Ordeal of Mansart*, the militant W. E. B. DuBois has described the manner in which intelligent freedmen sought salvation with the assistance of Southern aristocrats.

As his personal experiences freed him from bitterness towards Caucasians as a group, so his family's experiences relieved bitterness towards the South. The experiences of his parents in slavery probably had been milder than most. His father had been trained in a trade and had been taught to read, write, and compute. As a semi-skilled worker occasionally hired out, he fared better than the average field hand. Irony rather than bitterness is the dominant tone in "The Ingrate," a story Dunbar based on his father's life. Although Dunbar's mother had experienced unpleasantness (as what slave did not), her life as a house slave in Kentucky undoubtedly was easier than that of a slave in the deeper South.

Even had his experiences prompted protest against the South, his social and economic philosophies would have militated against it. Believing that America would prosper only if all citizens recognized their interdependence, he sought to win respect for Negroes by showing that, instead of sulking about the past, they were ready to participate in the joint effort to create a new America. In the poems of *Majors and*

Minors (1895) and the stories of *Folks from Dixie* (1898), he repeatedly emphasized the ability and willingness of Negroes to forgive white Americans for previous injustices.

Dunbar's noble sentiments and protagonists reveal not only a naive political philosophy but also a romantic and idealized concept of society. He believed in right rule by an aristocracy based on birth and blood which assured culture, good breeding, and all the virtues appropriate to a gentleman. He further believed that Negroes, instead of condemning such a society, must prove themselves worthy of a place in it by showing that they had civilized themselves to a level above the savagery which he assumed to be characteristic of Africa.[3] Furthermore, having been reared in Dayton, Ohio, he distrusted big cities and industrialization. Provincially, he assumed the good life for the uneducated to be the life of a farmer in a small western or mid-western settlement or the life of a sharecropper for a benevolent Southern aristocrat. Neither a scholar, political scientist, nor economist, he naively offered an agrarian myth as a shield against the painful reality of discrimination in cities.

Artistic ideals also restricted Dunbar's protest. Even Saunders Redding, generally extremely perceptive in his study of Dunbar, has regretted Dunbar's failure to criticize his society more frequently in his poetry.[4] Dunbar, however, regarded poetry—in standard English—as a noble language, best suited for expressing elevated ideas. Prose was his voice of protest. Protest is missing even from his first two books of poetry, which were privately printed.

In summary, Dunbar's experiences, his social and economic philosophies, and his artistic ideals limited his criticism of the South. This fact, however, should not imply, as some suppose, that Dunbar accepted the total myth of the plantation tradition. In reality, he was no more willing to assume the romanticized plantation to be characteristic of the entire South than he was willing to deny that some slaves had loved their masters or had behaved foolishly.

Nor should it be assumed that his hunger for fame and money silenced his protest against unjust treatment. Actually, he vigorously castigated conditions familiar to him in the North.

The legend of his enforced silence may have germinated from Dunbar's complaints about editors' reactions to his poetry. W. D. Howells had praised Dunbar's dialect poetry as his unique contribution to American literature. Dunbar subsequently felt that Howells' judgment

---

[3] See "One Man's Fortune," *The Strength of Gideon and Other Stories* (New York, 1900), p. 131.

[4] Redding, *To Make a Poet Black* (Chapel Hill, N.C., 1939), p. 60.

caused editors to underestimate the worth of his non-dialect poetry.[5] Dunbar complained also about his failure to improve as a writer. But no biographer has recorded a single complaint about restrictions in subject-matter or thesis. As candid as Dunbar was in correspondence, such silence implies an absence of restriction. In fact, evidence suggests occasional deference to Dunbar. An editor of *Century* sought Dunbar's judgment about whether the magazine over-emphasized the comic character of the Negro. Dunbar responded with his assurance that a laugh could not hurt the Negro, who has "a large humorous quality in his character."[6]

Significantly, Dunbar was least silent at the very time at which he depended most upon continuing popularity with editors and readers. During 1900 and 1901, he derived his only income from royalties and public readings. His medical expenses, the support of his mother, and the cost of maintaining an attractive wife and a home in Washington increased both his expenditures and his worry about his ability to sustain the expenses. At such a critical time, he frequently spoke out as vigorously as his idol, Frederick Douglass, had spoken and as bitterly as any Negro has.

From 1898 until 1903 he identified himself with protest in articles to newspapers. In 1898 in the Chicago *Record*, he condemned the murder of Negroes in the race riots in Wilmington, North Carolina. When the Denver *Post* requested an article in 1899, he wrote "The Hapless Southern Negro." In 1900 he defended the Negro's intellectual potential in the Philadelphia *Times;* and in 1903, in the *Chicago Tribune*, he pointed out the irony that America condemned Russia's treatment of prisoners yet ignored the lynching, the re-enslavement, the disfranchisement, the unemployment and the discrediting of American Negroes. Four articles of protest may seem too few, but they refute the reputed silence.

Even more significant is his fiction in 1900 and 1901. Previously, his protests had been mild. In *The Strength of Gideon and Other Stories* (1900), however, Dunbar slapped back. In "A Mess of Pottage" he pictured the Negro as an individual betrayed by both political parties. "A Council of State" is written in a similar tone. Intelligent Negro leaders have planned to campaign against the Republican administration which has made them "crushed men of a crushed race."[7] When advised to be moderate, one leader answers:

---

[5] Lida Keck Wiggins, *The Life and Works of Paul Laurence Dunbar* (New York, 1907), p. 109.

[6] Virginia Cunningham, *Paul Laurence Dunbar and His Song* (New York, 1947), p. 207.

[7] *The Strength of Gideon and Other Stories* (New York, 1900), p. 333.

"Conservatism be hanged! We have rolled that word under our tongues when we were being trampled upon; we have preached it in our churches when we were being shot down; we have taught it in our schools when the right to use our learnings was being denied us, until the very word has come to be a reproach upon a black man's tongue."[8]

Their efforts are futile. Betrayed by a mulatto who has no sympathy for the Negroes she professes to represent, they are crushed by the white machine.

Another story is even more acerbate. Having worked faithfully for the Republican party in Alabama, Mr. Cornelius Johnson (in "Mr. Cornelius Johnson, Office-Seeker") comes to Washington to obtain the minor political appointment he expects as a reward for his service. As the Congressman repeatedly postpones inquiry into the matter, Johnson is progressively stripped of the dignity in which he has cloaked his image. Insulted by white clerks who call him by his first name, forced to save money by moving from his hotel into a boarding house and by eating snacks in his room rather than dining out, compelled to secure money by pawning his clothes, Johnson finally mortgages his home in Alabama so that he may remain in Washington. His despair intensifies because "a body feels as if he could fight if only he had something to fight. But here you strike out and hit—nothing."[9] After a year's delay he is informed that the Senate has refused to confirm his appointment. Ruined financially and emotionally, he cries to Washington, "Damn your deceit, your fair cruelties; damn you, you hard white liar."[10]

Dunbar's characteristic irony occasionally seeps through the bitterness. In "Mr. Cornelius Johnson," he mused wryly:

> In Alabama one learns to be philosophical. It is good to be philosophical in a place where the proprietor of a cafe fumbles vaguely around in the region of his hip pocket and insinuates that he doesn't want one's custom.

In "A Council of State" he mocked the elasticity of the word "colored" and the credulity of white people who accept as a leader of Negroes anyone who professes to be. Irony accompanies humiliation as "Mr." Cornelius Johnson is reduced to "Cornelius" in the office of his Congressman, and the mulatto "leader" of her people is assigned servant's errands by the white boss of the Republican machine. The irony, however, does not lighten the tone. These stories cannot be called pessi-

---

[8] *Ibid.*, p. 331.
[9] *The Strength of Gideon and Other Stories* (New York, 1900), pp. 223-224.
[10] *Ibid.*, p. 227.

mistic. The confirmed pessimist at least perceives an alternative outcome even while he positively affirms the inevitability of the un-desired outcome. In these stories Dunbar, however, saw only destruction.

Dunbar recognized economic as well as political problems. The most thought-provoking story on the theme is "One Man's Fortune," which Dunbar drew from his experiences in Dayton. Having graduated from a Northern college, Bertram Holliday seeks his fortune confident that he is "master of his fate" and "captain of his soul." Applying for employment as a clerk in the office of a white lawyer, he is advised to start at the bottom, to accept a position as waiter in a hotel. When Bert protests that waiting on tables will not provide legal experience, he is warned that, unprotected by the sympathy which Northerners once felt for Southern slaves, Negroes of a later generation can expect no justice in the North. Applying to an office which had advertised for a clerk, preferably with a high school education, he is told to seek a job in the shipping room. Similar rebuffs teach him that "all the addresses and all the books written on how to get on are written for white men. We blacks must solve the question for ourselves."[11] Bert does not desire to go South to teach school. He believes that, since the South is training its own teachers, jobs for educated Northern Negroes must be developed in the North.

After taking work as a janitor in a factory, he is hired as a clerk by the lawyer who previously had rejected him. Now campaigning for a judiciary post, the lawyer wants Bert to solicit votes from Negroes in the community. After the lawyer has been elected, Bert is replaced by a white youth. Defeated, Bert accepts a teaching position in the South.

Contrasted with the fate of the idealistic protagonist is the success of his more realistic classmate, Davis, who argues that the Negro has no real opportunity in North America. Because his ancestors, savages two hundred years earlier, had been taught civilization in the lowest and most degrading contact with it, the Negro cannot assume the psychology which makes white men respond eagerly to challenges. The Anglo-Saxon heritage of seven centuries teaches, Davis insists, a love for struggle in a normal battle. The Negro, who lacks this frenzy, is forced into an abnormal battle. Instead of fighting to secure a position befitting his education, Davis works in a hotel until he saves enough money to purchase a barber shop, which he operates success-fully by concealing his intelligence from his white customers.

In *The Strength of Gideon and Other Stories*, economic problems and injustice also harass the uneducated. In "The Finish of Patsy

---

[11] *Ibid.*, p. 147.

Barnes," Patsy and his mother have come North hoping to support themselves more easily than they had in Kentucky. His mother's illness forces Patsy to seek employment as a jockey. In this story, as in "One Man's Fortune," Dunbar contrasted the Negroes' failure with the success of Irish immigrants already possessed of authority to employ or reject Negroes whose ancestors had populated America for generations. In "An Old-Fashioned Christmas," Jimmy Lewis, a young newsboy, is arrested on Christmas Eve for shooting dice with a friend for five-cent stakes. Confined overnight, the tearful child is brought before a judge who explains that he must send Jimmy to jail to demonstrate New York City's intolerance of gambling. To free him, Jimmy's mother pays his fine with money she had saved to buy food appropriate for an old-fashioned Christmas dinner. Written in 1899, the story anticipates current condemnations of police brutality and money-blinded courts.

Dunbar also examined injustices in the South. The popularity of lynchings inspired the ironic "The Tragedy at Three Forks." Inflamed by editorial innuendo, townspeople lynch two Negroes for a crime committed by a white girl. However, when one white man kills another in the ensuing struggle for souvenirs, he is spared because the crowd agrees with an observer that a white man must be given a chance to explain his actions. Dunbar concluded his tale of the lynching.

> Conservative editors wrote leaders about it in which they deplored the rashness of the hanging but warned the Negroes that the only way to stop lynching was to quit the crimes of which they so often stood accused.[12]

In the following year Dunbar wedded his social criticism of Negroes and of America in a novel, *The Sport of the Gods,* published first in *Lippincott's Magazine.* His savage attack upon stereotypes and myths of the plantation tradition has been blunted by critics who, observing the melodramatic occurrences and the diatribes against city life, fail to perceive the abject despair suggested by the ending.

Having remained in Virginia after emancipation, Berry Hamilton worked faithfully for twenty years for Colonel Oakley. His only compensation was $30 per month, a small cottage, $15 per month for his wife's service, discarded clothes, and food which the Colonel did not need. Although he remained in the small slave cabin, he managed to transform it into a "typical Negro house," decently, tastefully, and conservatively furnished. By living frugally, he also saved $1300 from his meager income.

---

[12] *Ibid.,* p. 282.

When Oakley's younger brother alleges that he has been robbed of $800, the Colonel immediately suspects Berry, who has never been accused of any previous crime. Colonel Oakley rationalizes that Negro slaves had stolen only food because they had not known the value of money; the more knowledgeable freed Negro would steal money too. Far different from the beautiful heroine of the plantation myth, his wife is an insipid, brainless creature who echoes her husband's thoughts and weeps at the glorious nobility which her brother displays when he offers to shake Berry's hand. Berry is arrested and sentenced to ten years in prison although no evidence is offered to support the charge against him. Unfortunately, Dunbar says, he lived in a community in which only one white man ever doubted Berry's guilt. Part of the community thought is reflected by another man, renowned for his kindness to Negroes, who defends Berry by insisting that, because Negroes have no concept of right and wrong, they should not be imprisoned for stealing. Insisting that America has mistreated Negroes by freeing them before they were ready for civilization, he expects Negroes to ask to be re-enslaved. The spokesman for the other part of the white community contends that Berry's theft evidences the total depravity of the Negro.

Ostracized by the Negro community, dispossessed by the Oakleys, and robbed of $500 by the police, who claimed it as part of the stolen money, the Hamiltons move to New York, where for the first time in her life Fannie Hamilton hears herself addressed as "Mrs. Hamilton." That, however, is the only profit from five years in New York. Quickly corrupted by his desire to belong, her son Joe imitates the parasites who waste their days and night. Joe subsequently is imprisoned for having murdered an actress who had ended their affair because he had become an alcoholic. Dazzled by the glamor of the stage, his sister becomes an actress. (Despite, or perhaps because of, his familiarity with actors and actresses for the musical shows which he helped write, Dunbar judged actresses to be doomed to damnation.) Even Mrs. Hamilton is victimized by New York. Although she cannot be deluded by the false values which ensnare her children, she is tricked into a marriage ceremony with a gambler who persuades her that Berry's imprisonment automatically divorced her from him.

During four of these five years, Colonel Oakley has known of Berry's innocence. After receiving a letter in which the younger brother confessed to having invented the theft to conceal his gambling losses, Oakley unhesitatingly places the Oakley family honor above the freedom of one Negro. Distraught from the strain of his guilty secret, however, Oakley weakens physically and mentally.

When a fantastic series of circumstances exposes the injustice to Berry Hamilton, the town and the state of Virginia must reconsider the issue. Had there been no national publicity, the town would preserve the Oakley honor by leaving Berry in jail. The spokesman noted for kindness to Negroes argues that since imprisonment is the closest approach to the enslavement which Negroes need and want, Berry will probably cry when he is forced from prison. Even the state will not admit an error in Berry's conviction by twelve good men and true (and white). Instead, the governor pardons Berry. Seeking his family in New York, Berry learns the grim sport the gods have played, rescues his wife from her sadistic lover, and returns to Virginia.

Some critics argue that the attack on the evils of New York and the return to the South evidence Dunbar's inability to avoid the plantation tradition.[13] Dunbar's ending, however, is far more bitter and hopeless than that. The alternatives he offers are the restraint of the body in the South and the festering of the soul in the North. Confronted with these alternatives, Berry returns to his old Virginia cabin to live out his days

> listening to the shrieks of the madman [Colonel Oakley] across the yard and thinking of what he had brought to them and to himself.
>   It was not a happy life, but it was all that was left to them, and they took it up without complaint, for they knew they were powerless against some will infinitely stronger than their own.

If these two books had been published anonymously, they would be considered bitter protests and the author would be heralded as the first major ironist in literature by Negroes. Several reasons underlie the failure of many readers to recognize these qualities. Dunbar often phrased ideas ambiguously; consequently, his most successful irony is that which is heavily and fully developed. Second, some of his subtlety may have been overlooked by critics. Finally, his dark acerbity may have been missed by readers blinded by his bright image as a comic writer.

The Sport of the Gods, however, ended Dunbar's major work as a social critic. One can merely conjecture the extent to which Dunbar's later writing was affected by his drinking, his separation from his wife, and his failing health. When he next published a collection of stories, he seemed determined to prove only that he could write Thomas Nelson Page's plantation tales better than Page himself.

A muted voice of protest, however, was sounded in his poetry collection, *Lyrics of Love and Laughter,* published in the same year, 1903. In two poems, "The Haunted Oak" and "To the New South," he attacked lynchings and the ingratitude of the South.

---

[13] See Hugh M. Gloster, *Negro Voices in American Fiction* (Chapel Hill, 1948); Bone, *The Negro Novel in America* (New Haven, 1958).

In his final two works of protest fiction, "The Wisdom of Silence" and "The Lynching of Jube Benson,"[14] he continued his criticism of the South. "The Wisdom of Silence" is ironic. By refusing assistance and by succeeding despite the efforts of loan sharks, Jeremiah Anderson angers his ex-master. As Dunbar says, nothing angers a person more than to be frustrated when he is prepared to say, "I told you so." Fortunately for the ex-master, Jeremiah's crops and barn are burned by persons unknown. Jeremiah is forced to receive and acknowledge help from his ex-master, "Thank e' Mas' Sam." In "The Lynching of Jube Benson," a Southern doctor unsuccessfully attempts to explain why he lynched a faithful servant whom he suspected of rape.

> "Why did I do it. I don't know. A false education, I reckon, one false from the beginning. I saw his black face glooming there in the half light, and I could only think of him as a monster. It's tradition. At first I was told that the black man would catch me, and when I got over that, they taught me that the devil was black, and when I had recovered from the sickness of that belief, here were Jube and his fellows with faces of menacing blackness. There was only one conclusion: This black man stood for all the powers of evil, the result of whose machinations had been gathering in my mind from childhood up."[15]

His writings evidence Dunbar's protests against both the South and the North. His position, however, is difficult to appraise exactly because he vacillated and assumed seemingly contradictory stances. Some of his attitudes are difficult to explain. Although the illustrations in his collections of stories seem to caricature Negroes, Dunbar appreciated them so much that he secured an original for his home. Many readers disparage Page's plantation tales, which idealize a genteel, aristocratic society which never existed. Yet, Dunbar apparently considered the Negroes authentic, or at least conceivable. In "Negro Life in Washington," he described a living Negro whom he imagined to have emerged from one of Page's stories.

Perhaps the simplest explanation which offers any consistency is that readers have demanded too much of Dunbar as a symbol. Commanding him to speak for the Negro, they forget that Negroes speak with hundreds of different voices. Dunbar is merely one. Insensitive to the implications of creating comic Negro figures, he was extremely sensitive to the insults which a Northern society might inflict upon an educated Negro. Willing to criticize injustices of Northern or Southern

---

[14] Both stories were published in *The Heart of Happy Hollow* (New York, 1904).

[15] *Ibid.*, p. 236.

society, he, nevertheless, supported outmoded economic and social ideals. Occasionally conscious of the ridiculous postures of white Americans, he was even more conscious and less tolerant of ridiculous behavior of Negro Americans. Ignorant of historical truths about Africa and about slavery, he respected as fact the myths current in his time. Because he recognized distinctions between Negroes he knew and Negro stereotypes of the plantation stories, he inferred the race's remarkable progress within a generation. In short, Paul Laurance Dunbar was a talented, creative, high school graduate whose views reflect the limited knowledge of many historians, economists, and social philosophers of his day.

WILLIAM STANLEY BRAITHWAITE

The

Novels

of

Jessie Fauset

JESSIE FAUSET (1884?-1961) WROTE NOVELS OF MANNERS ABOUT THE black middle class—the "Black Bourgeoisie." Her fiction frequently deals in the trials of domestic society: housekeeping and dressmaking, flirtations and dinner engagements. This was natural for Fauset, the daughter of an old, distinguished Philadelphia family and one of the most "traditional" participants in the Harlem Renaissance. During the twenties as a literary editor of *The Crisis*, the NAACP's house organ, Fauset did much to encourage young black writers, even though she often disagreed with what they were trying to do.

Although it is true that her themes sometimes are, as William Stanley Braithwaite suggests, in the tradition of Jane Austen, there is a significant difference. The feminine characters who became her chief subjects are black; their social experience and concern with manners always occur within a cultural context that places them at a disadvantage because of their race. The word "race" is important here, because one can be a "Negro" in the American culture without being "black." Due to a long tradition of racial intermixture (much of it by white coercion) many Afro-Americans are as "white" as the blondest descendents of Northern European immigrants. (Indeed, many *are* the descendents of such immigrants.) Faced with a society that offers immense advantages to white-skinned citizens and incredible difficulty to their black countrymen, light-skinned Negroes have often been tempted to "cross the color line" and "pass" as white.

Black novelists have frequently explored the "passing" theme and Fauset treats it, in one way or another, in all four of her novels. Her interest, however, seems to be part of a more general concern with the difficulties of living a "normal," middle class life amid a society irrationally obsessed with color prejudice. Her first novel, *There is Confusion* (1924), describes the difficulties of Negro life in the United States for two families, the Byes and Marshalls, and how they affect the generation coming of age during World War I, especially the beautiful Joanna Marshall and the sensitive Peter Bye. Her second novel, *Plum Bun* (1929), deals with the same well-bred class of eastern Negroes and tells of the discovery by the light-skinned Angela Murray that passing is an unsatisfactory response to being black in America. *The Chinaberry Tree* (1931) charts the effects of fathers' sins upon their offspring, specifically on two cousins, Laurentine Strange and Melissa Paul, who suffer greatly for their illegitimacy until they eventually find happiness with respected, middle-class husbands. *Comedy: American Style,* Fauset's fourth novel, describes the obsessive efforts of the light-skinned Olivia Cary to free herself and her family from the disadvantages accruing to color in the United States.

It is appropriate that a Negro critic like William Stanley Braithwaite (1878-1962) should analyze Fauset's achievement. The Austen analogy came naturally to him, for his interest in manners—especially literary manners—was great. Braithwaite brought an ornate, self-conscious rhetoric to the practice of criticism that was part of a nineteenth century conception of the *litterateur.* He also maintained a belief in the gentility of art that was fairly common among many early black critics and which is reflected in his favorable, but not overly specific, evaluation of Fauset. For many years a member of the literary staff of the Boston *Evening Transcript,* Braithwaite annually edited *The Anthology of Magazine Verse and Yearbook of American Poetry,* an anthology he collected for sixteen consecutive years between 1913 and 1929. He also published three books of poetry, all illustrative of the poetical conventions of the nineteenth century lyric.

WILLIAM STANLEY BRAITHWAITE

The Novels of Jessie Fauset

I DON'T AT ALL MIND LOOKING BACK—A STATEMENT I AM BOLD TO MAKE, in face of the implied challenge of some of my readers—over thirty-five years, and publicly embrace an era, the *first* era, of creative literature by Negro writers. We have crossed a turbulent, roaring, treacherous, aesthetic Steam of Time between 1898 and 1933: between Chesnutt's "The Marrow of Tradition" say, and Jessie Fauset's "Comedy: American Style," in the growth and development of the Negro novelist.

Our creative literature, chiefly poetry and fiction, has carried the Race across this stream—a bridge, girder and gable and solid granite piers and towers, suspended fairylike in the mist of misunderstanding and calumny, dazzlingly unsubstantial in the sunlight of sympathy and encouragement—from the shores of a "backward," "inferior" people of the eighteen-nineties, to, well, to the shores of cultural and spiritual equality with our fellow-citizens of today. A magic structure and an alluring journey! Yes, by all the precepts and paradoxes of an elusive and deceptive opportunity: no, by all the confluent, Promethean flames of biological urgencies and gifts which the bloods of Europe have poured into the original stream-source from Africa. The "gay nineties" was a tragic era, the "mauve decade," of the critical fancy, was a jaundiced vision, where the Negro was concerned; and in them, the Negro was a passionate root, that sent its first fragile stems above the aesthetic soil along the borderlands of the old and the new century.

There was a girlhood at this time whose wistful dreams must have sent her bright, brown eyes staring in the direction of far horizons, where lay hidden the secrets of a peoples' pride of spirit, secrets that were miraculously endowed with *beauty*; a girlhood that was to grow into womanhood; a searcher after the lure whose priceless possession made her a bright, enchanting blossom on the literary plant that has grown so magically in the last decade.

Within a few months, a decade will have been reached since the publication of Jessie Fauset's first novel "There is Confusion." In 1928, appeared "Plum Bun," in 1931, "The Chinaberry Tree," and in November of this year, "Comedy: American Style." Four novels in not quite ten years. Only one Negro novelist has equalled this output, Dunbar. Our other novelists, Chesnutt, DuBois, McKay, Nella Larsen, Walter White, Rudolph Fisher, Wallace Thurman, G. S. Schuyler, Langston Hughes, Countee Cullen, and Arna Bontemps, have produced three,

Reprinted from *Opportunity*, XII (January 1934), 24-28, by permission of The National Urban League. Copyright © 1934 by *Opportunity*.

two, and one novel, respectively. These eleven writers have described and interpreted Negro life and experience with an art built, with two or three exceptions, to the same pattern. There has not been much variation to the theme nor to the *milieu.*

Miss Fauset has done otherwise, and done it with superb courage. She stands at the head of the procession; and I deliberately invite the objection of critical opinion when I add, that she stands in the front rank of American women novelists in general. Glance at the procession of American women novelists, and their names will register the quality and character of their art, both as an expression, the rendering of human experience, the delineation of human character and nature, and environmental influences. Sara Orne Jewett, Mary E. Wilkins Freeman, Margaret Deland, Edith Wharton, Dorothy Canfield Fisher, Willa Sibert Cather, Ellen Glasgow, Kathleen Norris, Gertrude Atherton, Julia Peterkin, Zona Gale, to name a few, the most conspicuous and successful of the last two generations. If my claim is extravagant, that Miss Fauset assumes a natural and spontaneous association in this company, I am quite willing to take an immediate chastisement, and leave to posterity the relish of honoring with reiterated quotation this morsel of critical extravagance.

Can one by any extension of the critical yardstick credit any of these women novelists with the extraordinary imaginative perception of discovering a new world of racial experience and character, hitherto without psychological and spiritual map and compass, and with poignant surprise find it buffeted, baffled, scorned and rejected, by the pressure of an encircling political, economic, social and spiritual society, as with an intangible wall of adamant, through which it had to break for the means of survival, and more than mere survival, *progress,* and return from the discovery with both a tragedy and comedy of manners? No, Miss Jewett's Maine folk in her 'country of the pointed firs,' are fundamentally of the same dramatic substance in motive and experience as Miss Cather's Nebraska pioneers; Miss Wharton's Knickerbocker aristocrats are essentially one with the same pride and mellow grace of mind and habit as Miss Glasgow's Virginia 'first families,' the only difference that, with the former the *nouveau riche* gave a surface glitter to the jewel raping its purity, while with the latter a 'lost cause' took the sheen from the once proud texture of a feudal regime. Also these white novelists could afford to toy with some solid virtues and traditions of their craft, which often, and in several cases amongst them, mitigated their value and sincerity as literary artists. Strange as it may seem to all except those of cultivated taste and a broad knowledge of the history and traditions of aesthetic values, many of these novelists, in spite of their reputations and the authoritative praise given them, are scarcely more than deft craftsmen, manipulating the profoundest emotions of humanity for the sake of capturing their readers' attention and interest.

When Miss Fauset tremulously stepped across the threshold of American literature with "There is Confusion," in 1924, she did more than tell the story of a segment of a neglected group of American citizens of color, whose family, social and economic life, on the plane on which she placed it, was new material for the novelist; she unrecognizably made her entrance upon the American scene of letters as the potential Jane Austen of Negro literature. How is one to make clear the subtle distinction between Negro and American literature? Is Negro literature determined by the material or by the color and race of the author who creates it? If by the former, then there are a countless number of white Americans who are *Negro writers*; and yet obviously they cannot be, because by every evidence of proof these authors are known to be white men and women; if by the latter, here we have a paradox as confusing as the other circumstances, because the author of obvious Negro blood is dealing with individuals who, though they are likewise Negroes, are now, after several centuries of transportation and transformation from the native soil of the race—just as the English, the Italian, the French, the Spanish, or German, whose lives went into the colonization of these western lands, and also into the foundations of the American Republic—speaking the common language, and in the custom of living, dressing, eating, working, depend upon the same means and methods as all other Americans; thus it is not merely a question of rationality, but of truth, that the shaper of their individual and collective destinies upon the patterns of creative literature, though racially of Negro extraction or descent, is first and foremost an American author and the creator of American literature.

Thus, if it is convenient to speak of Negro literature as a classification of American literature, it is essential to insist that the standards are one and the same. And if comparisons are made, it is the character and not the quality of the material that is the chief object of appraisal and analysis. With some modification then, I repeat, that Miss Fauset, when she started her novelistic career with "There is Confusion," as the potential Jane Austen of Negro literature, after many decades of authorship by white women novelists, became the first American woman novelist to wrap her shoulders in the scarf of rare and delicate embroidery that Jane Austen's genius bequeathed to the American woman who could wear it most gracefully.

I daresay, as a novelist Miss Fauset would be credited with many a virtue by certain eminent critics, if she were but obliging enough to ignore the *conventional* ideals and triumphs of the emerged group of the Race. She has been infinitely more honest with her characters than her critics have cared to acknowledge, indeed, to have even suspected. After all, her purpose, whether conscious or unconscious, has been to create in the pages of fiction a society which outside the Race simply did not and preferably, in accordance with granted assumption, could not be allowed to exist. The spirit, the consciousness of pride, dignity, a new quality of moral idealism, was breathed into this darker body of human nature by her passionate sympathy and understanding of its ironic position in the flimsy web of American civilization. Only recently a review of Miss Fauset's latest novel, "Comedy: American Style," in one of the leading Negro papers, resented what the reviewer charged was a lack of climax and philosophy in the recital of Olivia Cary's color obsession and the pain it brought her family. The philosophy in this latest novel, as in the three earlier ones, is not, and never was intended to be, an imposed thesis upon the surface of the story. Miss Fauset is too good an artist to argue the point; to engrave a doctrine upon so intangible an element as Truth, or to array with a misfitting apparel of rhetoric the logic which like a pagan grace or a Christian virtue should run naked as the wind through the implications that color and shape the lives of her characters and their destinies. I am afraid that Negro critical eyes as well as white critical eyes have quite often failed to discern these implications in which are contained the philosophy of a tremendous conflict; the magnificent Shakesperean conflict of *will* and *passion* in the great tragedies from "Titus Andronicus" to "Coriolanus"; for in this Negro society which Miss Fauset has created imaginatively from the realities, there is the *will*, the confused but burning *will*, to master the *passion* of the organized body of lusty American prejudice.

Philosophy, indeed! If we trace the range of American fiction—so spotty in its genuine qualities—we do not find since Hawthorne a similar, and singular, devotion of the philosophy of *rebuke* to an inhuman principle, elevated to an institution and safeguarded by both law and public opinion, as we find in these novels of Jessie Fauset's. Hawthorne's novels were the vehicle for, and presented types of human lives as, a brooding, passionate rebuke to the hard, callous Puritan spirit, which denied earthly happiness and fulfillment, the sense of joy and beauty, to the people. So in the novels of Miss Fauset, we find underlying the narrative, this same philosophy of rebuke, brooding and passionate also, against the contemporary spirit of the American people, who have elevated prejudice into an institution, safeguarded also by law and public sentiment, denying the freedom of development, of the inherent right to well-being, and the pursuit of happiness. It comes as a strange, mysterious echo out of the pages of the great romancer, to hear Miss Fauset's women, Joanna Marshall, Angela Murray and Olivia Cary (is it singular that her men are less given to this articulate yearning?) cry, in Angela's words: "Doesn't anyone think that we have a right to be happy, simply, naturally?" And Joanna, in the first of the novels, at the very end of her story in which she is drawn as a somewhat selfish, ambitious, and unintentionally hard girl, while building her career, after being twitted by Peter her lover, about her desire for greatness, replied, "No, . . . my creed calls for nothing but happiness."

Happiness and—*beauty*! these are the overtones, vibrating from the ordinary drama of men and women, young and old, acting out their tense and colorful destinies in the pages of these four novels, aloof at the core of their interests and intentions from the broad currents of American life. These people want, most of all, to be themselves. To satisfy the same yearnings and instincts, which God has given them in the same measure bestowed upon other people. When some of their members "cross over" into the white world, to enjoy the advantages and privileges for which they are fitted and worthy, as Angela Murray, and her mother Mattie, in temporary spells of adventure, Anthony Cross, and Olivia Cary did, it was not because they desired to be "white," but because a cruel, blind, and despising tradition had taught them it was wiser and more profitable "not to be colored." So far Miss Fauset has nicely balanced her survey of this extraordinary scene and the people who compose it. "There is Confusion," the first of her novels, deals with the clear-cut background and its atmosphere of a rising racial social group in New York, the action taking place largely in the pre-war years. It is mainly the story of Joanna Marshall's artistic ambition to fulfill her talents in the larger world of universal recognition and appreciation. The Marshall family is typical of many Negro families of the period, rising by hard work and moral principles to a position of respectability and influence among their own. Peter Bye, Joanna's lover, though he was careless of the distinction, brings into the story the pride of ancestry from an old Philadelphia family. That [Though] Joanna, in the end, was defeated in her purpose to achieve greatness—it is interesting to reflect upon the parallel story of Maggie Ellersley, poor and unfavored by opportunity, who strove so earnestly and honestly to be respectable in the sense that the Marshalls were, and who built her own sturdy ambitions upon the materials and services designed entirely along racial lines—she remains a more significant figure in the late realization of her love for Peter.

"Plum Bun," Miss Fauset's second novel is, perhaps, her most perfect artistic achievement, and the most balanced force of interracial experience. Its heroine, Angela Murray, not so profoundly and vividly drawn as Laurentine Strange or Melissa Paul, in "The Chinaberry

ROBERT BONE

Zora Neale Hurston

ZORA NEALE HURSTON (1903-1960) HAS NOT ENJOYED THE LITERARY reputation she deserves. Her fictional achievement falls just short of Wright and Ellison, and this makes all the more tragic her death at the age of 57, forgotten, sick, tired, and poor. Hurston's novels are about women without being feminist; she is interested in the female condition generally and black womanhood in particular; in the loves, joys, frustrations, and tragedies which attend the female condition, complicate it, and endow it with such rich possibility.

A professional folklorist as well as a novelist, Hurston spent much of her life gathering Negro folklore in the rural South. Her findings were published in *Mules and Men* (1935) and in a number of articles for professional folklore journals. Her interest in the anthropological sources of superstition and myth also led her to publish an account of Jamaican voodoo in *Tell My Horse* (1938) and a semi-fictional, semi-satirical study of the legend of Moses entitled *Moses Man of the Mountain* (1939).

Her folklore researches frequently inform her fiction, and all of her novels create a rich atmosphere of the rural South. Hurston could easily have taken her Barnard degree in anthropology and forgotten her folk roots; she was too aware of their significance to do so, however, and her fiction tells the complex story of the simple life of rural people without sentimentality or special pleading.

Robert Bone, author of *The Negro Novel in America* (New Haven, 1958), is Professor of Languages and Literature in the Teachers College of Columbia University.

ROBERT BONE

Zora Neale Hurston

ZORA NEALE HURSTON . . . WAS BORN AND RAISED IN AN ALL-NEGRO town in Florida—an experience with "separate-but-equal" politics which deeply affected her outlook on racial issues, as well as her approach to the Negro novel. Her father was a tenant farmer and jackleg preacher whose colorful sermons were an important influence on Miss Hurston's style. Her mother urged her to "jump at the sun," and at the first opportunity she left home, employed as a maid in a traveling Gilbert and Sullivan company. An ambitious reader in secondary school, she set her sights on college, achieving this aim largely through her own efforts. She attended Morgan State College in Baltimore, Howard University, and Columbia University, where she studied anthropology under Franz Boas.

At Howard she joined the Stylus, an undergraduate literary society sponsored by Alain Locke. Drawn at once into the vortex of the Negro Renaissance, she published several stories in *Opportunity*, and collaborated with Langston Hughes and Wallace Thurman on the editorial board of *Fire*. In the early 1930's a prize story called "The Gilded Six-Bits" appeared in *Story* magazine, leading to an invitation from Lippincott's to do a novel. The result was *Jonah's Gourd Vine* (1934). Her second and more important novel, *Their Eyes Were Watching God*, appeared in 1937, while a third novel, *Seraph on the Suwanee*, was published in 1948. In addition to her short stories and novels, Miss Hurston has written three books of folklore, an autobiography, a one-act play, one or two librettos, and several magazine articles.

Jonah's Gourd Vine has style without structure, a rich verbal texture without dramatic form, "atmosphere" without real characterization. It is the story of John Buddy, a field hand turned preacher whose congregation accepts him as "a man amongst men," but is unprepared to find him also a man amongst women. A great preacher (the author introduces a ten-page sermon to prove it), John Buddy is no less a lover. An erratic tension arises between folk artist and philanderer, but it is not carried forward to a suitable denouement. In its emphasis on atmosphere and local color, in its exploitation of the exotic, and especially of exotic language, and in its occasional hint of primitivism, *Jonah's Gourd Vine* expresses a sensibility molded predominantly by the Negro Renaissance.

Reprinted from Robert Bone, *The Negro Novel in America*, rev. ed. (New Haven: Yale University Press, 1958), pp. 126-32, by permission of the publisher and the author. Copyright © 1958, 1965, by Yale University.

The style of the novel is impressive enough. Zora Neale Hurston, whom Langston Hughes has described as a rare *raconteuse,* draws freely on the verbal ingenuity of the folk. Her vivid, metaphorical style is based primarily on the Negro preacher's graphic ability to present abstractions to his flock. Take the opening sentence of the novel: "God was grumbling his thunder and playing the zig-zag lightning through his fingers"; or such an image as "the cloud-muddied moonlight"; or the small-town flavor of "Time is long by the courthouse clock." The danger is that these folk sayings may become the main point of the novel. Overdone, they destroy rather than support authentic characterization. In *Jonah's Gourd Vine* they are too nonfunctional, too anthropological, and in the end merely exotic. Miss Hurston has not yet mastered the form of the novel, but her style holds promise of more substantial accomplishment to come.

The genesis of a work of art may be of no moment to literary criticism but it is sometimes crucial in literary history. It may, for example, account for the rare occasion when an author outclasses himself. *Their Eyes Were Watching God* (1937) is a case in point. The novel was written in Haiti in just seven weeks, under the emotional pressure of a recent love affair. "The plot was far from the circumstances," Miss Hurston writes in her autobiography, "but I tried to embalm all the tenderness of my passion for him in *Their Eyes Were Watching God.*" Ordinarily the prognosis for such a novel would be dismal enough. One might expect immediacy and intensity, but not distance, or control, or universality. Yet oddly, or perhaps not so oddly, it is Miss Hurston's best novel, and possibly the best novel of the period, excepting *Native Son.*

The opening paragraph of *Their Eyes Were Watching God* encompasses the whole of the novel's meaning: "Ships at a distance have every man's wish on board. For some they come in with the tide. For others they sail forever on the horizon, never out of sight, never landing, until the Watcher turns his eyes away in resignation, his dreams mocked to death by Time. That is the life of man" (p. 9). For women, the author continues, the dream is the sole reality. "So the beginning of this was a woman, and she had come back from burying the dead."

Janie has been gone for almost two years as the action of the novel commences. The townspeople know only that she left home in the company of a lover much younger than herself, and that she departed in fine clothes but has returned in overalls. Heads nod; tongues wag; and the consensus is that she has played the fool. Toward the gossiping women who, from the safety of a small-town porch "pass nations through their mouths," Janie feels only contempt and irritation: "If God don't think no mo' 'bout 'em than Ah do, they's a lost ball in de high grass." To Pheoby, her kissing-friend, she tells the story of her love for Tea-Cake, which together with its antecedents comprises the main body of the novel.

Janie's dream begins during her adolescence, when she is stirred by strange wonderings as she watches a pear tree blossom. No sooner is her dream born, however, than it is desecrated by her grandmother. Nanny, who has witnessed her share of the sexual exploitation of Negro women, declares firmly: "[Neither] de menfolks white or black is makin' a spit cup outa you." Seeking to protect Janie from the vicissitudes of adolescent love, she puts her up on the auction block of ·marriage. To Nanny, being married is being like white folks: "You got yo' lawful husband same as Mis' Washburn or anybody else." Against her better judgment, therefore, Janie acquiesces in an early marriage with Logan Killicks, a hard-working farmer considerably older than herself.

"There are years that ask questions and years that answer: Did marriage compel love like the sun the day?" Janie soon realizes her mistake. She aspires to more than sixty acres and an organ in the parlor, and refuses to barter her fulfillment as a woman in exchange for property right: "Ah ain't takin' dat ole land tuh heart neither. Ah could throw ten acres of it over de fence every day and never look back to see where it fell" (p. 42). Affairs reach a crisis with the appearance of Jody Starks, a younger man who offers Janie a fresh start in a neighboring county. "Janie pulled back a long time because he did not represent sun-up and pollen and blooming trees, but he spoke for far horizon." Her first dream dead, she runs off with Jody to the all-Negro town of Eatonville.

Janie's second dream scarcely fares better than the first. Although her husband becomes "a big voice," a property owner, and eventually mayor of the town, Janie remains restless, unfulfilled. Asked by Jody how she likes being "Mrs. Mayor," she replies: "It keeps us in some way we ain't natural wid one 'nother. Youse always off talkin' and fixin' things, and Ah feels lak Ah'm jus' markin' time" (p. 74). A widening rift develops in the marriage as a fundamental clash of values becomes apparent. Janie can no more reconcile herself to Jody's store than to Logan Killicks' sixty acres: "The store itself was a pleasant place if only she didn't have to sell things." On one occasion, when the townsfolk playfully take off from work for the mock funeral of a dead mule, Jody remarks, "Ah wish mah people would git mo' business in 'em and not spend so much time on foolishness." Janie's reply is caustic: "Everybody can't be lak you, Jody. Somebody is bound tuh want tuh laugh and play."

By this time, the wider meaning of the novel has begun to emerge. A dramatic tension has arisen between the sound business instincts of Janie's two husbands and her own striving toward a full life, which is later to take on flesh in the person of Tea-Cake. At first glance, what seems to be taking shape in the dramatic structure of the novel is the familiar cultural dualism of the Negro Renaissance. Although this Renaissance pattern is definitely present, Miss Hurston pitches her theme in a higher key. Janie rejects the Nanny-Killicks-Jody way of life because of its cramped quarters and narrow gauge: "Nanny belonged to that other kind that loved to deal in scraps." It is Janie's urge to touch the horizon which causes her to repudiate respectability.

Meanwhile, Janie's second marriage moves toward a culmination in Jody's illness and death. For many years their relationship has been purely perfunctory: "The spirit of the marriage left the bedroom and took to living in the parlor." Only on his deathbed does Janie confront her husband with the bitter knowledge of an inner life which she has been unable to share with him: "You done lived wid me for twenty years and you don't half know me atall." Taking stock after Jody's death, Janie senses in this repressed phase of her life an unconscious preparation for her great adventure: "She was saving up feelings for some man she had never seen."

If the first half of the novel deals with the prose of Janie's life, the latter half deals with its poetry. Not long after Jody's death, Tea-Cake walks into her life. First off, he laughs; next he teaches her how to play checkers. One afternoon he urges her to close up shop and come with him to a baseball game. The next night, after midnight, he invites her on a fishing expedition. Their relationship is full of play, of impulsiveness, of informality, and of imagination. Easy-going, careless of money, living for the moment, Tea-Cake is an incarnation of the folk culture. After a whirlwind courtship, he persuades Janie to leave Eatonville and to try his way.

On a deeper level, Tea-Cake represents intensity and experience. As Janie puts it in summing up her two years with him: "Ah been a delegate to de big 'ssociation of life." Their new life begins with a trip to Jacksonville, "and to a lot of things she wanted to see and know." In the big city, Tea-Cake deserts Janie for several days, while she suffers the torments and anxieties of a middle-aged lover. Upon his return she learns that he had won a large sum in a crap game and had immediately given a barbecue for his friends, in order to find out how it feels to be rich. When she protests at being left out, he asks with amusement, "So you aims tuh partake wid everything, hunh?" From that moment, their life together becomes an unlimited partnership.

From Jacksonville, Janie and Tea-Cake move "down on the muck" of the Florida Everglades for the bean-picking season. Janie goes to work in the fields in order to be with Tea-Cake during the long working day. They share the hard work and the hard play of the folk, laughing together at the "dickty" Negroes who think that "us oughta class off." In this milieu of primitive Bahaman dances, of "blues made and used right on the spot," and of "romping and playing . . . behind the boss's back," Janie at last finds happiness. In true Renaissance spirit, it is the folk culture, through Tea-Cake, which provides the means of her spiritual fulfillment.

One night, "the palm and banana trees began that long-distance talk with rain." As the winds over Lake Okechobee mount to hurricane force, the novel moves to a swift climax. Janie and Tea-Cake find themselves swept along with a crowd of refugees, amid awesome scenes of destruction and sudden death. In the midst of their nightmarish flight, Tea-Cake is bitten by a dog and unknowingly contracts rabies. Some weeks later, suffering horribly, he loses his senses and attacks Janie when she refuses him a drink of water. In the ensuing melee, Janie is compelled to shoot Tea-Cake to protect her own life. "It was the meanest moment of eternity." Not merely that her lover dies, but that she herself is the instrument—this is the price which Janie pays for her brief months of happiness. Her trial and acquittal seem unreal to her; without Tea-Cake she can only return to Eatonville to "live by comparisons."

As the reader tries to assimilate Janie's experience and assess its central meaning, he cannot avoid returning to a key passage which foreshadows the climax of the novel: "All gods dispense suffering without reason. Otherwise they would not be worshipped. Through indiscriminate suffering men know fear, and fear is the most divine emotion. It is the stones for altars and the beginning of wisdom. Half gods are worshipped in wine and flowers. Real gods require blood" (p. 215). Through Tea-Cake's death, Janie experiences the divine emotion, for her highest dream—to return to the opening paragraph of the novel—has been "mocked to death by Time." Like all men, she can only watch in resignation, with an overpowering sense of her own helplessness.

Yet if mankind's highest dreams are ultimately unattainable, it is still better to live on the far horizon than to grub around on shore. Janie does not regret her life with Tea-Cake, or the price which is exacted in the end: "We been tuhgether round two years. If you kin see de light at daybreak, you don't keer if you die at dusk. It's so many people never seen de light at all. Ah wuz fumblin' round and God opened de door" (p. 236). As the novel closes, the scene returns to Janie and her friend in Eatonville. Pheoby's reaction to the story she has heard is a clinching statement of the theme of the novel: "Ah done growed ten feet higher from jus' listenin tuh you, Janie. Ah ain't satisfied with mahself no mo'."

DARWIN T. TURNER

Frank Yerby

as

Debunker

As Darwin T. Turner indicates, Frank Yerby (1916–   ) has long been a puzzle to students of the American novel. A graduate of Paine College in Augusta, Georgia, Yerby took an M.A. at Fisk and did graduate work at the University of Chicago. He taught English at Florida A & M and at Southern University, quitting the latter school to take an assembly-line job at a wartime Ford plant in Detroit. His writing during his early years was in the protest tradition and dealt exclusively with the black experience; his short story, "Health Car," an account of racial injustice perpetrated by military police, won the O. Henry Memorial Award in 1944.

With the publication of *The Foxes of Harrow* in 1946, Yerby gave his talents to the writing of "costume novels," escapist romances designed to appeal to public tastes which seldom mention racial issues at all. Immensely popular, these novels have permitted him to live in Europe in comfortable circumstances. This European life style, his admitted willingness to court the middle-class housewife mentality, and his reluctance to lend his pen to the black revolution in the United States have all brought him severe reproach, and Yerby's own statements have encouraged censure from both literary and social critics. He once told a New York *Times* columnist that the novelist has no right to inflict on the public his private ideas on politics, religion, or race; at another time he suggested that the novelist's concern should be what interests his readers; at still another, he rhetorically asked an interviewer what some novelists would write about when the biological accident of a man's color became unimportant.

With this knowledge, it is fascinating to discover that the normal Yerby novel often contains a covert element of protest. It suggests either that Yerby has been fooling his public, or that he is not certain himself of his fictional purpose. At the very least, Darwin T. Turner's essay indicates the importance of the popular novel as a revelation of submerged social and authorial psychology and reminds us that there is usually more to popular literature—even to the costume novels of Frank Yerby—than most critics are willing to admit.

DARWIN T. TURNER

Frank Yerby as Debunker

SCHOLARS NO LONGER READ FRANK YERBY. OR IF THEY DO, THEY REFUSE to admit the fact publicly. They have reason to ignore him, for he has refused to fit comfortably into any of the cherished stereotypes.

They tried him first as a symbol. Within two years after he flared to fame with a best seller, *Foxes of Harrow* (1946), a Negro critic boasted that Yerby had demonstrated the Negro writer's ability to free himself from "the shackles of race."[1] But Yerby did not prove effective as a symbol. He refused to plead for the race; he abandoned America without shrieking that bigotry had exiled him from home; he earned a fortune writing books, and spent his time racing sportscars and lolling on beaches. So corpulent an achiever of the American dream can never personify the Negro intellectual, for the charm of the symbol is its aura of failure.

For the same reason, champions of the oppressed could not plead his cause, for he seemed to have none. They could not denounce publishers who rejected his works; obviously, Dial Press impatiently awaited his annual manuscript. They could not castigate an unenlightened public for denying him a hearing; sales figures proved that more readers bought his books than bought those of William Faulkner.

The university critics could not use him. Who looks for myths, archetypes, ironies, absurdism, existentialism, or complicated personae in a writer so transparent that ordinary people read him voluntarily? And why read a writer whom everyone can understand? It was better to dismiss him quickly as a "prince of pulpsters," who would not be considered seriously if he were not Negro.[2] Perhaps, if ignored, he, like television, might go away.

Surely, however, a novelist who has produced twenty books, most of them best sellers, in twenty years deserves at least cursory examination, if for no reason but that he is the first to prove that a Negro American can write fiction which consistently sells well.

Yerby's plot construction reveals artistic weakness. Despite his skillful tangling and untangling of exciting narratives which mesmerize even many sophisticated readers, Yerby too often depends on contrived endings. Even more dangerously for a spinner of thrillers, he frequently

---

[1] Hugh Gloster, "The Significance of Frank Yerby," *The Crisis*, IV (1948), 13.
[2] Robert Bone, *The Negro Novel in America* (New Haven, 1958), pp. 167-168.

Reprinted from *The Massachusetts Review*, IX, No. 3 (Summer 1968), 569-77, by permission of the publisher and the author. Copyright © 1968 by *The Massachusetts Review*, Inc.

snarls his plots with digressive essays on customs, language, philosophy, and history.

Such strengths and weaknesses are the trademark of an entertainer. Possessing only these, Yerby probably would deserve a place in the company of James Fenimore Cooper and Alexandre Dumas, père, of the past, and Erle Stanley Gardner and Ian Fleming of the present. Surprisingly, however, Yerby's costume novels exhibit another dimension, disregarded by the readers who lament his failure to write an historical novel and by the others who condemn his refusal to write an overtly polemical treatise on the plight of the American Negro. Ideas—bitter ironies, caustic debunkings, painful gropings for meaning—writhe behind the soap-opera facade of his fiction.

Significantly, Frank Yerby, a Georgia-born Negro exile from America, has concentrated on the theme of the outcast who, as in existentialist literature, pits his will against a hostile universe. By intelligence and courage, he proves himself superior to a society which rejects him becaue of his alien, inferior, or illegitimate birth. After he has carved his niche, he secures himself there, or tries to secure himself, by marrying someone of the dominant culture. Class and national hatreds disappear within these marital unions.

But Yerby discounts the possible amalgamation of certain groups. Regardless of talent, beauty, or wealth, the quadroons of Louisiana remain outcasts (*The Foxes of Harrow;* and *Captain Rebel,* 1956). Beautiful Mexican Belen bears Roak Garfield's son but cannot marry him (*The Garfield Honor,* 1961). Dr. Mose Johnson, a Negro, risks lynching because he dared to attempt to save a white child's life (*The Serpent and the Staff,* 1958). Zenobia, a slave girl, comforts Pietro, but he returns to his noblewomen (*The Saracen Blade,* 1953). If, apparently, Frank Yerby sees intermarriage and amalgamation as the ultimate solution to all animosities, but recognizes that some societies prohibit that solution, there is little reason to wonder why he taints his tales with the somber hint that man's life is a joke played by a merciless and senile deity.

Furthermore, despite his avowed respect for his readers' prejudices, Yerby repeatedly has violated his own dictum that a writer should neither preach nor instruct. Driven by emotions which inspired him to write fiction of social protest in his early years, Frank Yerby now writes anti-romantic, existentialist melodrama which is frequently as satirical as Voltaire's *Candide.*

In typical romances the hero, after perilous adventures, wins the virgin and lives happily ever after. Yerby, however, doubts the "one man-one woman" romantic myth upon which such stories depend.

Therefore, his hero, after Herculean struggles, often wins only a stained Cunegonde.

Contrary to the pattern of conventional romance, disaster does not merely threaten, it happens—and to the best people. Stephen Fox's lovely ex-mistress Desiree is raped by his son. Fancy Williamson has no choice but to continue to live with her husband even though she knows his infidelity. Kit Gerardo fails to avenge either the betrayal which ended his mother's life or the rape which soiled his sweetheart's virginity. Jean-Paul Marin repeatedly is betrayed and humiliated by the woman he loves and to whom he repeatedly returns. His next sweetheart is raped by fifteen soldiers. His pretty face is scarred grotesquely when he is slashed with a chain. James Jarrett's first sweetheart becomes pregnant after she has been seduced by her obscene and repulsive stepfather, who, after cheating and killing her father, had taken her mother as mistress. Determined to have a son, Jarrett hires a concubine, who later deserts him. Roak Garfield's mortal enemy marries Belen, the only woman Roak loves; by rearing Belen's child as his own, he prevents Roak's learning of the existence of the son he wants. Having neither love nor a son, Roak has sought pleasure in horseback riding; but an accident cripples him so badly that he can no longer ride.

Yerby inflicts such severe physical and mental tortures upon his protagonists that a thoughtful reader searches for a reason. Although Yerby may have wished merely to gratify his American readers' avidity for sadism or to imitate the bloody, tragic incidents abundant in the dramas of Shakespeare, whom he admired and frequently quoted, another possibility must be considered—that Frank Yerby, who now admits that discrimination compelled his exile, has avenged himself vicariously by punishing his American protagonists who, unrestricted by skin color, can attain the status denied to him.

Although such an explanation does not account for the sufferings of Pietro Donati, a Sicilian, or Marin, a Frenchman, significantly, in the novels between 1946 and 1958, only one American protagonist enjoys untainted happiness at the conclusion of the story. That one, Duncan Childers, appeared in 1958 in a novel which Yerby dedicated to his second wife, Blanquita, perhaps as a testament to her easing of a tension and a bitterness which he had sought to purge through his writings.

The other American protagonists suffer such miserable ends that few readers can envy the materialistic successes which precede.

True, the American protagonists suffer less disastrously after 1958, but no wise mortal would volunteer to live one of the roles. A Tory in Georgia, James Jarrett (*Jarrett's Jade,* 1959) dies fighting against

American patriots, who have recruited his son. Crippled Roak Garfield lives with neither love nor a son. Paris Griffin of Mississippi remembers the rape and massacre of his older brother's family, the murder of his younger brother, and his murdered wife's adultery (*Griffin's Way*, 1962). Only Michael Ames (*Gillian*, 1960) enjoys wealth and happy marriage, but he, like Childers, is an educated man and a scientist.

In addition to maintaining his own disbelief by creating anti-romantic stories, Frank Yerby teaches more than a careless reader would suspect. Although he has alleged that Dial Press excises 99 and 99/100 percent of his history,[3] he has debunked historical myths relentlessly. Perhaps this crusade eventually will be considered Yerby's major contribution to American culture. For most people do not derive their history from scholars. Instead, they accept, believe, and repeat the myths transmitted orally from generation to generation or the interpretations gathered from popular literature. Yerby has provided many to remember. One wishes that all were accurate.

Chiefly, of course, he has attacked America, in particular the South. Until recent years this section of America has received literary glorification as a region of culture and gentility. The males reputedly were aristocratic, cultured, brave, and honorable. The females were gentle and chaste. Savagely, Yerby has ridiculed these myths.

The South, he has pointed out, was founded by adventurers, outcasts, and failures who migrated to America because they had nothing to lose; the actual aristocrats, having nothing to gain by emigration, remained on the continent. By exploiting people and the land, these immigrants amassed fortunes. Accustomed only to indolence and luxury, their children and grandchildren created the legends about aristocratic heritage.

Second-generation Americans, Yerby has shown, did not resemble the idealized stereotypes of the myth. Educated in the North, which housed the only worthwhile non-military schools, young gentlemen, like Etienne Fox, learned to drink, gamble, and wench while they were receiving "the gentleman's C." Returning to the South, they hunted and entertained; they read books infrequently and speculated philosophically even less frequently. Occasionally, they illogically assumed that they could defend their honor by shooting straight. Socially, their sisters towered above Fancy Williamson of the Carolina hills or Laurie

---

[3] Yerby has protested against the editorial interference. Recently, Yerby has argued that *An Odor of Sanctity* (1965) would have been great if Dial "had had the guts to publish that novel the way I wrote it." (In an interview by Hoyt Fuller—"Famous Writer Faces a Challenge," *Ebony*, xxi (June, 1966), p. 193.)

Griffin of Mississippi peasantry, but morally they were equal. While being raped by James Jarrett, Mary Knox of Georgian aristocracy realizes that she is enjoying herself. Impoverished Cecile Fox of Louisiana buys medical supplies with her body, her only barterable resource. Louisiana-born socialite, Susan Drake, a married woman, shamelessly pursues the man she loves.

Yerby has charged that even the houses and towns have been idealized in the myth. Instead of being tastefully appointed, Neo-Grecian mansions, houses of the early planters were rambling frame structures in yards littered with farm implements and livestock. Later houses often were architectural monstrosities (*Floodtide*, 1950). Supposedly the cultural mecca of the ante-bellum South, New Orleans was a pigsty ravaged by disease and exploited by corrupt governments.

Unlike a typical propagandist, however, Yerby has not restricted his attack to one group. He has also castigated Americans above the Mason-Dixon line. In *Floodtide*, Morgan Brittany, a Northern emigrant, mouths platitudinous protests against slavery; soon, however, she gratifies her perverted lusts by beating her chained slaves. Most of the sadistic overseers, Yerby has alleged, were reared in the North. New Yorkers evidenced their bigotry when they slaughtered Negroes whom they blamed for the North's involvement in the Civil War. Northern businessmen exploited white laborers as shamefully as Southern planters had exploited slaves (*Pride's Castle*, 1949). During Reconstruction, carpetbaggers from the North ignobly amassed fortunes by preying upon the conquered people. (*The Vixens*, 1947).

Yerby has not spared Negroes. Depicting cringing slaves who fawn upon their masters and betray their fellows, he has argued that the American slaves rarely rebelled because the traders wisely selected them predominantly from tribes made docile by centuries of bondage in Africa. In contrast, the slaves of Haiti, carelessly selected from proud and warlike tribes, overthrew their French masters.[4] Furthermore, having been restricted to childlike existence devoid of formal education, dignity, or opportunity to assume responsibility for their welfare, American slaves, when freed suddenly, could not govern themselves. Few, consequently, proved capable of governing wisely in the Southern legislatures.

Regardless of their wealth or talent, free Southern Negroes, he has argued, were excluded from society, denied dignity, and robbed even

---

[4] See *The Foxes of Harrow*. Zora Neale Hurston, in *Tell My Horse*, explained differently. Because Africans, she reported, killed their princes rather than sell them into bondage, all American Negroes were commoners devoid of the nobler characteristics of those who remained on the African continent. The arguments of Miss Hurston and Mr. Yerby are more persuasive than factual.

of the power to protect their women—those who acted like men were shot *(The Foxes of Harrow)*. Yet, unwilling to identify themselves with slaves, they often compensated for their own humiliation by abusing darker-skinned Negroes *(Captain Rebel)*. Educated Northern Negroes doubted the educability of Southern Negroes and sometimes adjudged themselves inferior to less-educated white men *(Griffin's Way)*.

Relentlessly condemning the senselessness of war, Yerby has exploded many myths which glorify heroes and causes. The colonists, he has alleged, did not arise with a universal shout to carry the banner of freedom against the cannons of tyranny. Many colonists fought with the British; others used the war as a pretext for rape and looting *(Jarrett's Jade,* 1959, and *The Bride of Liberty,* 1954).

American invaders of Mexico were not avengers of gallant Texans but butchers deluded into war by cunning Southern legislators who hoped to annex new slave territories so that pro-slavery Congressmen would outnumber anti-slavery Congressmen *(Benton's Row,* 1954). The South did not fight the Civil War to preserve a way of life enjoyed by one-half of the nation, for only four percent of the families in the South owned as many as ten slaves *(The Foxes of Harrow)*. Actually, the war began because wealthy plantation owners mistakenly believed that the North would not fight or would perish without agricultural imports from the South *(Captain Rebel)*. Southern soldiers did not always prove to be gallant lads in gray. Frightened Southerners deserted; unscrupulous Southerners pillaged; uniforms, except among the officers, were butternut brown. And it did not matter whether one Southern soldier could equal three Northern soldiers; for every Southern soldier, the North had five, each armed with ten times the firepower of a Southern soldier. The North did not win the war because God approved a just cause. It won because Lincoln finally found a general willing to send wave after wave of numerically superior forces against Lee until the Southern force was depleted *(The Foxes of Harrow, The Vixens,* and *Captain Rebel)*.

Reconstruction, Yerby has suggested was a farce. By passing "black codes" intended to re-establish slavery, the South provoked Northern Congressmen into establishing military control, which, in turn, supported new Southern legislatures dominated by ignorant Negroes and by unscrupulous scalawags and carpetbaggers. Instead of a single group of high-minded aristocrats united to safeguard the chastity of their women and to free their land from despotic ex-slaves, the Klans comprised men of all classes, who intimidated or tortured anyone whom they disliked *(Griffin's Way)*. In 1898, Americans did not fight to rid the Western Hemisphere of Spanish tyranny. The Spanish-American War merely climaxed a half-century of agitation by Southerners anxious for more slave-holding territory *(Floodtide)*.

Turning from America, Yerby has debunked myths of other lands. A currently popular idea, best described in Charles Silberman's *Crisis in Black and White*, attributes the ignominious position of the American Negro to Anglo-Saxon inexperience with slavery. Briefly, the thesis is that Spaniards and Frenchmen, accustomed to temporary slavery, attached no shame to the condition. Unfamiliar with it, the Anglo-Saxons justified it by arguing the natural inferiority and the predestined enslavement of Negroes. In rebuttal, Yerby has revealed that the Spanish massacred their slaves *(The Golden Hawk,* 1948, and *Floodtide)*.

Crusaders did not preserve the faith of the Prince of Peace. One crusade was directed against a group of people who sinned only by refusing to be either Catholic or warlike. Another crusade provided a pretext for ravaging wealthy Christians. A third resulted in the massacre and enslavement of numbers of youths *(An Odor of Sanctity)*.

Yerby is no misanthrope; he has heroes: Thomas Jefferson, who freed his slaves; George Washington, who led American revolutionists heroically despite his incompetence as a military tactician; Henri Christophe, who helped free Haiti from French authority. Moreover, Yerby has struggled to evolve a positive philosophy. Significantly, he has repudiated the patient goodness frequently held before Negroes as a desirable standard. Yerby persists in showing that men succeed and are extolled because they are smarter, stronger, bolder, and braver than other men. Sometimes, they act morally and honorably; more often they do not. But neither their contemporaries nor their descendants evaluate the morality of the successful, the heroes. The minority groups in Yerby's stories suffer because they are ignorant, weak, and cowardly. Foolishly, they beg for help from a deity, which, according to Yerby, if it exists, views mankind hostilely, indifferently, or contemptuously. Life has meaning only when man—frail and insignificant —sparkles as brightly as possible in his instant of eternity.

After twenty years of best-sellers, Frank Yerby has not improved significantly as a craftsman. He mars exciting plots with contrived endings and digressive essays. He stereotypes heroes and heroines. He reveals verbal facility in exposition and description but astonishing ineptness in dialogue. He may use historical materials convincingly, or he may direct undue attention to his research. Despite his artistic weaknesses, however, Frank Yerby deserves to rank at least with Alexandre Dumas père, Sir Walter Scott, and James Fenimore Cooper as a romancer. Possibly, his delightful burlesque and his satire of historical personages, customs, and events place him a level or two higher, at least for the twentieth-century reader.

Rumblings, however, indicate that Frank Yerby does not wish to be identified with such company. Recently, he has stated that, after he finishes *Goat Song*, his current recipe-product, he intends to write "the most ambitious novel" of his career. Centering his attention on Yeshu'a, Yerby will explore "the relationship of man to the quality of evil in this world."[5] Yerby believes he will succeed: "I am going to put into it everything I know about writing, which, by now is a considerable amount."[6] Others are not as optimistic. In a very perceptive profile of Yerby, Hoyt Fuller has commented:

> It is quite a challenge for a writer whose career has been built on the facile rendering of fantasy and romance, and it may be a greater challenge than the author suspects. The shifting of creative gears from the merely entertaining to the profoundly serious could be as difficult for Yerby as surely it would be for a writer like, say, James Baldwin to accomplish the exact reverse. The working habits and perspectives of a lifetime are involved in such a move, and such habits and viewpoints are not, ordinarily, so easily changed.[7]

Skepticism is justifiable because Yerby seems oblivious to the actual reasons for his literary reputation. He believes that critics automatically dismiss his novels as mere entertainment because of the melodrama and formula writing which he candidly admits providing. He blames his publishers for excising his historical material and for demanding more sex. He implies that, if he publishes the next novel under a pseudonym so that critics will evaluate it objectively and if Dial Press publishes everything that he writes, his next work will be acclaimed a masterpiece. But neither critics nor editors have contributed to his weaknesses in language or in plot structure. Furthermore, it is doubtful that Yerby will improve his work significantly merely by developing a serious theme. He has written profound passages in many works; and, in *An Odor of Sanctity*, he concerned himself with a serious issue. He has not yet demonstrated, however, that he can make a significant theme emerge credibly from the interaction of characters. Unless he does this, the philosophy will stand out as incongruously and as absurdly as a candle on a fallen cake.

It is to be hoped that, questing for the Grail of significance, Yerby will not tarnish his golden luster as an entertaining debunker of historical myths.

---

[5] Fuller, *op. cit.*, p. 193.
[6] *Ibid.*
[7] *Ibid.*

NATHAN A. SCOTT, JR.

The Dark

and

Haunted Tower

of

Richard Wright

RICHARD WRIGHT (1908-1960) WAS THE FIRST BLACK AMERICAN NOVELIST to write a "best seller" in the classic sense. *Native Son,* published in 1940, almost immediately went into a second edition, became a Book of the Month Club selection, and subsequently has sold over a million copies. This success brought Wright money and fame but did little to ease his life as an Afro-American. Still the subject of white discrimination, he exiled himself in 1947 and lived in France until his death.

Wright's fiction consistently presents an angry, apocalyptic warning: mutual protection and common purpose are impossible in the United States so long as we deny each other humanity; so long as Bigger Thomases or Cross Damons (the respective heroes of *Native Son* and *The Outsider*) are created, the forces of chaos are immediate and certain. The usual Wright protagonist is driven, sometimes blindly, to acts of rebellion in order to assert his freedom. The victim of an environment intent on destroying him, he strikes out in affirmation of selfhood, angrily questing for a more meaningful existence than white America is willing to grant. As a result, Richard Wright perhaps most clearly defines the violence inherent in the black condition in white America.

Wright gave particular expression to the violence which shaped his own life in a famous autobiography, *Black Boy* (1945). Born and raised in Mississippi, Wright fled the South for Chicago in the 1920's and became a postal worker, insurance collector, struggling writer and Communist Party member. He later repudiated the party for much the same reason that he spent a lifetime of writing protesting the existence forced upon black Americans: he believed that limitations on individual freedom were humanly and politically self-destructive.

Nathan A. Scott, Jr. is Professor of Theology and Literature in the Divinity School of the University of Chicago and also holds a professorship in the University's English Department. Dr. Scott is a priest of the Episcopal Church and serves as Canon Theologian of the Cathedral of St. James in Chicago. He is also a Fellow of the School of Letters of Indiana University. His most recent books are *Negative Capability: Studies in the New Literature and the Religious Situation* (Yale University Press, 1969) and *The Unquiet Vision: Mirrors of Man in Existentialism* (World, 1969). His previous books include *Modern Literature and the Religious Frontier* (1958), *Albert Camus* (1962), *Samuel Beckett* (1965), *The Broken Center: Studies in the Theological Horizon of Modern Literature* (1966), and *Craters of the Spirit: Studies in the Modern Novel* (1968).

NATHAN A. SCOTT, JR.

The Dark and Haunted Tower of Richard Wright

THE EXISTENTIALIST OVERTONES AND THE EXPLICIT ALLUSIONS TO NIETZ-sche and Heidegger in *The Outsider* led some of the reviewers of his book of 1953 to conclude that Richard Wright was misguidedly experimenting with intellectual traditions outside his actual experience and that he had taken a wrong turning. This was a judgment, however, which surely had to require as its basic premise something like the rather incomprehensible *mystique* about the Negro intellectual which is occasionally invoked by fools and professional obscurantists, that he is somehow ancestrally fated to exclusion from the general Atlantic community of cultural exchange simply because his racial identity does itself, in some ineffable way, consign him to a permanent ghetto of the mind. But, if this *mystique* is abandoned as the nonsense that it really is, there should have been no occasion for surprise at the expression which *The Outsider* provided of the extent to which Mr. Wright, after several years of residence in France, had been influenced by the secular modes of European existentialism. For here is a philosophical movement which has found its basic subject matter not so much in the history of philosophy as in the crises and distempers of human existence in the twentieth century. The fundamental reality about which it has very often wanted to speak is that of "the extreme situation"—the situation, that is, in which man's essential dignity is radically challenged by an unconscionable subversion of justice and an intolerable distance between master and slave. And this is precisely the reality that stirred Mr. Wright's imagination into life—from the time of his first forays into the literary life, under the sponsorship of the Communist Party, while still a Chicago postal employee in the 'thirties, up to the time of his sudden death in Paris in November of 1960.

So there was nothing at all unnatural in this American Negro writer having responded affirmatively to the *Angst*-ridden accents and idioms of Jean-Paul Sartre and Georges Bataille and Maurice Blanchot. For, among those Negro intellectuals of his time whose gift of expression enabled them to have a "voice," it may well be that there was none for whom the reality of their "extreme situation" constituted so great a burden. The social statisticians today are busy, of course, in their notations of the steadily increasing improvement in what they call "race relations," and it is probably the case that the moral quality of

Reprinted from *Black Expression,* ed. Addison Gayle, Jr. (New York: Weybright and Talley, 1969), pp. 296-311, by permission of the author and publisher. Copyright © 1969 by Weybright and Talley, Inc.

our life is, in this dimension, something less of an embarrassment than it was a decade or so ago. But the tokens of acceptance that the Negro has won here and there are not yet so great as to make it impossible for others to imagine that he, when he is sensitive and discerning, still feels his status to be precarious and undecided. He has only to contemplate the bitter intransigence of the South and the subtle but firmly maintained exclusions of the North to be reminded of how meagre and insubstantial is the new ground that he has recently gained. Though it is only in the occasional pockets of Southern depravity that he is still exposed to the nakeder forms of violence and intimidation, he knows that the actuality of the American experience continues to involve for him that most unhinging kind of frustration which is a result of the glitter and promise of life in a great country being near enough for the mind to be dazzled by the sense of their availability, and yet far enough away to exact a sense of defeat more exacerbating than anything a slave could possibly feel. When this bitter irony is explored by a radical imagination, the nature of the human material is surely such as will permit its being seized by way of the image of Tantalus: for all of the bland notations of achieved progress that may be offered by the social scientist, there is still an *agonia* here whose gall partakes of the "extreme situation"—and this was the perspective by which Richard Wright was consistently guided in all his efforts to shape the story of the American Negro into something whose tragic sorrow might quicken the conscience of our time.

Though he had numerous minor predecessors, Mr. Wright was the first American Negro writer of large ambitions to win a major reputation in our literary life. *Uncle Tom's Children,* his first collection of stories, achieved a limited currency in the late 'thirties among readers of leftist social sympathies, but it was not until *Native Son* burst upon the scene in 1940 that he won access to the kind of forum that Sunday Supplement reviewers and a national book club could give. Within a month after its publication tens of thousands of copies were moving across book dealers' counters all over the land; it frequently was being said that nothing so comparable to the great tragic fictions of Dostoievski had yet appeared in our literature; and hordes of Mr. Wright's readers were enjoying that great thrilling shiver of delight that the intellectual middle class in this country during the 'thirties had come to find in what Eric Bentley has called "the fun-world of proletarian legend," particularly when the fun involved the tabooed exoticism of the Negro. The very simplicity and violence of the novel's didacticism did, in a way, permit many people to envisage themselves as in league with Mr. Wright and with Christ in the harrowing of a Hell full of all the forces of reaction and illiberality; and, in this way perhaps, the illusion grew that *Native Son*, by itself and quite suddenly, had very greatly enlarged and deepened our imaginative understanding of a whole dimension of American experience.

This was, however, an illusion, and when one reads today the story of Bigger Thomas, one cannot but be struck by how little the novel gives us of the bite and flavor either of social actuality or of the particular kind of human individual of whom Bigger is offered as an *exemplum.* To read such a book, for example, as Ralph Ellison's brilliant novel of 1953, *Invisible Man,* is to find, among one's richest satisfactions, the sense of immersion in all the concrete materialities of Negro life. One hears the very buzz and hum of Harlem in the racy, pungent speech of his West Indians and his native hipsters, and all the *grotesquerie* in his opening account of the dreary little backwater of a remote Southern Negro college has in it a certain kind of empirically absolute rightness. Indeed, the book is packed full of the acutest observations of the manners and idioms and human styles that comprise the ethos of Negro life in the American metropolis; and it gives us such a sense of social fact as can be come by nowhere in the stiffly pedantic manuals of academic sociology.

But, at its center, *Native Son* exhibits nothing other than a socially discarnate and demoniac wrath. In the moments before her "little death," the Negrophile Joanna Burden in *Light in August* cries out to her Negro lover Joe Christmas, "Negro, Negro," as if, in the instant of sexual transport, his human particularity were of no account; and, in the same novel, a lynch mob, Faulkner tells us, "believed aloud that it was an anonymous Negro crime committed not by a Negro but by Negro. . . ." And this is the character whom we find to be the protagonist of Richard Wright's novel of 1940—called, yes, for the sake of the novelistic convention, Bigger Thomas, but really Negro, *Negro.* Thus it is that, for all of the anger the novel directs at the moral imagination that has been poisoned by racism, its own pathos is, finally, a consequence of the degree to which it is overwhelmed by the cancer it wants to cauterize. From the moment, on its first page, when Bigger is awakened by the *Brrriiiinnng!* of his alarm clock, until his "faint, wry, bitter smile" of farewell at Mr. Max on the final page, the novel is controlled by precisely those hopeless assumptions about Negro life which elicited its rage, and its protagonist's sense of his own identity is formed by just that image of himself which, as it lives in the larger culture, has caused his despair. So, in its entirety, the novel moves wholly within the envenomed abstractions of racial myth.

In one of the stories in *Uncle Tom's Children,* "Long Black Song," the husband of a Negro woman who has been seduced by a white salesman says: "The white folks ain never gimme a chance! They ain

never give no black man a chance! There ain nothing in yo whole life
yuh kin keep from em! . . . Ahm gonna be hard like they is! So hep me
Gawd, Ahm gonna be *hard!* When they come fer me Ahm gonna *be*
here!" Not only is this the posture of all but one of his protagonists in
the stories that make up his first collection, it is also the posture of the
young Chicago Negro whose story Mr. Wright tells in *Native Son.* He,
too, is one who intends to "be hard"; indeed, as he says, "Every time I
think about it I feel like somebody's poking a red-hot iron down my
throat." So it is with a sullen suspiciousness that he faces the Chicago
philanthropist who takes him off the relief rolls by hiring him as a
chauffeur. And it is with an even greater scepticism that he views his
employer's daughter and her Communist sweetheart who make gestures of fraternity toward him by inviting him to join them in a café as
an equal. But this is a relation that never becomes genuinely complicated, for, at the end of their first evening together, the girl is so
intoxicated that Bigger, having been entrusted with seeing her home,
has to carry her bodily from the family automobile to her bedroom—
into which her blind mother comes suddenly, just in the moment when
he is contemplating taking Mary sexually. And, in order to prevent the
mother's knowing that he and Mary are in the room, he smothers the
girl and then, in his panic, stuffs her body into the furnace. This, in
turn, leads eventually to his second crime, against his mistress Bessie,
to whom he confesses the first deed and whom he must finally remove
to prevent her betraying him to the police. But he cannot ultimately
avoid his nemesis and is at last captured on a South Side tenement
rooftop, as a raging mob clamors for his life in the street below.

Now the engine that Mr. Wright desperately relied upon to whip
this lurid fairy-tale into some semblance of probability was the court-
room defense of Bigger by his Jewish lawyer, Mr. Max. And here is
what we are told, that Bigger

> . . . murdered Mary Dalton accidentally, without thinking, without
> plan, without conscious motive. But, after he murdered, he accepted
> the crime. And that's the important thing. It was the first full act of
> his life; it was the most meaningful, exciting and stirring thing that
> had ever happened to him. He accepted it because it made him
> free, gave him the possibility of choice, of action, the opportunity
> to act and to feel that his actions carried weight. . . .
>
> Let me tell you more. Before this trial the newspapers and the
> prosecution said that this boy had committed other crimes. It is
> true. He is guilty of numerous crimes. But search until the day of
> judgment, and you will find not one shred of evidence of them. He
> has murdered many times, but there are no corpses. Let me explain.
> This Negro boy's entire attitude toward life is a *crime!* The hate and
> fear which we have inspired in him, woven by our civilization into

the very structure of his consciousness, into his blood and bones, into the hourly functioning of his personality, have become the justification of his existence.

Every time he comes in contact with us, he kills! It is a physiological and psychological reaction, embedded in his being. Every thought he thinks is potential murder. . . . Every desire, every dream, no matter how intimate or personal, is a plot or a conspiracy. Every hope is a plan for insurrection. Every glance of the eye is a threat. *His very existence is a crime. . . .*

And, what is more, we are told that we have only to "multiply Bigger Thomas twelve million times, allowing for environmental and temperamental variations, and for those Negroes who are completely under the influence of the church, and you have the psychology of the Negro people."

Thus it is, I say, that the novel is, paradoxically, controlled by precisely the assumptions about Negro life that elicited its rage, for the astonishing thing that it finally does is to offer a depraved and inhuman beast as the comprehensive archetypal image of the American Negro.

The imagination that we meet here, in other words, is extremist and melodramatic, feeding on the horrific themes of alienation and violence and abysmal fear, and its single occupation is with the racial tragedy. But all the great ones have had what was two hundred years ago called a "ruling passion," and it does indeed seem to be very much a part of the kind of brilliance and assertiveness that we associate with major art. That Mr. Wright should have had his ruling passion is not, therefore, something that we shall hold against him; what was unfortunate in him was his utter defenselessness before it. And here I mean that, despite his cursory tutelage under European existentialism in the late 'forties and 'fifties and despite the attention which he gave to the literature of modern psychology and social science, he never won such a point of purchase in the realm of systematic ideas as might have afforded his mind some protection against the deracinative force of the tragic encounters which it had had with the world. After reading, for example, the heartrendingly poignant story that is told in *Black Boy*, his autobiography of 1945—which is one of the great human testaments in modern American literature—it would surely take an exceedingly sluggish moral imagination for one not to perceive how inevitable it was that this man should bear to his grave the scars of the scalding humiliations that, as a Negro, he was subjected to in his youth in the state of Mississippi. Here, indeed, was a man who knew the insidious day-by-day intimidation, the fear that is in the air, and the atrocious brutality that make up the moral stench of the concentration camp; and, unlike the German Jew under Hitler, he lived this infernal life of the damned and the rejected not just for a few night-marish years that were known to be absurdly discontinuous with the normal state of things, but he lived it as the historic inheritance of his people; this was all that he knew, from infancy until he was old enough to risk the journey of flight from Memphis to Chicago. So we accept the authenticity of the rage and the anger which were the emotions with which he impulsively faced the world. But, when some such extremity as this constitutes his basic situation, whatever the needs of the existing human being, the artist needs to be equipped with some defense against the intensity of his own experience, for, unless he has some means of supporting or controlling it, the great likelihood is that his work will then express not a coherent ordering of human experience in objective form but only the emotional tics of his own incipient hysteria. And it was just some such vantage point as this that might have enabled him to distance himself from his *agonia* and to be re-leased to the sheer labor of composition itself—it was just this that Mr. Wright never managed. In his famous essay on "Technique as Dis-covery," Professor Mark Schorer has, of course, proposed that it is in the dynamism of the creative process itself, and through his wrestling with the medium of his language, that the artist comes by those major insights into the meaning of his experience that enable him to take control of it. But the logic whereby *technique* is assigned so decisive a role in the formation of *vision* is something that still escapes me. So mine, therefore, is the older axiom, that an artist needs to know a very great deal *before* he puts pen to paper; and, if he does not, he may then, I take it, be expected to provide us with some variety of what the late R. P. Blackmur called "the fallacy of expressive form."

Now this was, I believe, at bottom, Mr. Wright's crucial failure: he simply did not *know* enough about the labyrinthine interiorities of the human soul. His own life-experience conditioned him, of course, to keep a lively awareness that (as W. H. Auden says) "Ubiquitous within the bond/Of one impoverishing sky,/Vast spiritual disorders lie." Yet these were not really *spiritual* disorders, since he made no allowance for human existence having anything other than a purely social-historical dimension. In the *New Year Letter* Mr. Auden sug-gests that

> *There are two atlases: the one*
> *The public space where acts are done,*
> *In theory common to us all. . . .*
> *The other is the inner space*
> *Of private ownership, the place*
> *That each of us is forced to own,*
> *Like his own life from which it's grown,*
> *The landscape of his will and need. . . .*

But so obsessed was Mr. Wright with the demonic aberrations that disfigure "the public space" that he lost any deep sense of what wretchedness there is within "the inner space," within what Mr. Auden calls "our parish of immediacy." T. S. Eliot once said of Ezra Pound's *Cantos* that they posit a Hell for other people, not for Mr. Pound or his readers. It might also be said of the books of Richard Wright that, though theirs is a Hell for most of Mr. Wright's readers (who are white), it is not a Hell for Mr. Wright himself and his racial kinsmen; both he and they bear upon themselves the stigmata of its fury, but both he and they are exempted from that which is generally problematic in the human soul, and from which the fury proceeds. The complex relations between the "two atlases" are not explored. And, in this way, it was possible for Mr. Wright to envisage the human community as though it were split into two opposed camps, the one black and the other white. But, in this way, it was never possible for him even to approximate the Baudelairean astringency—"*Hypocrite lecteur,—mon semblable,—mon frère!*"

And it is also this exclusive and simplistic concentration upon the one atlas, "the public space," which enabled Mr. Wright so disastrously to insist upon racial humiliation as the ultimate suffering, the ultimate indignity. And I speak of the disastrousness of it, because, however thumpingly tautologous it may be to assert that evil is evil, whatever its aspect, this is, nevertheless, the fact of the matter; and to assert that some special evil is the ultimate evil, simply because this is that by which one has oneself been most hurtfully victimized, is merely to indulge in a desperate kind of sentimentality. This was, however, the unpromising position that consistently controlled Mr. Wright's way of performing the act of self-definition as an artist, and, for all of the ardor, it is this sentimentality which makes so humanly impertinent a body of writing than which there is none in our time that ought to have greater pertinence to those like ourselves, who are drenched in the particular American experience that gave to Mr. Wright his ruling passion.

In his review of *Native Son* in March of 1940, Malcolm Cowley, having in mind the consistency with which Mr. Wright's executive design, both in the stories of *Uncle Tom's Children* and in his novel, had been a design of violence, suggested that his "sense of the indignities heaped on his race" might well go so deep as to make it his unconscious tendency in his fiction to revenge himself "by a whole series of symbolic murders." And though Mr. Cowley may at this point have been somewhat overstating things, the propensity for violence cannot, it is true, be gainsaid: Mr. Wright may not have been bent on symbolic murder, but at least it can be asserted that he was eager to sound a hue and a cry and had something of a penchant for "holding a loaded pistol at the head of the "white world while he [muttered] between clenched teeth: 'Either you grant us equal rights as human beings or else this is what will happen.' "* But, of course, the unfortunate consequence of his taking this kind of position was that, inevitably, it compelled him to practice a terrible brutalization upon his characters: he had, as in the wronged husband of "Long Black Song," to make them "hard," in order to give dramatic substance to the threat he wanted to utter; and, in thus sweeping them into the raging abysses of violent criminality, he forged an image of *la présence noire* that is in no great way removed from the wild and lickerish nigger who inhabits the demented imagination of the racial paranoiac. For all of the new sophistications that appeared in *The Outsider*, this is as true of his novel of 1953 as it is of his early work of the 'thirties.

Cross Damon is a half-educated intellectual who bears the Negro's ancestral burden of rejection and marginality, but his concern with what is socially problematic in his situation is but one phase of a deeper concern with what is metaphysically problematic in human life. He is a man whose sense of the world has been formed by that tradition of philosophic radicalism that runs from Nietzsche to contemporary existentialists like Heidegger and Sartre, and so he is particularly alert to the religious vacuum which this tradition has asserted to be at the heart of modern experience. He regards the old "myths" as a mischievous and archaistic legacy bequeathed us by the primitive ages of human history in which man,

> naked and afraid, found that only one thing could really quiet his terrors: that is *Untruth*. He . . . was afraid of the clamoring world of storms, volcanoes, and heaving waves, and he wanted to change the world. His myths sought to recast that world, tame it, make it more humanly meaningful and endurable. The more abjectly frightened the nation or race of men, the more their myths and religions projected out upon the world another world in *front* of the real world, or, in another way of speaking, they projected another world *behind* the real world they saw, lived, suffered, and died in. Until today almost all of man's worlds have been either preworlds or backworlds, *never* the real world. . . .

But in this "real world" in which modern man must live today the non-existence of God is not to be argued; it is simply to be taken for granted, and the theistic hypothesis is simply to be understood as "something projected compulsively from men's minds in answer to

---

* Glicksberg, Charles I.: "Negro Fiction in America," *The South Atlantic Quarterly* 45:482 (Oct.) 1946.

their chronic need to be rid of fear, something to meet the obscure needs of daily lives lived amidst strange and threatening facts." And this means, in Cross Damon's analysis of the modern predicament, that the dreadful burden which man must bear today is the burden of freedom, the burden, as he says, of being "nothing in particular," except what man chooses through his actions to become. This is why panic sometimes drapes the world which Cross looks out upon, for what he knows himself to confront is "the empty possibility of action," the necessity of actually making something of himself, and the knowledge that he can do what he damn well pleases on this earth, that everything is permitted, and that he must discover

> good or evil through his own actions, which were more exacting than the edicts of any God because it was he alone who had to bear the brunt of their consequences with a sense of absoluteness made intolerable by knowing that this life was all he had and would ever have. For him there was no grace or mercy if he failed.

He has, in other words, undergone the most expensive denudation that a man can suffer, for to Cross Damon God is dead. And, being thus stripped of that which might alone furnish some objective warrant for the human enterprise, there is nothing else to which he owes any loyalty; he is on his own, a pure *isolé*, and he gives his suffrage to neither family nor tradition nor church nor state; nor does he give it to race. "My hero," said Mr. Wright, "could have been of any race."

When we first meet Cross he is a clerk in a Chicago post office, and his personal life, like that of Sartre's Mathieu in the initial phase of his drama, is in a state of messy disorder. As a result of an early and unsuccessful marriage, he is having to support a wife with whom he no longer lives and three children. And then there is little Dot, his mistress, whom he had supposed to be seventeen years of age but whom he discovers, after the onset of her pregnancy, to be not quite sixteen. Gladys refuses to give him a divorce so that he may marry the girl, and Dot, desperately hoping somehow to trap him into a marriage, intends to seek legal counsel. When Gladys learns of this, she begins to be fearful that Cross may be jailed and that she and the children may be robbed of his support: so she demands that he sign over the house and the car to her. She further demands that he borrow eight hundred dollars from the Postal Union on his salary, so that the titles on both the house and the car may be cleared, and she tells him that, if he refuses, she will go to the police with Dot and assist her in filing charges of rape against him. So Cross has no alternative but to accede to her requests.

But, then, on that fateful night when he is returning home after having just received from the Postal Union the eight hundred dollars which he is to deliver to Gladys on the following morning, he is involved in a subway accident in which it is supposed that he has lost his life, the smashed body of another man being identified as his. This is, of course, Cross' great chance, and he is quick to seize it, for it means an opportunity to gain release from the inauthenticity of his existence, an opportunity to escape all those pledges and promises to his wife and his mother and his mistress "which he had not intended to make and whose implied obligations had been slowly smothering his spirit." By this "stroke of freakish good luck" he is able to "rip the viscous strands" of that "vast web of pledges and promises . . . and fling them behind him." Now, for the first time, this young man feels that his life is determined by a really valid project—namely, that of making something of himself and of giving some vital definition to his human identity.

So he takes a train out of Chicago for New York City, where he quickly becomes involved in a phantasmagoric drama of the Communist underworld which culminates in his committing murder three times and in the suicide of Eva Blount, the widow of one of his victims, who, after falling in love with him, cannot bear the truth, when she finally learns of the terrible deeds that he has performed. And Cross at last is destroyed by the Party's assassins.

Now, when the novel is thus summarized, it may appear to be only a rather lurid sort of potboiler; and, to be sure, there is no minimizing the harshness of its violence. Yet, for all of its melodramatic sensationalism, it is an impressive book. Indeed, it is one of the very few American novels of our time that, in admitting into itself a large body of systematic ideas, makes us think that it wants seriously to compete with the major philosophic intelligence of the contemporary period. And it may well be that the strange kind of indifference or even outright denigration that the book elicited at the time of its appearance demands to be understood in terms of the easy assumption which is habitually made in our literary life, that the difference in method and intention between poetry and philosophy ordains the impropriety of a work of fiction being complicated by the dialectical tensions of systematic thought. But this is a kind of finickiness notably unsupported by the European tradition exemplified by such books as Mann's *Doktor Faustus* and Malraux's *La Condition Humaine* and Camus' *La Peste*. And it was toward this tradition that Mr. Wright was reaching in *The Outsider*, which, though it is a very imperfect work, is yet (after *Black Boy*) his finest achievement and, as the one emphatically existentialist novel in contemporary American literature, a book that deserves to have commanded a great deal more attention than it has.

Though Mr. Wright insisted that his hero "could have been of any race" and that his primary quality was the metaphysical horror he

felt before the yawning emptiness in things created by the demise of
the old "myths," the fact remains, however, that Cross is a Negro. And,
as such, he is dubiously privileged to have what the prosecutor Ely
Houston calls "a dreadful objectivity," the kind of "double vision," that
is, which belongs to one who is "both inside and outside of our culture." But, given the ardency of his commitment to atheistic premises,
the actual content of this "double vision" proves to be the conviction
of Ivan Karamazov, that therefore "everything is permitted," not even
murder being debarred. And so that night when he walked into the
room where the Fascist nigger-hater Herndon and the Communist
Blount were fighting and bludgeoned them both to death, he was "not
taking sides . . . not preferring the lesser evil," for, in the world as it
was apprehended by Cross, there were no sides to be taken; he no
longer slept in the old myths of the Greeks and the Jews, and he knew
that nothing was to be preferred to anything else. So his act was simply
"a sweeping and supreme gesture of disdain and disgust with both of
them!" The logic, in other words, is this, that to be a Negro is to be
an outsider, not only in a sociological sense but also, and more deci-
sively, in a moral sense as well. And the mission of the outsider, like
that of Camus' Caligula, is to reveal to mankind that the human City
is really a jungle and that all the disciplines and restraints of civilization are "just screens which men have used" to throw a kind of "veneer
of order" over the disorder that still seethes beneath the surface. But
since, as it appears, this is a mission that cannot be accomplished apart
from terrorism, Mr. Wright's conclusion of 1953 entailed essentially the
same mischievousness that had been implicit thirteen years earlier in
Native Son, the notion that the natural life-movement of the Negro
who bears the full burden of his situation is toward a great blasting
moment of supreme destruction. Bigger Thomas is an inarticulate proletarian who enacts his role unthinkingly, whereas Cross Damon, having
read his Nietzschean primers, accepts his mission with deliberation
and in the spirit of a kind of inverted messianism—but this is the only
significant difference between them, for both aim, as it were, at getting
outside of history altogether, through an act of consummate violence.
Like Conrad's Kurtz, Cross does, to be sure, behold at last "the horror,"
as he gaspingly admits to Houston a moment before his death; but he
has, nevertheless, tasted the terrible joy of his murderous orgasm: he
has burst the belt and been "hard" and won through at least to the
unhistorical realm of the dream—which is of revenge.

    Mr. Wright was always too impatient with what Henry James called
the "proving disciplines" of art to win the kind of genuine distinction
as a writer for which his talents qualified him. And, like George Orwell,
for him the greatest uses of art were not those by which we distance

ourselves from the world in order to contemplate more strenuously its pattern and meaning. They were, rather, those by which we seek a more direct entry into the world for the sake of redeeming it from the brutality and the indecencies by which it must otherwise be overwhelmed. So it is rather a sad irony that his own art did in point of fact so often drift toward a definition of man, and particularly of the American Negro, that deeply undercut his conscious intention to make it serve a genuinely humane vision. As James Baldwin has said, the real tragedy of Bigger Thomas "is not that he is cold or black or hungry, not even that he is American, black, but that he has accepted a theology that denies him life, that he admits the possibility of his being subhuman and feels constrained, therefore, to battle for his humanity according to those brutal criteria bequeathed him at his birth."* And this is precisely what it is that renders so ambiguous many of the other chief protagonists in Mr. Wright's fiction.

His last years, unhappily, were not, it seems, a period of rich fulfillment and harvest. Mr. Baldwin has reported† on some of the asperities that increasingly isolated him from friends and acquaintances and young American Negro and African intellectuals who were living in Paris. And I suspect that his crotchetiness was not unconnected with the fortunes of his reputation in the literary life. Though *The Outsider* won a respectful reception in some quarters, it by no means achieved any large *succès d'estime* in the critical forum; and the novel of 1958, *The Long Dream,* met little more than polite indifference. So it was the publication in 1945 of *Black Boy* which had brought him to the zenith of his success. Thereafter his fiction and his political criticism, though no different in tone and emphasis from his earlier work, seemed to be nettling in their effect, and the reputation of the early 'forties has today become merely a minor datum of that earlier time. This is, of course, in part, I suspect, but a particular case of the more general demise of the naturalism of the American nineteen-thirties. At the beginning of the decade Edmund Wilson had suggested in *Axel's Castle* that this was an idiom which could survive only by consenting to be complicated by disciplines of intelligence and imagination that he somewhat clumsily denominated as "Symbolism," but this was a challenge that did not begin to be responded to until the early 'fifties, by the generation of Ralph Ellison and Saul Bellow and William Styron. And, however robust our respect may still be for the Dos Passos of the *U.S.A.* trilogy or the Steinbeck of *The Grapes of Wrath* or the Wright of *Native Son,* we find them today to be writers with whom it

---

* Baldwin, James: *Notes of a Native Son,* p. 23. Boston: The Beacon Press, 1961.

† Baldwin, James: *Nobody Knows My Name,* pp. 200-215. New York: The Dial Press, 1961.

is virtually impossible any longer to have a genuinely reciprocal relation, for the simple fact is that the rhetoric of what once used to be
called "reportage" proves itself, with the passage of time, to be a
language lacking in the kind of amplitude and resonance that *lasts*.
This may not be the precise judgment which the cunning of history,
in its ultimate justice, will sustain, but it is, at any rate, *ours*.

It may, of course, be that this is a kind of verdict on our fiction of
twenty-five or thirty years ago that has sometimes been applied with
too alacritous a facility by the high priests of our present dispensation,
and I am prepared even now to confess to the irritation that I recently
felt when I came again upon the patrician hauteur of a sentence of the
late R. P. Blackmur's in which it is asserted that "*Native Son* is one of
those books in which everything is undertaken with seriousness except
the writing." But whatever may in turn be history's ultimate verdict on
our present way of dealing with the American naturalism of the recent
past, there is, quite apart from the line that in this respect we want
now to take, a more specific and more cogent reason for the revision
that we may want to practice on the accolades of the early 'forties for
Mr. Wright's work (the enthusiastic equations of the author of *Native
Son* with Dostoevski, etc.), and it is a reason which is clarified by the
collection of stories entitled *Eight Men* that appeared a few weeks
after his death.

At least three of the stories of which this book is composed were
written before 1945, but, since the collection was supervised by the
author himself, we are justified in assuming that they do all reflect his
final sense of life—and what is most remarkable about the book is the
summation that it provides of the consistencies which, throughout his
career, formed Richard Wright's personal signature. In each of the
eight stories which comprise this volume the central figure is a black
isolé whose crucifixion by a hostile world is offered as type and
example of a collective suffering and a collective fate. And all these
various statements are marked by an immoderate and melodramatic
imagination of the world as "split in two, a white world and a black
one, the white one being separated from the black by a million psychological miles." The last of the eight pieces, "The Man Who Went to
Chicago"—which is, I take it, autobiographical—ingeniously inter-
weaves narrative and essay, and, at one point, in recounting his experience in the early 'thirties "as an orderly to a medical research institute
in one of the largest and wealthiest hospitals in Chicago," Mr. Wright
says:

> Each Saturday morning I assisted a young Jewish doctor in slitting
> the vocal cords of a fresh batch of dogs from the city pound. The
> object was to devocalize the dogs so that their howls would not

disturb the patients in the other parts of the hospital. I held each dog as the doctor injected Nembutal into its veins to make it unconscious; then I held the dog's jaws open as the doctor inserted the scalpel and severed the vocal cords. Later, when the dogs came to, they would lift their heads to the ceiling and gape in a soundless wail. The sight became lodged in my imagination as a symbol of silent suffering.

And though the image comes toward the close of this collection, once it is encountered it seems then to resonate backward across the entire book, indeed across the entire *oeuvre*, and we feel that the human presence at the center of Mr. Wright's dramatic world has itself somehow been converted into a howling dog whose wails are soundless. In one instance, the long story called "The Man Who Lived Underground," this is an extremism which makes for a wonderfully scarifying and improbable piece of Gothicism which is absolutely self-contained and brilliant. And the piece called "Man of All Work" is a beautifully constructed account of a man who, not being able to find any employment, disguises himself as a woman and, in his wife's clothes, hires himself out as a domestic, being certain that, since Negroes are never really looked at anyway, he'll be able to carry the stunt off—a situation which enables Mr. Wright, with a remarkable deftness and irony, to probe the kind of demasculinization of the male and the kind of resulting rupture of the primitive bonds of the family which have often occurred in Negro life; nor does he also fail, with a savage funniness, to suggest what is outrageous in the sexual panic of American whites. But in every other case, as we move through the stories in *Eight Men*, though we are kept going from page to page and though the writing has the minor virtues of a professionally skillful naturalism, we are dealing with a body of work which totters and collapses under the pressure of a radical imagination unequipped with any defense against its own radicalism; and nowhere else is there a fully achieved work of art.

But, when we have done, it may be that we ought to remember that there are in human experience issues weightier and more exacting than the issues of aesthetics and literary criticism. And it may also be that, in whatever kingdom of the spirit Richard Wright now dwells, as he broods over this uncongenial world of earth, he finds it sufficient merely to say, "I am the man, I suffer'd, I was there." Of this I am reminded, as I glance now at the Dedication of *The Outsider*—"For Rachel, my daughter who was born on alien soil."

RICHARD KOSTELANETZ

The Politics

of Ellison's Booker:

Invisible Man

as

Symbolic History

RALPH ELLISON's *Invisible Man* IS ACKNOWLEDGED BY MANY AS ONE OF the supreme achievements of the modern American novel. It received the National Book Award in 1953; critics continually praise it and persistently endeavor to explicate its subtleties. It has become the one Afro-American novel read widely in both the secondary school and the university.

Born and raised in Oklahoma, Ellison (1914–   ) attended Tuskegee Institute and studied music before coming to New York in the 1930's. Encouraged to write by his friend Richard Wright, he contributed to *The New Masses*, worked with the New York Federal Writers Project and served as an editor of *The Negro Quarterly*. In 1945 he began work on the novel which would become *Invisible Man*.

Published in 1952 after years of careful re-writing, *Invisible Man* has been followed only by a collection of essays (most of which were previously published elsewhere) under the title *Shadow and Act* in 1964. Ellison's long-awaited second novel has not yet appeared.

Included in *Shadow and Act* is an essay entitled "The World and The Jug" which was written during a famous dispute of late 1963 and early 1964 between Ellison and the critic Irving Howe. In an essay for *Dissent* called "Black Boys and Native Sons," Howe had condemned both Ellison and James Baldwin for their lack of militancy as writers of fiction. Ellison's reply, in essence, was that protest was not necessarily art, even though all art constituted protest of some sort; moreover, that his artistic purpose was the same as Wright's and Baldwin's: to "affirm the broad possibility of personal realization," to satisfy the "impulse to celebrate human life."*

These statements suggest at least one theme basic to *Invisible Man*. The anonymous black narrator of the novel is offered a series of life styles in the form of a succession of masks, all designed to delude him into believing that people can identify his substance when they recognize his mask. Obviously, the masks fail because they deny the reality they conceal—the black self that struggles to assert its humanity amidst a racist America. The fact about this process which is often overlooked is that the *telling* of his story—from the security of an underground room—enables the hero to end the novel with an affirmation of self; his cognizance that masks must be rejected will enable him to leave the underground for the world. Richard Kostelanetz believes that this entire process is symbolic of black American history, and if he is correct, Ellison's novel assumes the shape of an Afro-American myth: an ordering of fact and emotion that defines and explains the total black experience in this country.

A well-known critic and anthologist, Richard Kostelanetz is the author of *The Theatre of Mixed Means* (1968); he has edited a number of books, including *On Contemporary Literature* (1964) and *The Young American Writers* (1967). His critical essays have frequently appeared in literary magazines and journals of opinion.

RICHARD KOSTELANETZ

The Politics of Ellison's Booker: *Invisible Man* as Symbolic History

> Invisible Man *is* par excellence *the literary extension of the blues. It was as if Ellison has taken an everyday twelve-bar blues tune (by a man from down South sitting in a manhole up North in New York singing and signifying about how he got there) and scored it for a full orchestra.*—ALBERT L. MURRAY.

I

IN HIS COLLECTION OF ESSAYS, *Shadow and Act* (1964), RALPH ELLISON defines the purpose of novelistic writing as "converting experience into symbolic action," and this phrase incidentally captures the particular achievement of his novel, *Invisible Man,* in which he creates a nameless narrator whose adventures, always approximate and unspecific in time and place, represent in symbolic form the overall historical experience of the most politically active element of the American Negro people.

"It is through the process of making artistic forms" Ellison adds elsewhere, "that the writer helps give meaning to the experience of the group," a statement which, especially in its tactile imagery, echoes Stephen Dedalus's ambition, in James Joyce's *Portrait of the Artist as a Young Man,* "to forge in the smithy of my soul the uncreated conscience of my race." In the major sequences of *Invisible Man,* the narrator confronts a succession of possible individual choices which, as they imply changes in group behavior, have a symbolic political dimension for Negro people. When an alternative seems adequate enough to win the narrator's favor, his acceptance becomes, in effect, a pragmatic test of its viability. After he discovers the posited solution is inadequate to his needs, as all of them are, he samples another. Although Ellison does not have his narrator confront every known political possibility, the novel is still the most comprehensive one-volume fictional—symbolic—treatment of the history of the American Negro in the twentieth century.

In the opening quarter of the novel, the narrator eagerly tests opportunities for Negro existence within the Southern system, and just as

Reprinted from *The Chicago Review,* XIX, No. 2 (1967), 5-26, by permission of the author and publisher. Copyright © 1967 by *The Chicago Review.*

Voltaire's *Candide* innocently embraces philosophical optimism, so the young Negro assumes the notions prevalent in the early twentieth century of how the colored people can best succeed in the South—those of Booker T. Washington. From a vantage point later in time, the narrator remembers that as a young man about to graduate high school, "I visualized myself as a potential Booker T. Washington," who hoped to follow his idol's advice and perhaps emulate his career.[1] The most successful Negroes, he believed, were those who proved themselves essential to white society, either because they had an employable trade or because they helped to keep order within the Negro communities.

The whole future of the Negro rested largely upon the question of whether or not he should make himself, through his skill, intelligence and character, of such undeniable value to the community in which he lived that the community could not dispense with his presence.

From this proposition stemmed Washington's major corollary: since the South offered the Negro greater social and economic opportunities, the Southern Negro would be wise to remain where he was born. "Whatever other sins the South may be called to bear," he wrote, "when it comes to business, pure and simple, it is in the South that the Negro is given a man's chance in the commercial world." At the base of Washington's politics, then, was a faith that Southern whites would give the respectable Negro a fair opportunity to succeed, and honor whatever success a Negro achieved for himself.

From these positions, Washington, as history and Ellison's narrator saw him, derived the three major lines of conduct implemented at Tuskegee Institute (which distinctly resembles the college in *Invisible Man*). First, Washington believed that to make himself as appealing as possible to white society, the Negro must be industrious in his work, respectful in his dealings with his white superiors, responsible for his family and to his community, and, perhaps most important, scrupulously clean. In *Up from Slavery*, his most influential book, Washington never ceased proclaiming the advantages of an immaculate appearance. For Tuskegee's students, instruction in hygiene was as important as book- and trade-learning:

---

[1] What Washington actually believed and said, it should be pointed out, differ slightly from the ideas generally ascribed to him by both followers and enemies. In fact, he spoke out against the grandfather clause, protested lynching, and urged legal action against discrimination. However, since the narrator of Ellison's novel as a high school student subscribes to the prevailing popular image, the following summary deals with the myth, rather than the fact of Washington. History remembers Washington as having primarily urged his fellow Negroes to lead an honest and industrious life within the framework of Southern segregation.

It has been interesting to note the effect that the use of the tooth-brush has had in bringing about a higher degree of civilization among the students. With few exceptions, I have noticed that, if we can get a student to the point where, when the first or second toothbrush disappears, he of his own motion buys another, I have not been disappointed in the future of that individual. Absolute cleanliness of the body has been insisted upon from the first. The students have been taught to bathe as regularly as to take their meals. . . . Most of the students came from plantation districts, and often we had to teach them how to sleep at night; that is, whether between the two sheets . . . or under both of them. The importance of the use of the nightgown received the same attention.

Thus, in the daily schedule at Tuskegee, Washington allocated one-half hour for cleaning one's room, and school officials made periodic inspection tours of the dormitories. A central aim of Tuskegee's education was to take a back-country Negro and, metaphorically, soak him with whitewash.

Secondly, if the Negro were to succeed, he must not challenge the system of white supremacy. In Washington's pet phrase, he must campaign for "responsibility," not "equality." A demand for equal rights, he feared, could only violently disrupt the stability of the South; and not only would revolt have little chance of success, but also the cost in Negro lives would be too exhorbitant to make it worthwhile. "The wisest among my race understand that the agitation of questions of social equality is the extremist folly," he wrote, for the Negro must, following Washington's own example, "deport himself modestly in regard to political claims." Political rights, he argued, "will be accorded to the Negro by the Southern people themselves, and they will protect him in the exercise of those rights," only if the Negro treads the path of humility, impresses white society with his conscientiousness, and contributes to their material prosperity.

Thirdly, the Negro must measure his success in tokens of recognition from white society, rather than in terms of respect of his own people. This is the major lesson Washington drew from his own life, and in the latter half of his autobiography he catalogues the honors he received from white America. He especially enjoyed lecturing before groups of white Southerners, and he saved his most important speeches for the racially mixed audiences of large Southern expositions. Among his deepest desires was to have the President of the United States visit Tuskegee; and when the possibility arose, he twice journeyed to Washington, D.C., to persuade McKinley to come. Furthermore, few things pleased him more than encountering a group of white people who, like some Georgia men mentioned in his book, "came up and introduced [themselves] to me and thanked me earnestly for the work that I was trying to do for the whole South." (Whether they addressed him by his Christian name or "Mr. Washington," he does not disclose.) What a Negro's peers thought of his own work was not as important as what the white folks judged; again, Washington felt that Negroes could best succeed in America by conforming to the prescriptions of entrenched white authority.

Ellison's narrator so thoroughly and innocently subscribes to the Washingtonian ethic that, when he is selected to give the valedictory address at his high school, he echoes both Washington's ideas and his rhetoric. Telling his Negro classmates to cultivate friendly relations with their white neighbors, the narrator quotes the key line of Washington's Atlanta Proclamation Address, "Cast down your bucket where you are," for, it is implied, if the colored southerners look for water elsewhere, they may die of thirst. Likewise, the narrator uses the Washingtonian phrase "social responsibility" to define the role the Negro should play in the South. Upon his graduation the narrator believes that he can rise through the Southern system, perhaps becoming, like his idol, an educational leader or, more modestly, a doctor or lawyer in the Negro South.

The narrator, along with other class leaders, is invited to a gathering of the local white dignitaries; and at the occasion, they ask the narrator to repeat his valedictory address. When he arrives at the meeting, he is first directed to join his classmates in a free-for-all "battle royal" that is a feature of the evening's entertainment. Although he instinctively shies away from bodily contact with boys bigger than himself, the narrator consents to the ordeal to please the white audience. Along with the other Negro youths, he is blindfolded with white cloth; when the bells ring, he is pushed into the ring and throughout the fight, the white citizens on the sidelines encourage the Negro school boys to "knock" each other's "guts out." This incident, like most of the major scenes in the book, embodies a symbolic dimension that complements the literal action; that is, the scene stands for something larger in the experience of the Southern Negro. Here, Ellison shows how the white powers make the Negroes channel their aggressive impulses inward upon their own race instead of upon their true enemy, who remains on the sidelines, supervising the fray to make sure the violence is directed away from themselves.

To pay for the "entertainment," the hosts put numerous coins and bills upon a rug and encourage the Negroes to pick up "all you grab." Once this new contest starts, they discover the rug is electrified. The shocks lead the boys to jump and shriek, in animal-like movements, to the amusement of the white audience. "Glistening with sweat like a circus seal and . . . landing flush upon the charged rug," one boy "literally dance[d] upon his back, his elbows beating a frenzied tattoo upon the floor, his muscles twitching like the flesh of a horse stung by many flies." In other words, before the Negro receives the pay he earned, he must overcome unnecessary hazards, often arbitrarily imposed, and publicly make a fool of himself. Between the Negro and the money he earns from white society are, symbolically, all the galvanic terrors of an electrified rug; and the price of the white man's pay is the Negro's debasement of his humanity.

After the other boys are paid their pittances and excused, the narrator delivers his speech. Again, he voices the platitudes of Booker T. Washington, feigning the air of sincerity and accents of emphasis. When he mentions the phrase "social responsibility," they ask him to repeat it again and again, until in a moment of mental exhaustion he substitutes the word "equality." Challenged by the audience, he quickly reverts to the traditional, unrevolutionary phrase. Ellison here illustrates that as the speaker's censor relaxes, his true desires are revealed; but as soon as he remembers the power of Southern authority, he immediately represses his wish. At the end of the meeting, the superintendent of the local schools presents the narrator with a briefcase; in it is a scholarship to the state college for Negroes. Again, the political meaning is that the Negro must publicly debase himself and suppress his true desires before he will receive the rewards of Southern society. Washington's guidance would seem to underestimate the price of Negro success in the South.

In the second sequence of the novel, the narrator discovers what kinds of Negroes receive rewards totally disproportionate to their work. As a student, the narrator is assigned to act as a chauffeur for a white trustee, Mr. Norton (whose name at once echoes "Northern" and Charles Eliot Norton, the first professor of art history at Harvard and heir to a certain kind of New England Brahmin liberalism). Responding to Norton's commands, the narrator drives the old man to the Negro slum down below the "white-washed" college on the hill. At his passenger's request, he stops the car before the log cabin of Jim Trueblood, who, as his name suggests, represents the primitive, uneducated Negro unaffected by the values of white culture. Norton, discovering to his horror that Trueblood has impregnated his daughter, asks the Negro whether he feels "no inner turmoil, no need to cast out the offending eye?" Refusing Oedipus's response to a similar sin, the Negro uncomprehendingly replies, "My eyes is allright," adding, "When I feels po'ly in my gut I takes a little soda and it goes away." Prompted by Norton's queries, Trueblood tells how the officials at the Negro college responded to his misdeed: "[They] offered to send us clean outta the country, pay our way and everything and give me a hundred dollars to git settled with." To the "whitewashed" Negroes, Trueblood represents that elemental humanity that college education must eliminate; and Trueblood's presence near the campus serves as a reminder of the primitive past the college community wants to repudiate.

To escape their strategy of alternate threats and enticements, Trueblood enlists the aid of his white boss who, in turn, refers him to the local sheriff. That official and his cronies so relish Trueblood's tale of sexual indiscretion that they ask him to repeat all the details, giving him food, drink and tobacco in return for their second-hand pleasure.

> They tell me not to worry, that they was going to send word up to the school that I was to stay right where I am. It just goes to show yuh that no matter how biggity a nigguh gits, the white folks always cut him down.

In the days following, Trueblood becomes a celebrity, attracting the interest of white people he had never encountered before.

> The white folks took to coming out here to see us and talk with us. Some of 'em was big white folks, too, from the big school way 'cross the State. Asked me lots 'bout what I thought 'bout things, and 'bout my folks and kids, and wrote it all down in a book.

Presumably, these men were Southern scholars who intended to use Trueblood's confessions as evidence of the inherent immorality of the Negro. Moreover, Trueblood reports, the local white people now give him more work. "I'm better off than I ever been before," he says. "I done the worse thing a man can do in his family and 'stead of things gittin bad, they got better." In short, Trueblood's experience contradicts Washington's belief that white society would reward only those Negroes who live by its expressed morality. Instead, they eagerly appreciate a Negro who conforms to the traditional stereotype of the immoral savage in black skin.

After leaving Trueblood, the narrator follows Norton's command to take him to a roadside bar. Here they encounter a group of hospitalized Negro veterans, mostly psychiatric patients, going to the ironically named "Golden Day" for their weekly round of drinks and whores. Their shepherd is the hospital attendant Supercargo who, as his name suggests, functions as their collective super-ego. Not only does he impose the repressive forces of white society upon them, but he also represents obedience internalized into their own consciences. Therefore, as soon as he disappears to fetch a drink upstairs, the men "had absolutely no inhibitions." A brawl ensues, directed largely against

Supercargo and the social forces he represents. As the "veterans" air their complaints, the narrator discovers that they are the dispossessed Negro middle-class. One is an ex-surgeon who was dragged from his home by white men and beaten, it is implied, for saving the life of a white person. Another is a composer on the borderline of lunacy, "striking the [piano] keyboard with fists and elbows and filling in other effects in a bass voice that moaned like a bear in agony." A third "was a former chemist who was never seen without his shining Phi Beta Kappa key." The lesson of their experience is that Southern society destroys Negro talent and genuine accomplishment. Once again, Washington's advice on how the Negro should live in the South proves an inadequate guide.

Back on the campus, the narrator is summoned into the office of the college president to be reprimanded for taking Norton down to the slum, for letting him talk to Trueblood, for leading him to the Golden Day, and for allowing the benefactor to hear complaints of the dispossessed Negroes. He blames the narrator for innocently following Norton's commands and, even worse, for honestly answering his queries. The heart of the young man's error, Bledsoe says, is that "You forgot to lie." "But," the narrator replies, "I was only trying to please him. . . ." To this Bledsoe retorts in anger, "Why, the dumbest black bastard in the cotton patch knows that the only way to please a white man is to tell him a lie! What kind of education are you getting around here?" Bledsoe believes, echoing some cynical implications in Washington's thought, that the Negro college should preach the attainment not of dignity and self-achievement but of surface obsequiousness and underlying cynicism. Had not, the narrator remembers, Bledsoe himself been a model of such behavior. Had not he illustrated how the Negro should play the role of the second-class man.

Since Bledsoe's authority within the college is absolute, the narrator decides to accept punishment for the mistakes his innocence engendered—expulsion; and armed with several of Bledsoe's letters of recommendation, the young man heads for New York. He recognizes that his ethics cannot cope with the reality he finds:

> How had I come to this? I had kept unswervingly to the path placed before me, had tried to be exactly what I was expected to be, had done exactly what I was expected to do—yet, instead of winning the expected reward, here I was stumbling along. . . . For, despite my anguish and anger, I knew of no other way of living, nor other forms of success available to such as me.

Rather than succumb to the new reality he discovers, the young man who scrupulously followed the suggestions of Booker T. Washington, is forced to disobey his idol's advice and leave the South.

Perhaps the final commentary on Booker T. Washington's ideas is the address given in the college chapel by a Rev. Homer Barbee, a visitor from Chicago. Barbee presents all the optimistic platitudes, predicting the improvement of conditions in the South and greater opportunity for his people to fulfill their worldly ambitions. Instead of bitterness or notions of emigration, revolt and racial conflict, he offers the hope of success within the Southern system—a "bright horizon" through self-improvement. His ideas offer a certain appeal to the narrator and his classmates, until the young man realizes that Barbee wears dark glasses. He is blind, both in the physical sense and in his awareness of political realities. To the Negro in quest of self-fulfillment, the South in fact offers no hope, except to the blind, the immoral, and the cynical. This is the political meaning of the first section of the book.

II

Before he lets his narrator explore much of the North, Ellison introduces a scene which serves as a symbolic portrait of the underlying reality of Negro-white relations in America. Ostensibly, the chapter describes the operation of a paint factory; but the remark that the factory "looks like a small city" indicates symbolic dimensions. The narrator is assigned to mix ten drops of black paint into every can of "Optic White." When he protests that the black would discolor the pure white, his white foreman replies, "Never mind how it looks. You just do what you're told and don't try to think about it." Unaware of the physical principle that mixing small amounts of black paint into white paint actually makes white whiter, the narrator scrupulously follows directions. This process for enriching white paint symbolically parallels the interplay of racial colors in America. The black Negro makes the white world whiter; for since his values and aspirations emulate those of the white world, he reinforces the white American's eschatology and, like the black in the can of paint, embellishes the whiteness of American public life. The company's motto is, ironically, "Keep America Pure with Liberty Paints," and, since the paint will be used on a national monument, the passage suggests that all of American history has a similar color composition. Although Negroes have contributed to the American achievement, their effort, like the ten drops, enriches the existing texture. When the narrator inadvertently takes his refill from the wrong tank, the mixture he produces is "not as white and glassy as before; it had a grey tinge." If put on the national monument, it would reveal the heretical truth that American life, underneath the white surface, is, like the color grey, a mixture of black and white. For this mistake, the narrator is removed from his paint-mixing job. If he had likewise revealed the actuality beneath the white-washed surface of America, it is implied, he would have been exiled from the country.

In the second quarter of the novel, the narrator arrives in New York to test the opportunities open to the Negro in the North. He carries seven sealed letters of introduction from President Bledsoe to philanthropic white liberals who are patrons of the college. At six of the offices, the narrator asks to see the man to whom the letter is addressed. The letter is taken from him and delivered; and every time, the secretary returns and informs the narrator that the important man will contact him later. None fulfill his promise; for unbeknownst to the narrator, Bledsoe's letter tells the businessmen that this student has seriously violated some undisclosed rule of the school:

> This case represents one of the rare, delicate instances in which one for whom we held great expectations has gone grievously astray, and who in his fall threatens to upset certain delicate relationships between certain interested individuals and the school.

However, in his concluding sentence, Bledsoe, perhaps disingenuously, asks each recipient to help the young man. The lesson this episode portrays is that the Northern philanthropists will aid "Negroes" in the South, but they will not rescue an individual needy Southern Negro in the North. They suffer from hyperopia: Pain in the distance can be seen clearly, while that close at hand is blurred.

Since one of the businessmen is away from New York, the narrator postpones calling at his office. Finally getting an interview, the narrator meets the son of "Mr. Emerson," an heir to the American liberal tradition. He speaks in platitudes, often using a second platitude that doubles back on the first: "Ambition is a wonderful force," he tells the narrator, "but sometimes it can be blinding . . . On the other hand, it can make you successful—like my father . . . The only trouble with ambition is that it sometimes blinds one to realities." He is also extremely self-conscious. "Don't let me upset you," he tells the narrator, "I had a difficult session with my analyst last evening and the slightest thing is apt to set me off." When he makes a slip of the tongue, Emerson stops to ponder its significance. He boasts of the number of Negro acquaintances he has—artists and intellectuals all—and of his regular attendance at an important Negro club. Being, as he says, "incapable of cynicism," he reveals to the narrator the deceitful contents of Bledsoe's letter. However, because he is afraid to disobey his father's wishes, young Emerson does not hire the narrator and warns him not to reveal their conversation to anyone. The Northern Emersonian liberal, the novel tells us, is too torn by neurosis, self-doubt and compromise to help the Negro in need.

Recognizing that those who support him in principle offer him few opportunities in practice, the narrator seeks a job as a laborer at Liberty Paints. He is hired, he later discovers, as a "scab," because the company wants to replace its unionized white workers with cheaper non-union Negro labor. The narrator is assigned to the foreman named Kimbro, described as a "slave driver." Assuming this traditional role, Kimbro instructs his Negro workers in their jobs. When a worker makes an error, as does the narrator, Kimbro exercises an overseer's authority and assigns him to another task. After his mistake in mixing the colors, the narrator is assigned to assist Lucius Brockway in the third sub-basement of the plant. Since his job is to control and service the machines that mix the base of the paint, the whole operation of paint-making depends upon his talents. The company has in the past frequently attempted to replace Brockway with white labor—during Brockway's illness an engineer of Italian ancestry was assigned to the job—but it discovered that no one else could do his work. Fearing that someone else will intrude on his domain, Brockway is fanatically anti-union. Entirely subservient to white authority, he takes a childish delight in the company's dependence on him and his special relationship with the boss. When Brockway retired, the Old Man discovered the paint was losing its excellence and personally persuaded Brockway to return to his job. Underpaid and underpraised, Brockway survives in the industrial system by embracing the existing authority and by having indispensible talents.

One day, the narrator inadvertently enters a union meeting in the locker-room. The white workers, assuming that he is applying for membership, at once suspect that he is a company spy. One member proposes that the narrator prove his loyalty to the union before he be permitted "to become acquainted with the work of the union and its aims." Although the novel does not develop the theme of this encounter, the incident suggests that before the labor movement will accept the Negro, he must go to inordinate lengths to justify his right to belong. Once the union people identify him as suspect, they make no effort to ascertain his actual attitude toward unions. "They had made their decision without giving me a chance to speak for myself." As the narrator departs, the meeting chairman tells him, "We want you to know that we are only trying to protect ourselves. Some day we hope to have you as a member in good standing."

What the sequence illustrates is that to both white industry and white unions the Negro is acceptable only if he is either more loyal or more competent than a white; and business would prefer that his labor be less expensive. "The existence of racial prejudice in both employee and employer groups is of course an indisputable fact," wrote

Horace R. Cayton and George S. Mitchell in 1939, in *Black Workers and the New Unions.* "If there were no economic advantages in employing Negroes, most employers would prefer a white labor force." This situation creates what the sociologist Robert Merton christens the self-fulfilling prophecy: "In the beginning, a *fake* definition of the situation [evokes] a new behavior which makes the originally false conception come true." If the dominant majority decides that Negroes are unfit to become union members because, it reasons, their lower standard of living allows them to take jobs at less than the prevailing wage, then the Negroes, as a result of exclusion, will become strike-breakers, accepting the lower wage and, it follows, necessarily adjusting their existence to the lower standard of living. Similarly if an employer rules that the Negroes are incapable of doing important work, then, acting upon their own false belief, they give Negroes only menial jobs. If the Negro, having no other choice, accepts the distasteful labor and handles it competently, then, in the employer's eyes, the Negro has "proved" he is fit only for menial work. Both employers and unions, then, exploit the Negro's second-class position in American society; and neither offers the Negro an acceptable solution. Later in the novel, a misunderstanding, coupled with a difference in attitude, produces a fight between the narrator and Brockway. An explosion occurs, and the narrator finds himself in a hospital. Here he undergoes an unidentified operation somewhat resembling a lobotomy, from which, the doctor promises, he will emerge with a "complete change of personality."

III

In the development of the novel, this chapter and the one following it serve a transitional function; for whereas the narrator once accepted the conventional solutions to the Negro's dilemma, now he is emancipated from this narrow sense of possibility and prepared to sample more radical alternatives. Upon returning to his boarding house, a residence for more ambitious Negroes in New York, he recognizes that his house-mates display the vanities and deceits of those who either failed to climb through the existing system or deluded themselves with artificial tokens of success:

> The moment I entered the bright, buzzing lobby of Men's House I was overcome by a sense of alienation and hostility. My overalls were causing stares and I knew that I could live there no longer, that that phase of my life was past. The lobby was the meeting place for various groups still caught up in the illusions that had just been boomeranged out of my head: college boys working to return

to school down south; older advocates of racial progress with utopian schemes for building black business empires; preachers or-
dained by no authority except their own, without church or
congregation, without bread or wine, body or blood; the community
"leaders" without followers; old men of sixty or more still caught
up in post-Civil War dreams of freedom within segregation; the
pathetic ones who possessed nothing beyond their dreams of being
gentlemen, who held small jobs or drew small pensions, and all
pretending to be engaged in some vast, though obscure, enterprise,
who affected the pseudo-courtly manners of certain Southern congressmen and bowed and nodded as they passed like senile old
roosters in a barnyard; the younger crowd for whom I now felt a
contempt such as only a disillusioned dreamer feels for those still
unaware that they dream—the business students from southern
colleges, for whom business was a vague, abstract game with rules
as obsolete as Noah's Ark but who yet were drunk on finance.

This complements the lobotomy; for just as the narrator assumes a
new identity (the operation having caused him to forget his name), so
he emerges from his residence hotel with a different set of inclinations.

Soon after, when the narrator discovers some poor old Negroes being
evicted from their flat, he makes a speech on their behalf; and as his
efforts attract a Harlem crowd, the narrator is accosted by a red-
bearded man who introduces himself as "Brother Jack," who says of the
narrator's extemporaneous speech: "*History* has been born in your
brain." Jack explains that he belongs to a radical action group; and
once the conversation becomes more relaxed the narrator accepts Jack's
request to see him in the evening. That night, the narrator is introduced to the "Brotherhood," persuaded to become a salaried organizer
for the movement, and assigned to a "theoretician" who will educate
him in its aims and method. The "Brotherhood" is the American Communist Party in a thin fictional disguise.

This third major section of the novel portrays the narrator's discovery that this radical movement understands neither his existence nor
that of his people. From his opening conversation, Brother Jack speaks
a language strange to the Negro experience. Addressing the narrator
as "Brother," Jack offers him cheese cake, a white delicacy wholly
foreign to Negro taste. Furthermore, he muses on how "history has
passed by" the old evicted Negroes who are, he adds, "agrarian types,
you know. Being ground up by industrial conditions. Thrown on the
dump heaps and cast aside. They's like dead limbs that must be pruned
away so that the tree may bear young fruit or the storms of history
will blow them away." To this the narrator responds, "Look, I don't
know what you're talking about. I've never lived on a farm and I
didn't study agriculture." Later with an inappropriateness that is typical

of him, Jack predicts that the Brotherhood will transform the narrator into "the new Booker T. Washington." A conciliator like Washington is precisely the opposite of the kind of leader a radical group needs; a reference to, say, Frederick Douglass would have been more appropriate. Moreover, the Brotherhood's images of Negro Americans come from the storehouse of bourgeois stereotypes. When one "Brother" asks the narrator to sing a spiritual, the narrator replies that he cannot sing. The Brother's reply is, "Nonsense, *all* colored people sing." Yet, although he senses the Brotherhood's lack of understanding, the narrator is flattered enough to cast his lot with them.

From his earliest contact with the movement, the narrator is aware that he must assume a pre-cast role. When he accepts the job, he is outfitted with a new identity—on a slip of paper is written his new name. At a Brotherhood party, he overhears a female leader say, "But don't you think he should be a little blacker," and the statement prompts him to think, "What was I, a man or a natural resource?" Later, the Brotherhood suggests that he move to a new address and discontinue writing to his relatives for a while. When Jack introduces him to the larger circle under his new identity, the narrator notices, "Everyone smiled and seemed eager to meet me, as though they all knew the role I was to play." Though the narrator senses that the Brotherhood's aims and methods may not coincide with his, he accepts the role they thrust upon him for two reasons—because it offers him a key to understanding his experience and "the possibility of being more than a member of a race."

What the narrator fails to see at this point—and what he discovers later—is that "being more" than a member of his race means being less of a Negro. After he joins the Brotherhood, the narrator symbolically attempts to sever connections between himself and his Southern Negro past. In a boarding house in Harlem, he discovers an object of much ulterior meaning:

> The cast-iron figure of a very black, red lipped and wide mouthed Negro, whose white eyes stared up at me from the floor, his face an enormous grin, his single large black hand held palm up before his chest. It was . . . the kind of bank which, if a coin is placed in the hand and a lever pressed upon the back, will raise its arm and flip the coin into the grinning mouth.

The figurine represents an aspect of the historical past that the narrator now wants desperately to forget; it has become "a self-mocking image." When the steam pipe of his room emits a clanking sound, the narrator strikes it with "the kinky iron head," cracking the figurine whose parts scatter across the floor. To escape both the landlady's wrath and his own feelings of guilt, the narrator scrapes the parts into the leather briefcase he received from the Southern businessmen. He drops the package in a garbage can outside an old private house; but its owner demands that he retrieve it (and, all that its contents symbolize). He protests, but when she threatens to call the police, he digs his hand into the muck (that lies between him and his Negro past) and recaptures the load. Two blocks later, he drops it in the heavy snow; but a passerby brings it back to him. The narrator cannot dispose of the package or elements of his character its contents symbolize until near the novel's end. He later acquires from another Negro Brother a link from a work-gang chain which he puts into his pocket; whenever he touches it, he is reminded of his heritage. Through these symbolic devices, Ellison makes the point that not even the Brotherhood can separate the American Negro from his past.

These themes are reinforced by the narrator's introspective monologues. During his affiliation with the Brotherhood, he is haunted by fears of "becoming someone else." For example, just before he is to deliver his first important speech for the Brotherhood, he feels "with a flash of panic that the moment I walked out upon the platform and opened my mouth I'd be someone else. Not just a nobody with a manufactured name which might have belonged to anyone, or to no one. But another personality." The problem is not that the Brotherhood forces him to do things against his will, but that this political life is not an organic outgrowth of his own past. His present experience strikes the narrator as a meaningless series of tacked-on events, chance encounters, and sudden fortunes. He becomes aware of two identities in himself:

> The old self that slept a few hours a night and dreamed sometimes of my grandfather and Bledsoe and Brockway and Mary, the self that flew without wings and plunged from great heights; and the new public self that spoke for the Brotherhood and was becoming so much more important than the other that I seemed to run a foot race against myself.

A rigorous schedule prevents the narrator from thinking too much about this split; only when he is transferred to a less demanding job does this awareness of his divided personality oppress him.

If the Brotherhood has little sense of the needs of an individual Negro, it is even less aware of the actualities of American Negro life. Once the narrator becomes an organizer, he quickly rouses a strong, grass-roots movement among the Harlem populace; he makes speeches at public rallies and regularly visits all the important bars. His extraordinary success, however, makes his more experienced Negro Brothers jealous; and one, Brother Wrestum ("rest room"?), accuses him of individual opportunism and dictatorial aspirations. Although one

speech earns applause "like a clap of thunder," the narrator is condemned by his Brotherhood superiors, because his talk was "wild,
hysterical, politically irresponsible and dangerous, and worse than that,
it was *incorrect!*" The emphasis upon the last word suggests to the
narrator that, "The term described the most heinous crime imaginable."
They criticize him, he discovers, because he neglected to include the
ideology that would organize the Negro audience behind the Brotherhood. To prepare him more adequately for future speeches, they as-
sign him to an intensive indoctrination program. It is implied, though
not specifically illustrated, that these "correct" ideas and phrases are
incapable of moving the Harlem audience. After all, if Jack's favorite
clichés sound strange to the semi-educated ear of the narrator, they
would be more wholly foreign to the common Negroes. By not cor-
rectly gauging the attitudes of Harlem, the Brotherhood also destroys
the narrator's usefulness for its cause.

Once he is cleared of suspicions of both disloyalty and personal
opportunism, the narrator returns to Harlem to discover that in his
absence his personal following has disintegrated. In a symbolic passage, he enters a bar and addresses two old acquaintances as "Brothers."
The tall one replies inquisitively, "he is relative of yourn?" His cohort
adds, "Shit, he goddam sho ain't no kin of mine!" The first asks the
bartender, "We just wanted to know if you could tell us just whose
brother this here cat's supposed to be?" Since the bartender claims to
be the narrator's "Brother," an argument ensues, the tall one protesting
that since the narrator "got the white fever and left" for downtown—
revealed that his ultimate loyalties were not to Negroes and Harlem
—he was no longer a "brother" of the Negroes. Later, the narrator
discovers that in his absence the Brotherhood has abandoned its efforts
in Harlem. The work he did, the support he organized, have all disappeared and there seems little likelihood he can retrieve the lost ground.
His own labor for the Brotherhood, he deduces, accomplished nothing.
"No great change had been made."

In one comic interlude, the novel suggests that the Brotherhood
suffered because many of its organizers and sympathizers had motivations quite distant from politics. After he finishes his speech on the
"woman question," the narrator is accosted by an extremely sensual
woman who questions him on "certain aspects of our ideology." Since
the questioning will take a while, she invites him up to her apartment.
Innocently, he accepts her hospitality. She explains, as he enters her
sumptuous apartment, "You can see, Brother, it is really the spiritual
values of the Brotherhood that interest me." As he answers her questions, she moves closer to him and tells him how he embodies a "great

throbbing vitality." After he seduces her, he condemns her for "confusing the class struggle with the ass struggle."

The Brotherhood's failure to gauge the Negro's actual needs lies not so much in the confusion of motives exemplified by the seductive women as in the blindness intrinsic in the movement's approach to reality. The movement's ideology contains elements appealing to the impoverished Negroes. It offers colored members equal rights; yet it is unable to empathize with the people's needs and spiritual temper. The novel explains this failure in both symbolic and narrative terms. When the narrator is reprimanded by Brother Jack for not preaching the correct line at the proper time, the narrator retorts that Jack, a white man, cannot know "the political consciousness of Harlem." Jack insists that the committee is the ultimate judge of reality and that the narrator is disobeying its "discipline." The narrator rejoins that Jack wants to be "the great white father" of Harlem, "Marse Jack." A fight seems imminent; but before it starts, Jack snatches his glass eye from its socket. The eye, Jack explains, was lost in the line of duty—by implication, in following the "discipline." The passage suggests not only that Jack is half-blind to the realities of Harlem—with only one eye his perception is limited—but also that he is incapable of seeing Harlem *in depth*. The narrator himself recognizes the second implica-tion: "The meaning of discipline," he figures, "is sacrifice . . . yes, and blindness." Once he discovers this failure of perception, the narrator never again feels total loyalty to the Brotherhood.

Still, he accepts their command to see Hambro, the chief theoretician, who reveals more obviously why the Brotherhood is oblivious to the needs of Harlem. It has deserted its drive to recruit Negroes, because, the narrator is told, its emphasis has switched from national issues to international ones. When he asks Hambro, "What's to be done about my district," explaining the decline in membership and the threats from the black nationalists, the theoretician authoritatively informs him, "Your members will have to be sacrificed. We are making tempo-rary alliances with other poltical groups and the interest of one group of brothers must be sacrificed to that of the whole." When the narrator argues that exploiting the Negro people is cynical, Hambro replies, in characteristic double-talk, "Not cynicism—realism. The trick is to take advantage of them in their own best interests." The narrator asks what justifies the sacrifice of unwitting people, and Hambro replies "the laws of reality." Who determines the laws of reality? "The collective wisdom of the 'scientists' of the Brotherhood" is the reply. However, as the narrator perceives, the Brotherhood's science has little contact with hard facts. All they know is ideas about history's movements on the world stage; instead of trying to see Harlem as an individual entity, they see it only as an interdependent cog in a big machine. To the actual lives and hopes of American Negroes, the scientists are completely insensitive.

In talking with Hambro, the narrator concludes, "Everywhere I've turned somebody has wanted to sacrifice me for my good—only *they* were the ones who benefitted." This recognition unlocks the narrator's first general thesis about the relations of white people with the Negro. Both Hambro and Jack, he thinks, are incapable of seeing a human essence either black or white. They believe that only the political part of a man, that segment that could serve the interests of the movement, is worthy of attention; all other problems and aspirations, whether emotional or physical, are ignored. Men could just as well be invisible. "Here I had thought they accepted me," the narrator decides, "because they felt that color made no difference, when in reality it made no difference because they didn't see either color or men." He then recognizes that Jack and Hambro hardly differ from Emerson and Norton. "They were very much the same, each attempting to force his picture of reality upon me and neither giving a hoot in hell for how things looked to me. I was simply a material, a natural resource to be used." As the four white figures blend into one, the narrator discovers the core truth of his relationship with them: "I now recognized my invisibility."

The recognition means that the narrator implicitly accepts the warning Ras the Exhorter, the black nationalist, offered to him earlier in the book:

> Why you with these white folks? Why a good boy like you with them? You *my* brother, mahn. Brothers are the same color; how the hell you call these white men *brother*? Shit mahn Brothers the same color. We sons of Mama Africa, you done forgot? You black, BLACK! You got *bahd* hair! You got thick *lips!* They say you *stink!* They hate you, mahn. You African. AFRICAN! Why you with them? Leave that shit, mahn. They sell you out. That shit is old-fashioned. They enslave us—you forget that? How can they mean a black man any good? How they going to be your *brother?*

Ras's point—that all white men, whether enemy or friend, will use the Negro for their own purposes and finally betray him—is supported by the narrator's own understanding of his experience.

Ras himself proffers a political alternative for the American Negro, as he represents those Negro leaders who have espoused a racism that inverts the Manichean color symbolism traditional to the Christian West. Whereas the Western, which is to say American, mythos makes black synonymous with evil, the Negro racist makes black the color of all that is good. He attracts the support of Negroes by making them proud of their blackness. According to one scholar of black nationalism, C. Eric Lincoln,

> All black nationalist movements have in common three character-istics: a disparagement of the white man and his culture, a repudia-tion of Negro identity and an appropriation of "asiatic" culture symbols. Within this framework, they take shape in a remarkable variety of creeds and organizations.

The most prominent black nationalist in the period covered by Ellison's novel was Marcus Garvey, as the most famous exemplars in recent years are Elijah Muhammed and Malcolm X. However, there is little reason specifically to identify, as some critics have done, any of these figures with Ras the Exhorter. Although Ras is described as having, like Garvey, a West Indian accent, he favors resettlement in Abyssinia ("Ras" being Abyssinian for prince), whereas Garvey wanted to send American Negroes to West Africa. In this respect, one could say, Ras is closer to the historic Noble Drew Ali, the self-styled leader of the "Moors," who designated Morocco in North Africa as the Negro home-land; moreover, his name evokes a nod to the Ras Tafari movement of colored West Indians. What this multiple reference suggests is that Ras, like other important characters in the novel, is conceived as a fictional prototype embodying a utopian alternative that has been espoused by several historical figures; and sure enough, Ras's group embodies all three of the characteristics Professor Lincoln enumerates as typical of black nationalist movements.

The narrator never allies himself with Ras; for although he knows that Ras is capable of telling the truth about the Negro's relations with whites, the narrator also recognizes that the alternative Ras offers is unrealistic—absurd in everyday practice. Ras advocates a massive return to Africa which—given the costs, the lack of inhabitable space and the difficulties of resettlement—would be too hazardous for an average American Negro. For the United States, Ras preaches counter-violence, which the narrator discovers is ultimately self-destructive.

The Harlem battle Ras eventually wages is most thoroughly char-acterized by an anonymous Negro who tells his drinking cronies about the riot he has just witnessed. Through this device, Ellison reveals not only the absurdity of the battle itself but also the average Negro's bemused view of the fray:

> You know that stud Ras the Destroyer? Well, man, *he* was spit-ting blood. Hell, yes, man, he had him a big black hoss and a fur cap and some kind of old lion skin or something over his shoulders and he was raising hell. goddam if he wasn't a *sight,* riding up and

down on this ole hoss, you know one of the kind that pulls vegetable wagons, and he got him a cowboy saddle and some big spurs. . . .

Hell, yes! Riding up and down the block yelling, "Destroy 'em! Drive 'em out. Burn 'em out! I, Ras, commands you—to destroy them to the last piece of rotten fish!" And 'bout that time some joker with a big ole Georgia voice sticks his head out the window and yells, "Ride 'em cowboy. Give 'em hell and bananas." And man, that crazy sonofabitch up there on that hoss, looking like death eating a sandwich, he reaches down and comes up with a forty-five and starts blazing up at that window—and man, talk about cutting out! In a second wasn't nobody left but ole Ras up there on that hoss with that lion skin stretched out behind him. Crazy, man.

When he seen them cops riding up he reached back of his saddle and come up with some kind of old shield. One with a spike in the middle of it. And that ain't all; when he sees the cops he calls to one of his goddam henchmens to hand him up a spear, and a little short guy run out into the street and give him one. You know, one of the kind you see them African guys carrying in the moving pictures. . . .

Ras rides hard, "like Earle Sand in the fifth at Jamaica," into the mounted police; and although he manages to knock down two with his spear, a third policeman fells him with a bullet. Meanwhile, the onlookers of Harlem are looting the damaged stores. The political point is quite clear: To the typical Harlemite, Ras's actions are ludicrously ineffectual; for he is neither prepared for a modern battle nor able to win the support of the Negro people. Moreover, the violence he creates causes more deaths among the Negroes than the white enemies. In this respect, the riot echoes the battle royal fought at the beginning of the novel; for in both scenes, the Negroes vent their anger not against their oppressor but against their own people.

Against both Ras and Brother Jack is counterposed Rinehart, who represents the possibilities of Harlem life. As Ras's thugs are closing in upon the narrator, he steps into a drugstore and purchases a disguise of dark glasses and a wide-brimmed hat. Advancing down the street, he notices that several passers-by mistake him for a certain "Rinehart"; within moments, he discovers that Rinehart must be a desirable lover, a gambler, a numbers runner, a police briber, a male whore, a hipster, a zoot-suiter, and a self-ordained Reverend—"Spiritual Technologist." The narrator realizes why Rinehart can fill so many roles, for his own dark glasses reveal that the world of Harlem is "a merging fluidity of forms." In contrast to the Brotherhood, and also to Ras, who try to squeeze the world into rigid categories which limit the dimensions of existence, Rinehart sees that the Negro world in the North offers anonymity and possibility:

In the South everyone knows you, but coming North was a jump into the unknown. You could actually make yourself anew. The notion was frightening, for now the world seemed to flow before my eyes. All boundaries down, freedom was not only the recognition of necessity, it was the recognition of possibility. And sitting there trembling I caught a brief glimpse of the possibilities posed by Rinehart's multiple personalities. . . .

This recognition echoes the advice an anonymous veteran gave the narrator back in The Golden Day: "Be your own father, young man. And remember, the world is possibility if only you'll discover it." After this revelation, the narrator perceives that "Hambro's lawyer's mind was too narrowly logical" to understand Harlem.

After hastily departing from Hambro's, the narrator decides "to do a Rinehart," to face life with the most ironic of strategies. Remembering his childhood, he repeats to himself his grandfather's death-bed advice: "Live with your head in the lion's mouth. I want you to overcome 'em with yesses, undermine 'em with grins, agree 'em to death and destruction, let 'em swoller you till they vomit or bust wide open." He decides to master the trick of saying yes and no at the same time, yes to please and no to know. "For now I saw that I could agree with Jack without agreeing, and I could tell Harlem to have hope when there was no hope." To please his Brotherhood superiors he fabricates reports of a nonexistent growth in membership, and at the next Brotherhood gathering he entices Sybil, the wife of an organizational functionary, to come to his apartment. Although he knows that she sees him as just another hypersexual Negro, "expected either to sing 'Old Man River' and just keep rolling along, or do fancy tricks with my muscles," he decides this time to exploit his invisibility. However, when she makes "a modest proposal that I join her in a very revolting ritual," the narrator, sometimes a prig, is repelled by what he interprets as an assault on something deeper than mere sexuality. So, he spends the evening torn between the impulse to throw her out of his bed and wondering how Rinehart would have handled the situation. Though he imitates the motions he imagines to be Rinehart's, seducing the girl who calls him "boo'ful," he cannot play the role with the assurance of the master.

This experience with the Brotherhood, along with his recognition of the vanity of Ras's efforts, leads the narrator to a decisive decision: "I knew that it was better to live out one's own absurdity than to die for that of others." Later, he elaborates on the theme:

> I've never been more loved and appreciated than when I tried to "justify" and affirm someone's mistaken beliefs; or when I've tried to give my friends the incorrect, absurd answers they wished to hear.

> . . . Oh yes, it made them happy and it made me sick. So, I became ill of affirmation, of saying "yes" against the nay-saying of my stomach—not to mention my brain. . . . My problem was that I always tried to go in everyone's way but my own. I have also been called one thing and then another while no one really wished to hear what I called myself. So after years of trying to adopt the opinions of others I finally rebelled.

In the final sequences of the novel, the narrator confronts the problem of how to face what he takes to be the absurdity of society. In escaping from the police, he jumps through a manhole into a bin of coal. Unable to climb out, he experiences a "dark night of the soul," which includes a nightmare in which Norton, Emerson and Jack castrate him of his "illusions." Wading through the tunnels, he finds a large basement cavern which becomes his underground home; in his own way, the man who had Candide's innocence and questing energy eventually accepts Candide's final dictum, "That we must cultivate our [own] garden." Whereas Rinehart exploited absurdity for personal gain, the narrator as underground man accepts, as an expatriate, the condition through his own non-participation.

However, this escape, he discovers, is not satisfactory either. "I couldn't be still even in hibernation," he thinks, "because, damn it, there's the mind, the *mind*. It wouldn't let me rest." The narrator's conscience inspires him to write a book that will explain his experience. "Without the possibility of action," he thinks, existence takes on a meaninglessness, knowledge is forgotten, and the capacities to love and care are suppressed. The narrator achieves what Ellison described in his essay on Wright as the spirit of the blues: "They at once express both the agony of life and the possibility of conquering it through sheer toughness of spirit. They fall short of tragedy only in that they provide no solution, offer no scapegoat but the self." While he agrees with the wisdom of Louis Armstrong's song, "Open the window and let the foul air out," he also believes another song that says, "It was good green corn before the harvest." It is the latter belief that leads him to resolve to "shake off his old skin," to repudiate his form of expatriation, and to seek in the aboveground society an existence that allows him to live primarily for himself. He concludes his story affirming the desire to affirm. "There's a possibility that even an invisible man has a socially responsible role to play." With all his previous experiences and rejections, this becomes the most positive commitment that Ellison's narrator can justifiably make.

ROBERT BONE

The

Novels

of

James Baldwin

NO OTHER AFRO-AMERICAN NOVELIST HAS CAPTURED THE IMAGINATION of the American reading public like James Baldwin (1924–   ). Although still a relatively young man, Baldwin has been a national figure for the last fifteen years, one of the most articulate spokesmen about race that the country has ever known, as well as one of the important writers of his generation. He has increasingly become a figure of controversy, both praised and damned for his esthetic theories, his treatment of Richard Wright, his interest in homosexuality, his racial militancy (or lack of it), his commercial success, his very life style.

Many critics, Robert Bone included, feel that Baldwin is a much better essayist than novelist, and it has become fashionable to slight Baldwin's fictional achievement. However, anyone who has thought as much about the novel as Baldwin, and who has given such remarkable expression to that thinking, cannot be easily dismissed. One problem is that Baldwin's fiction seems to lack the emotional depth and intellectual significance illustrated in the essays. Too often Baldwin's characters appear to find simplistic solutions to their complex human problems; his novels never seem to meaningfully resolve themselves. In *Go Tell It On The Mountain,* young John Grimes ends the novel in religious conversion, but everything which attends that conversion makes it clear that Christ is an unsatisfactory solution to the real problem facing him: being black in America. In *Giovanni's Room* one of the two chief characters tragically attempts to flee from his homosexuality, the other kills a man and is executed. The survivors in *Another Country* end the novel searching for each other in heterosexual and homosexual love, but the novel has already suggested that love is suspect at best. Finally, in Baldwin's most recent novel, *Tell Me How Long the Train's Been Gone* (1968), the hero, a black actor named Leo Proudhammer, ends the novel in melancholy escape from the disaster area called the United States. Looking over San Francisco from a height the night before he is to leave for Europe to recover from a heart attack, Proudhammer laments the loss of the country that has taken itself away from him by its willful neglect of his people:

> We were on a height, and San Francisco unfurled beneath us, at our feet, like a many-colored scroll. I was leaving soon. I wished it were possible to stay. I had worked hard, hard, it certainly should have been possible by now for me to have a safe, quiet, comfortable life, a life I could devote to my work and to those I loved, without being bugged to death. But I knew it wasn't possible. There was a sense in which it certainly could be said that my endeavor had been for nothing. Indeed, I had conquered the city: but the city was stricken with the plague. Not in my lifetime would this plague end, and now, all that I most treasured, wine, talk, laughter, love, the embrace of a friend, the light in the eyes of a lover, the touch of a lover, that smell, that contest, that beautiful torment, and the mighty joy of a good day's work, would have to be stolen, each moment lived as though it were the last, for my own mortality was not more certain than the storm that was rising to engulf us all.*

Whether this statement reveals Baldwin's attitude toward his own relationship with his country is difficult to tell. But it is indicative of both the unfinished nature of James Baldwin's quest for meaning in life and art, and of the extraordinary literary talent that characterizes that search.

---

* Quoted from James Baldwin, *Tell Me How Long the Train's Been Gone* (New York, 1968) by permission of the publisher, The Dial Press, Inc.

ROBERT BONE

The Novels of James Baldwin

He made me a watchman upon the city wall,
And if I am a Christian, I am the least of all.
                        —NEGRO SPIRITUAL

THE MOST IMPORTANT NEGRO WRITER TO EMERGE DURING THE LAST decade is of course James Baldwin. His publications, which include three books of essays, three novels, and two plays, have had a stunning impact on our cultural life. His political role, as a leading spokesman of the Negro revolt, has been scarcely less effective. Awards and honors, wealth and success, have crowned his career, and Baldwin has become a national celebrity.

Under the circumstances, the separation of the artist from the celebrity is as difficult as it is necessary. For Baldwin is an uneven writer, the quality of whose work can by no means be taken for granted. His achievement in the novel is most open to dispute, and it is that which I propose to discuss in some detail. Meanwhile, it may be possible to narrow the area of controversy by a preliminary assessment of his talent.

I find Baldwin strongest as an essayist, weakest as a playwright, and successful in the novel form on only one occasion. For the three books of essays, *Notes of a Native Son* (1955), *Nobody Knows My Name* (1961), and *The Fire Next Time* (1963), I have nothing but admiration. Baldwin has succeeded in transposing the entire discussion of American race relations to the interior plane; it is a major breakthrough for the American imagination. In the theater, he has written one competent apprentice play, *The Amen Corner,* first produced at Howard University in 1955, and one unspeakably bad propaganda piece, *Blues for Mister Charlie* (1964). In the novel, the impressive achievement of *Go Tell It on the Mountain* (1953) has not been matched by his more recent books, *Giovanni's Room* (1956) and *Another Country* (1962). Perhaps a closer acquaintance with the author's life will help us to account for these vicissitudes.

James Baldwin was a product of the Great Migration. His father had come North from New Orleans; his mother, from Maryland. James was born in Harlem in 1924, the first of nine children. His father was a factory worker and lay preacher, and the boy was raised under the twin disciplines of poverty and the store-front church. He experienced

Reprinted from *Tri-Quarterly,* No. 2 (Winter 1965), pp. 3-20, by permission of the publisher. Copyright © 1965 by *Tri-Quarterly.*

a profound religious crisis during the summer of his fourteenth year, entered upon a youthful ministry, and remained in the pulpit for three years. The second crisis of his life was his break with this milieu; that is, with his father's values, hopes, and aspirations for his son. These two crises—the turn into the fold and the turn away—provide the raw material for his first novel and his first play.

Baldwin graduated from De Witt Clinton High School in 1942, having served on the staff of the literary magazine. He had already discovered in this brief encounter a means of transcending his appointed destiny. Shortly after graduation he left home, determined to support himself as best he could while developing his talent as a writer. After six years of frustration and false starts, however, he had two fellowships but no substantial publications to his credit. This initial literary failure, coupled with the pressures of his personal life, drove him into exile. In 1948, at the age of twenty-four, Baldwin left America for Paris, never intending to return.

He remained abroad for nine years. Europe gave him many things. It gave him a world perspective from which to approach the question of his own identity. It gave him a tender love affair which would dominate the pages of his later fiction. But above all, Europe gave him back himself. Some two years after his arrival in Paris, Baldwin suffered a breakdown and went off to Switzerland to recover:

> There, in that absolutely alabaster landscape, armed with two Bessie Smith records and a typewriter, I began to try to re-create the life that I had first known as a child and from which I had spent so many years in flight. . . . I had never listened to Bessie Smith in America (in the same way that, for years, I would not touch watermelon), but in Europe she helped to reconcile me to being a "nigger."[1]

The immediate fruit of self-recovery was a great creative outburst. First came two books of reconciliation with his racial heritage. *Go Tell It on the Mountain* and *The Amen Corner* represent a search for roots, a surrender to tradition, an acceptance of the Negro past. Then came a series of essays which probe, deeper than anyone has dared, the psychic history of this nation. They are a moving record of a man's struggle to define the forces that have shaped him, in order that he may accept himself. Last came *Giovanni's Room*, which explores the question of his male identity. Here Baldwin extends the theme of self-acceptance into the sexual realm.

Toward the end of his stay in Paris, Baldwin experienced the first symptoms of a crisis from which he has never recovered. Having exhausted the theme of self-acceptance, he cast about for fresh mate-

---

[1] *Nobody Knows My Name* (New York, Dial Press, 1961), p. 5.

rial, but his third novel stubbornly refused to move. He has described
this moment of panic in a later essay: "It is the point at which many
artists lose their minds, or commit suicide, or throw themselves into
good works, or try to enter politics."[2] Recognizing these dangers to his
art, Baldwin has not succeeded in avoiding them. Something like good
works and politics has been the recent bent of his career. Unable to
grow as an artist, he has fallen back upon a tradition of protest writing
which he formerly denounced.

Baldwin returned to America in 1957. The battered self, he must
have felt, was ready to confront society. A good many of the essays in
Nobody Knows My Name record his initial impressions of America,
but this is a transitional book, still largely concerned with questions of
identity. Protest, however, becomes the dominant theme of his next
three books. In *Another Country, The Fire Next Time,* and *Blues for
Mister Charlie,* he assumes the role of Old Testament prophet, calling
down the wrath of history on the heads of the white oppressor.

Baldwin's career may be divided into two distinct periods. His first
five books have been concerned with the emotion of shame. The flight
from self, the quest for identity, and the sophisticated acceptance of
one's "blackness" are the themes that flow from this emotion. His last
three books have been concerned with the emotion of rage. An apocalyptic vision and a new stridency of tone are brought to bear against
the racial and the sexual oppressor. The question then arises, why has
he avoided the prophetic role until the recent past?

The answer, I believe, lies in Baldwin's relationship to his father,
and still more, to his spiritual father, Richard Wright. Baldwin's father
died in 1943, and within a year Baldwin met Wright for the first time.
It is amply clear from his essays that the twenty-year-old youth adopted
the older man as a father-figure. What followed is simplicity itself:
Baldwin's habit of defining himself in opposition to his father was
transferred to the new relationship. If Wright was committed to protest
fiction, Baldwin would launch his own career with a rebellious essay
called "Everybody's Protest Novel."[3] So long as Wright remained alive,
the prophetic strain in Baldwin was suppressed. But with Wright's
death in 1960, Baldwin was free to *become* his father. He has been
giving Noah the rainbow sign ever since.

2

Go Tell It on the Mountain (1953) is the best of Baldwin's novels,
and the best is very good indeed. It ranks with Jean Toomer's *Cane,*
Richard Wright's *Native Son,* and Ralph Ellison's *Invisible Man* as a

---

[2] *Nobody Knows My Name,* p. 224.
[3] See *Notes of a Native Son* (Boston, Beacon Press, 1955), pp. 13-23.

major contribution to American fiction. For this novel cuts through the walls of the store-front church to the essence of Negro experience in America. This is Baldwin's earliest world, his bright and morning star, and it glows with metaphorical intensity. Its emotions are his emotions; its language, his native tongue. The result is a prose of unusual power and authority. One senses in Baldwin's first novel a confidence, control, and mastery of style which he has not attained again in the novel form.

The central event of *Go Tell It on the Mountain* is the religious conversion of an adolescent boy. In a long autobiographical essay, which forms a part of *The Fire Next Time*,[4] Baldwin leaves no doubt that he was writing of his own experience. During the summer of his fourteenth year, he tells us, he succumbed to the spiritual seduction of a woman evangelist. On the night of his conversion, he suddenly found himself lying on the floor before the altar. He describes his trance-like state, the singing and clapping of the saints, and the all-night prayer vigil which helped to bring him "through." He then recalls the circumstances of his life which prompted so pagan and desperate journey to the throne of Grace.

The overwhelming fact of Balwdin's childhood was his victimization by the white power structure. At first he experienced white power only indirectly, as refracted through the brutality and degradation of the Harlem ghetto. The world beyond the ghetto seemed remote, and scarcely could be linked in a child's imagination to the harrowing conditions of his daily life. And yet a vague terror, transmitted through his parents to the ghetto child, attested to the power of the white world. Meanwhile, in the forefront of his consciousness was a set of fears by no means vague.

To a young boy growing up in the Harlem ghetto, damnation was a clear and present danger: "For the wages of sin were visible everywhere, in every wine-stained and urine-splashed hallway, in every clanging ambulance bell, in every scar on the faces of the pimps and their whores, in every helpless, newborn baby being brought into this danger, in every knife and pistol fight on the Avenue."[5] To such a boy, the store-front church offered a refuge and a sanctuary from the terrors of the street. God and safety became synonomous, and the church, a part of his survival strategy.

Fear, then, was the principal motive of Baldwin's conversion: "I became, during my fourteenth year, for the first time in my life afraid— afraid of the evil within me and afraid of the evil without."[6] As the

---

[4] See *The Fire Next Time* (New York, Dial Press, 1963), pp. 29-61.
[5] *The Fire Next Time*, p. 34.
[6] *The Fire Next Time*, p. 30.

twin pressures of sex and race began to mount, the adolescent boy struck a desperate bargain with God. In exchange for sanctuary, he surrenderd his sexuality, and abandoned any aspirations which might bring him into conflict with white power. He was safe, but walled off from the world; saved, but isolated from experience. This, to Baldwin, is the historical betrayal of the Negro church. In exchange for the power of the Word, the Negro trades away the personal power of his sex and the social power of his people.

Life on these terms was unacceptable to Baldwin; he did not care to settle for less than his potential as a man. If his deepest longings were thwarted in the church, he would pursue them through his art. Sexual and racial freedom thus became his constant theme. And yet, even in breaking with the church, he pays tribute to its power: "In spite of everything, there was in the life I fled a zest and a joy and a capacity for facing and surviving disaster that are very moving and very rare."[7] We shall confront, then, in *Go Tell It on the Mountain*, a certain complexity of tone. Baldwin maintains an ironic distance from his material, even as he portrays the spiritual force and emotional appeal of store-front Christianity.

So much for the biographical foundations of the novel. The present action commences on the morning of John Grimes' fourteenth birthday, and before the night is out, he is born again in Christ. Part I, "The Seventh Day," introduces us to the boy and his family, his fears and aspirations, and the Temple of the Fire Baptized which is the center of his life. Part II, "The Prayers of the Saints," contains a series of flashbacks in which we share the inmost thoughts and private histories of his Aunt Florence, his mother, Elizabeth, and his putative father, Gabriel. Part III, "The Threshing-Floor," returns us to the present and completes the story of the boy's conversion.

Parts I and III are set in Harlem in the spring of 1935. The action of Part II, however, takes place for the most part down home. Florence, Elizabeth, and Gabriel belong to a transitional generation, born roughly between 1875 and 1900. *Go Tell It on the Mountain* is thus a novel of the Great Migration. It traces the process of secularization which occurred when the Negro left the land for the Northern ghettos. This theme, to be sure, is handled ironically. Baldwin's protagonist "gets religion," but he is too young, too frightened, and too innocent to grasp the implications of his choice.

It is through the lives of the adults that we achieve perspective on the boy's conversion. His Aunt Florence has been brought to the evening prayer meeting by her fear of death. She is dying of cancer, and

---

[7] *The Fire Next Time*, p. 55.

in her extremity humbles herself before God, asking forgiveness of her sins. These have consisted of a driving ambition and a ruthless hardening of heart. Early in her adult life, she left her dying mother to come North, in hopes of bettering her lot. Later, she drove from her side a husband whom she loved: "It had not been her fault that Frank was the way he was, determined to live and die a common nigger" (p. 92).[8] All of her deeper feelings have been sacrificed to a futile striving for "whiteness" and respectability. Now she contemplates the wages of her virtue: an agonizing death in a lonely furnished room.

Elizabeth, as she conceives her life, has experienced both the fall and the redemption. Through Richard, she has brought an illegitimate child into the world, but through Gabriel, her error is retrieved. She fell in love with Richard during the last summer of her girlhood, and followed him North to Harlem. There they took jobs as chambermaid and elevator boy, hoping to be married soon. Richard is sensitive, intelligent, and determined to educate himself. Late one evening, however, he is arrested and accused of armed robbery. When he protests his innocence, he is beaten savagely by the police. Ultimately he is released, but half hysterical with rage and shame, he commits suicide. Under the impact of this blow, Elizabeth retreats from life. Her subsequent marriage to Gabriel represents safety, timidity, and atonement for her sin.

As Gabriel prays on the night of John's conversion, his thoughts revert to the events of his twenty-first year: his own conversion and beginning ministry, his joyless marriage to Deborah, and his brief affair with Esther. Deborah has been raped by white men at the age of sixteen. Thin, ugly, sexless, she is treated by the Negroes as a kind of holy fool. Gabriel, who has been a wild and reckless youth, marries her precisely to mortify the flesh. But he cannot master his desire. He commits adultery with Esther, and informed that she is pregnant, refuses all emotional support. Esther dies in childbirth and her son, Royal, who grows to manhood unacknowledged by his father, is killed in a Chicago dive.

Soon after the death of Royal, Deborah dies childless, and Gabriel is left without an heir. When he moves North, however, the Lord sends him a sign in the form of an unwed mother and her fatherless child. He marries Elizabeth and promises to raise Johnny as his own son. In the course of time the second Royal is born, and Gabriel rejoices in the fulfillment of God's promise. But John's half brother, the fruit of the prophet's seed, has turned his back on God. Tonight he lies at home with a knife wound, inflicted in a street-fight with some whites. To

---

[8] All page references are to the Dial Press editions of the novels.

Gabriel, therefore, John's conversion is a bitter irony: "Only the son of the bondwoman stood where the rightful heir should stand" (p. 128).

Through this allusion, Baldwin alerts us to the metaphorical possibilities of his plot. Gabriel's phrase is from *Genesis* 21, verses 9 and 10: "And Sarah saw the son of Hagar the Egyptian, which she had born unto Abraham, mocking. Wherefore she said unto Abraham, Cast out this bondwoman and her son: for the son of the bondwoman shall not be heir with my son, even with Isaac." Hagar's bastard son is of course Ishmael, the archetypal outcast. Apparently Baldwin wants us to view Gabriel and Johnny in metaphorical relation to Abraham and Ishmael. This tableau of guilty father and rejected child will serve him as an emblem of race relations in America.

Baldwin sees the Negro quite literally as the bastard child of American civilization. In Gabriel's double involvement with bastardy, we have a re-enactment of the white man's historic crime. In Johnny, the innocent victim of Gabriel's hatred, we have an archetypal image of the Negro child. Obliquely, by means of an extended metaphor, Baldwin approaches the very essence of Negro experience. That essence is rejection, and its most destructive consequence is shame. But God, the Heavenly Father, does not reject the Negro utterly. He casts down only to raise up. This is the psychic drama which occurs beneath the surface of John's conversion.

The Negro child, rejected by the whites for reasons that he cannot understand, is afflicted by an overwhelming sense of shame. Something mysterious, he feels, must be wrong with him, that he should be so cruelly ostracized. In time he comes to associate these feelings with the color of his skin—the basis, after all, of his rejection. He feels, and is made to feel, perpetually dirty and unclean:

> John hated sweeping this carpet, for dust arose, clogging his nose and sticking to his sweaty skin, and he felt that should he sweep it forever, the clouds of dust would not diminish, the rug would not be clean. It became in his imagination his impossible, lifelong task, his hard trial, like that of a man he had read about somewhere, whose curse it was to push a boulder up a steep hill (p. 27).

This quality of Negro life, unending struggle with one's own blackness, is symbolized by Baldwin in the family name, *Grimes*. One can readily understand how such a sense of personal shame might have been inflamed by contact with the Christian tradition and transformed into an obsession with original sin. Gabriel's sermons take off from such texts as "I am a man of unclean lips," or "He which is filthy, let him be filthy still." The Negro's religious ritual, as Baldwin points out in an early essay, is permeated with color symbolism: "Wash me, cried the slave to his Maker, and I shall be whiter, whiter than snow! For black is the color of evil; only the robes of the saved are white."[9]

Given this attack on the core of the self, how can the Negro respond? If he accepts the white man's equation of blackness with evil, he is lost. Hating his true self, he will undertake the construction of a counter-self along the following lines: everything "black" I now disown. To such a man, Christ is a kind of spiritual bleaching cream. Only if the Negro challenges the white man's moral categories can he hope to survive on honorable terms. This involves the sentiment; everything "black" I now embrace, however painfully, as mine. There is, in short, the path of self-hatred and the path of self-acceptance. Both are available to Johnny within the framework of the church, but he is deterred from one by the negative example of his father.

Consider Gabriel. The substance of his life is moral evasion. A preacher of the gospel, and secretely the father of an illegitimate child, he cannot face the evil in himself. In order to preserve his image as the Lord's anointed, he has sacrificed the lives of those around him. His principal victim is Johnny, who is not his natural child. In disowning the bastard, he disowns the "blackness" in himself. Gabriel's psychological mechanisms are, so to say, white. Throughout his work Baldwin has described the scapegoat mechanism which is fundamental to the white man's sense of self. To the question, Who am I?, the white man answers: I am *white*, that is, immaculate, without stain. I am the purified, the saved, the saintly, the elect. It is the *black* who is the embodiment of evil. Let him, the son of the bondwoman, pay the price of my sins.

From self-hatred flows not only self-righteousness but self-glorification as well. From the time of his conversion Gabriel has been living in a world of compensatory fantasy. He sees the Negro race as a chosen people and himself as prophet and founder of a royal line. But if Old Testament materials can be appropriated to buttress such a fantasy world, they also offer a powerful means of grappling with reality. When the Negro preacher compares the lot of his people to that of the children of Israel, he provides his flock with a series of metaphors which correspond to their deepest experience. The church thus offers to the Negro masses a ritual enactment of their daily pain. It is with this poetry of suffering, which Baldwin calls the power of the Word, that the final section of the novel is concerned.

The first fifteen pages of Part III contain some of Baldwin's most effective writing. As John Grimes lies before the altar, a series of

---

[9] *Notes of a Native Son*, p. 21.

visionary states passes through his soul. Dream fragments and Freudian sequences, lively fantasies and Aesopian allegories, combine to produce a generally surrealistic effect. Images of darkness and chaos, silence and emptiness, mist and cold—cumulative patterns developed early in the novel—function now at maximum intensity. These images of damnation express the state of the soul when thrust into outer darkness by a rejecting, punishing, castrating father-figure who is the surrogate of a hostile society. The dominant emotions are shame, despair, guilt, and fear.

At the depth of John's despair, a sound emerges to assuage his pain:

> He had heard it all his life, but it was only now that his ears were opened to this sound that came from the darkness, that could only come from darkness, that yet bore such sure witness to the glory of the light. And now in his moaning, and so far from any help, he heard it in himself—it rose from his bleeding, his cracked-open heart. It was a sound of rage and weeping which filled the grave, rage and weeping from time set free, but bound now in eternity; rage that had no language, weeping with no voice—which yet spoke now, to John's startled soul, of boundless melancholy, of the bitterest patience, and the longest night; of the deepest water, the strongest chains, the most cruel lash; of humility most wretched, the dungeon most absolute, of love's bed defiled, and birth dishonored, and most bloody, unspeakable, sudden death. Yes, the darkness hummed with murder: the body in the water, the body in the fire, the body on the tree. John looked down the line of these armies of darkness, army upon army, and his soul whispered, *Who are these?* (p. 228).

This is the sound, though John Grimes doesn't know it, of the blues. It is the sound of Bessie Smith, to which James Baldwin listened as he wrote *Go Tell It on the Mountain*. It is the sound of all Negro art and all Negro religion, for it flows from the cracked-open heart.

On these harsh terms, Baldwin's protagonist discovers his identity. He belongs to those armies of darkness and must forever share their pain. To the question, Who am I?, he can now reply: I am he who suffers, and yet whose suffering on occasion is "from time set free." And thereby he discovers his humanity, for only man can ritualize his pain. We are now very close to that plane of human experience where art and religion intersect. What Baldwin wants us to feel is the emotional pressure exerted on the Negro's cultural forms by his exposure to white oppression. And finally to comprehend that these forms alone, through their power of transforming suffering, have enabled him to survive his terrible ordeal.

3

Give not thyself up, then, to fire, lest it invert thee.
                                        —MOBY DICK

. *Giovanni's Room* (1956) is by far the weakest of Baldwin's novels. There is a tentative, unfinished quality about the book, as if in merely broaching the subject of homosexuality Baldwin had exhausted his creative energy. Viewed in retrospect, it seems less a novel in its own right than a first draft of *Another Country*. The surface of the novel is deliberately opaque, for Baldwin is struggling to articulate the most intimate, the most painful, the most elusive of emotions. The characters are vague and disembodied, the themes half-digested, the colors rather bleached than vivified. We recognize in this sterile psychic landscape the unprocessed raw material of art.

And yet this novel occupies a key position in Baldwin's spiritual development. Links run backward to *Go Tell It on the Mountain* as well as forward to *Another Country*. The very furniture of Baldwin's mind derives from the store-front church of his boyhood and adolescence. When he attempts a novel of homosexual love, with an all-white cast of characters and a European setting, he simply transposes the moral topography of Harlem to the streets of Paris. When he strives toward sexual self-acceptance, he automatically casts the homosexual in a priestly role.

Before supporting this interpretation, let me summarize the plot. David, an American youth living abroad in Paris, meets a girl from back home and asks her to marry him. Hella is undecided, however, and she goes to Spain to think it over. During her absence, David meets Giovanni, a proud and handsome young Italian. They fall deeply in love and have a passionate affair. When Hella returns, David is forced to choose between his male lover and his American fiancée. He abandons Giovanni to the homosexual underworld which is only too eager to claim him. When Guillaume, whom Baldwin describes as "a disgusting old fairy," inflicts upon the youth a series of humiliations, Giovanni strangles his tormentor. He is tried for murder and executed by the guillotine. Meanwhile David, who has gone with Hella to the south of France, cannot forget Giovanni. Tortured by guilt and self-doubt, he breaks off his engagement by revealing the truth about himself.

At the emotional center of the novel is the relationship between David and Giovanni. It is highly symbolic, and to understand what is at stake, we must turn to Baldwin's essay on André Gide.[10] Published

---

[10] See *Nobody Knows My Name*, pp. 155-62.

toward the end of 1954, about a year before the appearance of *Giovanni's Room*, this essay is concerned with the two sides of Gide's personality and the precarious balance which was struck between them. On the one side was his sensuality, his lust for the boys on the Piazza d'Espagne, threatening him always with utter degradation. On the other was his Protestantism, his purity, his otherworldliness—that part of him which was not carnal, and which found expression in his Platonic marriage to Madeleine. As Baldwin puts it, "She was his Heaven who would forgive him for his Hell and help him to endure it." It is a drama of salvation, in which the celibate wife, through selfless dedication to the suffering artist, becomes in effect a priest.

In the present novel, Giovanni plays the role of Gide; David, of Madeleine. Giovanni is not merely a sensualist, but a Platonist as well: "I want to escape . . . this dirty world, this dirty body" (p. 35). It is the purity of Giovanni's love for David—its idealized, transcendent quality—that protects him from a kind of homosexual Hell. David is the string connecting him to Heaven, and when David abandons him, he plunges into the abyss.

We can now appreciate the force of David's remark, "The burden of his salvation seemed to be on me and I could not endure it" (p. 168). Possessing the power to save, David rejects the priestly office. Seen in this light, his love affair with Giovanni is a kind of novitiate. The dramatic conflict of the novel can be stated as follows: does David have a true vocation? Is he prepared to renounce the heterosexual world? When David leaves Giovanni for Hella, he betrays his calling, but ironically he has been ruined both for the priesthood and the world.

It is Giovanni, Baldwin's doomed hero, who is the true priest. For a priest is nothing but a journeyman in suffering. Thus Giovanni defies David, the American tourist, even to understand his village: "And you will have no idea of the life there, dripping and bursting and beautiful and terrible, as you have no idea of my life now" (p. 203). It is a crucial distinction for all of Baldwin's work: there are the relatively innocent—the *laity* who are mere apprentices in human suffering—and the fully initiated, the *clergy* who are intimate with pain. Among the laity may be numbered Americans, white folks, heterosexuals, and squares; among the clergy, Europeans, Negroes, homosexuals, hipsters, and jazzmen. The finest statement of this theme, in which the jazzman is portrayed as priest, is Baldwin's moving story, "Sonny's Blues."[11]

Assumption of the priestly role is always preceded by an extraordinary experience of suffering, often symbolized in Baldwin's work by the death of a child. Thus in *The Amen Corner* Sister Margaret becomes a store-front church evangelist after giving birth to a dead

---

[11] See *Partisan Review* (Summer, 1957), pp. 327-58.

child. And in *Giovanni's Room*, the protagonist leaves his wife, his family and his village after the birth of a still-born child: "When I knew that it was dead I took our crucifix off the wall and I spat on it and threw it on the floor and my mother and my girl screamed and I went out" (p. 205). It is at this point that Giovanni's inverted priesthood begins. Like Gide, he rebels against God, but the priestly impulse persists. He retreats from the heterosexual world, achieves a kind of purity in his relationship with David, is betrayed, and consigned to martyrdom.

The patterns first explored in *Giovanni's Room* are given full expression in *Another Country*. Rufus is a Negro Giovanni—a journeyman in suffering and a martyr to racial oppression. Vivaldo and the other whites are mere apprentices, who cannot grasp the beauty and the terror of Negro life. Eric is a David who completes his novitiate, and whose priestly or redemptive role is central to the novel. There has been, however, a crucial change of tone. In *Giovanni's Room*, one part of Baldwin wants David to escape from the male prison, even as another part remains committed to the ideal of homosexual love. In the later novel, this conflict has been resolved. Baldwin seems convinced that homosexuality is a liberating force, and he now brings to the subject a certain proselytizing zeal.

4

Another Country (1962) is a failure on the grand scale. It is an ambitious novel, rich in thematic possibilities, for Baldwin has at his disposal a body of ideas brilliantly developed in his essays. When he tries to endow these ideas with imaginative life, however, his powers of invention are not equal to the task. The plot consists of little more than a series of occasions for talk and fornication. Since the latter is a limited vehicle for the expression of complex ideas, talk takes over, and the novel drowns in a torrent of rhetoric.

The ideas themselves are impressive enough. At the heart of what Baldwin calls the white problem is a moral cowardice, a refusal to confront the "dark" side of human experience. The white American, at once over-protected and repressed, exhibits an infuriating tendency to deny the reality of pain and suffering, violence and evil, sex and death. He preserves in the teeth of human circumstance what must strike the less protected as a kind of willful innocence.

The American Negro, exposed to the ravages of reality by his status as a slave, has never enjoyed the luxury of innocence. On the contrary, his dark skin has come to be associated, at some buried level of the white psyche, with those forbidden impulses and hidden terrors which the white man is afraid to face. The unremitting daily warfare of American race relations must be understood in these symbolic terms. By projecting the "blackness" of his own being upon the dark skin of his Negro victim, the white man hopes to exercise the chaotic forces which threaten to destroy him from within.

The psychic cost is of course enormous. The white man loses the experience of "blackness," sacrificing both its beauty and its terror to the illusion of security. In the end, he loses his identity. For a man who cannot acknowledge the dark impulses of his own soul cannot have the vaguest notion of who he is. A stranger to himself and others, the most salient feature of his personality will be a fatal bewilderment.

There are psychic casualties on the Negro side as well. No human personality can escape the effects of prolonged emotional rejection. The victim of this cruelty will defend himself with hatred and with dreams of vengeance, and will lose, perhaps forever, his normal capacity for love. Strictly speaking, this set of defenses, and the threat of self-destruction which they pose, constitutes the Negro problem.

It is up to the whites to break this vicious circle of rejection and hatred. They can do so only by facing the void, by confronting chaos, by making the necessary journey to "another country." What the white folks need is a closer acquaintance with the blues. Then perhaps they will be ready to join the human race. But only if the bloodless learn to bleed will it be possible for the Negro to lay down his burden of hatred and revenge.

So much for the conceptual framework of the novel. What dramatic materials are employed to invest these themes with life? A Greenwich Village setting and a hipster idiom ("Beer, dad, then we'll split"). A square thrown in for laughs. A side trip to Harlem (can we be *slumming?*). A good deal of boozing, and an occasional stick of tea. Some male cheesecake ("He bent down to lift off the scarlet bikini"). Five orgasms (two interracial and two homosexual) or approximately one per eighty pages, a significant increase over the Mailer rate. Distracted by this nonsense, how can one attend to the serious business of the novel?

In one respect only does the setting of *Another Country* succeed. Baldwin's descriptions of New York contain striking images of malaise, scenes and gestures which expose the moral chaos of contemporary urban life. The surface of his prose reflects the aching loneliness of the city with the poignancy of a Hopper painting. Harrassed commuters and jostled pedestrians seem to yearn for closer contact. Denizens of a Village bar clutch their drinks with a gesture of buried despair. The whir of cash registers and the blatant glare of neon signs proclaim the harsh ascendancy of the commercial spirit. The tense subway crowds and the ubiquitous police convey a sense of latent violence. The furtive scribblings on lavatory walls provide a chilling commentary, in their mixture of raw lust and ethnic hate, on the scope and depth of our depravity.

Structurally speaking, the novel consists of two articulating parts. Book I is concerned to demonstrate how bad things really are in this America. Books II and III encompass the redemptive movement, the symbolic journey to "another country."

The central figure of Book I is Rufus Scott, a talented jazz drummer who is driven to suicide by the pressures of a racist society. Sensitive, bitter, violent, he sublimates his hatred by pounding on the white skin of his drums. With something of the same malice, he torments his white mistress, ultimately driving her insane. Crushed by this burden of guilt, he throws himself from the George Washington Bridge. Rufus, in short, is a peculiarly passive Bigger Thomas, whose murderous impulses turn back upon himself. Like Bigger, he was created to stir the conscience of the nation. For the underlying cause of Rufus' death is the failure of his white friends to comprehend the depth of his despair.

In the melting pot of Greenwich Village, Baldwin brings together a group of white Americans whose lives are linked to Rufus' fate. His closest friend is Vivaldo Moore, an "Irish wop" who has escaped from the slums of Brooklyn. Cass, a girl of upperclass New England stock, has rebelled against her background to marry an aspiring writer. Eric Jones, having left Alabama for an acting career in New York, has experienced a double exile, and is about to return from a two-year sojourn in France.

Each of these friends has failed Rufus in his hour of need. It is the moral obtuseness of the whites that Baldwin means to stress. Rufus stands in relation to his friends as jazzman to audience: "Now he stood before the misty doors of the jazz joint, peering in, sensing rather than seeing the *frantic* black people on the stand and the *oblivious*, mixed crowd at the bar" (p. 4-5, my emphasis). The audience simply refuses to hear the frantic plea in an insistent riff which seems to ask, "Do you love me?" It is a failure of love, but still more of imagination. Vivaldo and the others fail to transcend their innocence. They are blinded by their fear of self. Meaning well, they acquiesce in Rufus' death.

Having killed off Rufus early in the novel, Baldwin pursues the theme of vengeance and reconciliation through the character of Ida Scott. Embittered by the death of her brother, on whom she had counted to save her from the streets of Harlem, Ida takes revenge on the nearest white man. She moves in with Vivaldo, ostensibly in love, but actually exploiting the arrangement to advance her career as a blues singer. Toward the end of the novel, however, Vivaldo achieves a new sense of reality. This enables Ida, who has come reluctantly to love him, to confess to her deception. In a gesture of reconciliation, she slips from her finger a ruby-eyed snake ring—a gift from Rufus, and a symbol of her heritage of hate.

Books II and III are dominated by the figure of Eric Jones, the young actor who has gone abroad to find himself. His adolescence in Alabama was marked by a homosexual encounter with a Negro youth. In New York he has a brief, violent, and radically unsatisfying affair with Rufus, from which he flees to France. There he falls in love with Yves, a Paris street boy, and through a chaste and tactful courtship wins his trust and love. As Book II opens, they are enjoying an idyllic holiday in a rented villa on the Côte d'Azur. Eric must soon leave for America, however, where he has accepted a part in a Broadway play. After a suitable interval, Yves will join him in New York.

Since the love affair of Eric and Yves is the turning point of the novel, we must pause to examine its wider implications. Book II commences with a highly charged, symbolic prose:

> Eric sat naked in his rented garden. Flies buzzed and boomed in the brilliant heat, and a yellow bee circled his head. Eric remained very still, then reached for the cigarettes beside him and lit one, hoping that the smoke would drive the bee away. Yves' tiny black-and-white kitten stalked the garden as though it were Africa, crouching beneath the mimosas like a panther and leaping into the air (p. 183).

Like Whitman, his spiritual progenitor, Baldwin tends to endow his diffuse sexuality with mythic significance. Here he depicts, in this Mediterranean garden, what appears to be a homosexual Eden. Then, in an attempt to fuse two levels of his own experience, he brings into metaphorical relation the idea of homosexuality and the idea of Africa. Each represents to the "majority" imagination a kind of primal chaos, yet each contains the possibility of liberation. For to be Negro, or to be homosexual, is to be in constant touch with that sensual reality which the white (read: heterosexual) world is at such pains to deny.

The male lovers, naked in the garden, are not to be taken too literally. What Baldwin means to convey through this idyllic episode is the innocence of the unrepressed. He has been reading, one would surmise, Norman Brown's *Life Against Death*. "Children," Brown reminds us, "explore in indiscriminate fashion all the erotic potentialities of the human body. In Freudian terms, children are polymorphously perverse."[12] In this episode on the Mediterranean coast, we are back

---

[12] Norman Brown, *Life Against Death* (Wesleyan University Press, 1959), p. 27.

in the cradle of man, back in the sexually and racially undifferentiated human past; back in the lost paradise of the polymorphously perverse.

On these mythic foundations, Baldwin constructs a theory of personality. The primal stuff of human personality is undifferentiated: "He was, briefly and horribly, in a region where there were no definitions of any kind, neither of color nor of male and female" (pp. 301-2). One must face this formlessness, however, before one can hope to achieve form.

At the core of Baldwin's fiction is an existentialist psychology. In a passage whose language is reminiscent of *Genesis*, he describes Vivaldo's struggle to define himself: "And beneath all this was the void where anguish lived and questions crouched, which referred only to Vivaldo and to no one else on earth. Down there, down there, lived the raw unformed substance for the creation of Vivaldo, and only he, Vivaldo alone, could master it" (pp. 305-6). As music depends ultimately on silence, so being is achieved in tension with nothingness. Sexual identity—all identity—emerges from the void. Man, the sole creator of himself, moves alone upon the face of the waters.

We can now account for Eric's pivotal position in the novel. Through his commitment to Yves, he introduces an element of order into the chaos of his personal life. This precarious victory, wrested in anguish from the heart of darkness, is the real subject of *Another Country*. Images of chaos proliferate throughout the novel. Rufus leaps into chaos when he buries himself in the deep black water of the Hudson River. Cass encounters chaos in the strange, pulsating life of Harlem, or in an abstract expressionist canvas at the Museum of Modern Art. To Vivaldo, chaos means a marijuana party in a Village pad; to Eric, the male demi-monde which threatens to engulf him. Eric is the first of Rufus' friends to face his demons and achieve a sense of self. He in turn emancipates the rest.

From this vantage point, one can envision the novel that Baldwin was trying to write. With the breakdown of traditional standards—even of sexual normality—homosexuality becomes a metaphor of the modern condition. Baldwin says of Eric, "There were no standards for him except those he could make for himself" (p. 212). Forced to create his own values as he goes along, Eric is to serve "as a footnote to the twentieth century torment" (p. 330). The homosexual becomes emblematic of existential man.

What actually happens, however, is that Baldwin's literary aims are deflected by his sexual mystique. Eric returns to America as the high priest of ineffable phallic mysteries. His friends, male and female, dance around the Maypole and, *mirabile dictu*, their sense of reality is restored. Cass commits adultery with Eric, and is thereby reconciled to her faltering marriage. Vivaldo receives at Eric's hands a rectal revelation which prepares him for the bitter truth of Ida's confession. The novel ends as Yves joins Eric in New York, heralding, presumably, a fresh start for all and a new era of sexual and racial freedom.

For most readers of *Another Country*, the difficulty will lie in accepting Eric as a touchstone of reality. Let us consider the overall design. Rufus is portrayed as the victim of a white society which cannot face unpleasant truths. The redemptive role is then assigned to Eric. But few will concede a sense of reality, at least in the sexual realm, to one who regards heterosexual love as "a kind of superior calisthenics" (p. 336). To most, homosexuality will seem rather an invasion than an affirmation of human truth. Ostensibly the novel summons us to reality. Actually it substitutes for the illusions of white supremacy those of homosexual love.

In any event, it is not the task of a literary critic to debate the merits of homosexuality, but to demonstrate its pressure on the novel. Let us accept Baldwin's postulate that in order to become a man, one must journey to the void. Let us grant that homosexuality is a valid metaphor of this experience. We must now ask of Baldwin's hero: does he face the void and emerge with a new sense of reality, or does he pitch his nomad's tent forever on the shores of the burning lake? Then answer hinges, it seems to me, on the strength of Eric's commitment to Yves. Baldwin describes it as total, and yet, within a few weeks' span, while Yves remains behind in France, Eric betrays him with a woman and a man. How can we grant to this lost youth redemptive power?

One senses that Baldwin, in his portrait of Eric, has desired above all to be faithful to his own experience. He will neither falsify nor go beyond it. Central to that experience is a rebellion against the prevailing sexual, as well as racial mores. But on either plane of experience, Baldwin faces an emotional dilemma. Like Satan and the fallen angels, it is equally painful to persist in his rebellion and to give it up. Total defiance is unthinkable; total reconciliation only less so. These are the poles of Baldwin's psychic life, and the novel vacillates helplessly between them.

The drama of reconciliation is enacted by Ida and Vivaldo. Through their symbolic marriage, Ida is reconciled to whites; Vivaldo, to women. This gesture, however, is a mere concession to majority opinion. What Baldwin really feels is dramatized through Rufus and Eric. Rufus can neither be fully reconciled to, nor fully defiant of, white society. No Bigger Thomas, he is incapable of total hate. Pushed to the limits of endurance, he commits suicide. Similarly, Eric can neither be fully reconciled to women, nor can he surrender to the male demi-monde.

So he camps on the outskirts of Hell. In the case of Rufus, the suicidal implications are overt. With Eric, as we shall see, Baldwin tries to persuade us that Hell is really Heaven.

In its rhetoric as well, the novel veers between the poles of reconciliation and defiance. At times the butter of brotherhood seems to melt in Baldwin's mouth. But here is Rufus, scoring the first inter-racial orgasm of the book: "And shortly, nothing could have stopped him, not the white God himself nor a lynch mob arriving on wings. Under his breath he cursed the milk-white bitch and groaned and rode his weapon between her thighs" (p. 22). With what economy of phrase "the milk-white bitch" combines hostility to whites and women! Nowhere is Baldwin's neurotic conflict more nakedly exposed. On one side we have the white God and the lynch mob, determined to suppress sex. On the other, adolescent rebellion and the smashing of taboo, hardening at times into Garveyism.

By Garveyism I mean the emotional and rhetorical excess, and often the extravagant fantasies, to which an embattled minority may resort in promoting its own defense. *Another Country* is doubly susceptible to these temptations, for it was conceived as a joint assault on racial and sexual intolerance. Apparently prejudice encountered in either context will evoke a similar response. The arrogance of the majority has a natural counterpart in exaggerated claims of minority supremacy.

In the racial sphere, Baldwin employs defenses which go well beyond a healthy race pride or a legitimate use of folk material. His portrait of Ida, for example, leans heavily on the exotic, on that stereotype of jungle grace which flourished in the nineteen-twenties. To a touch of primitivism he adds flat assertions of superiority: Negroes are more alive, more colorful, more spontaneous, better dancers, and above all, better lovers than the pale, gray, milk-white, chalk-white, dead-white, ice-hearted, frozen-limbed, stiff-assed zombies from downtown. Well, perhaps. One does not challenge the therapeutic value of these pronouncements, only their artistic relevance.

Coupled with these racial sentiments are manifestations of sexual Garveyism. Throughout the novel, the superiority of homosexual love is affirmed. Here alone can one experience total surrender and full orgastic pleasure; here alone the metaphysical terror of the void. Heterosexual love, by comparison, is a pale—one is tempted to say, white—imitation. In many passages hostility to women reaches savage proportions: "Every time I see a woman wearing her fur coats and her jewels and her gowns, I want to tear all that off her and drag her someplace, to a *pissoir*, and make her smell the smell of many men, the

piss of many men, and make her know that *that* is what she is for"
(p. 210).

It may be argued that these are the sentiments of Yves and not of
Baldwin, but that is precisely the point. In *Another Country*, the sharp
outlines of character are dissolved by waves of uncontrolled emotion.
The novel lacks a proper distancing. One has the impression of Baldwin's recent work that the author does not know where his own psychic
life leaves off and that of his characters begins. What is more, he
scarcely cares to know, for he is sealed in a narcissism so engrossing
that he fails to make emotional contact with his characters. If his
people have no otherness, if he repeatedly violates their integrity, how
can they achieve the individuality which alone will make them
memorable?

In conclusion, I should like to view *Another Country* from the
perspective of the author's spiritual journey. Reduced to its essentials,
this journey has carried Baldwin from a store-front church in Harlem to
a Greenwich Village pad. His formative years were spent among the
saints, in an environment where repressive attitudes toward sex were
paramount. As a result, his sexual experience has always contained a
metaphysical dimension, bearing inescapably on his relationship to
God. To understand the failure of *Another Country*, we must trace the
connection between his sexual rebellion, his religious conceptions, and
his style.

Baldwin has described the spiritual geography of his adolescence in
the opening pages of *The Fire Next Time*. On a little island in the vast
sea of Harlem stood the saved, who had fled for their very lives into
the church. All around them was the blazing Hell of the Avenue, with
its bars and brothels, pimps and junkies, violence and crime. Between
God and the Devil an unrelenting contest was waged for the souls of
the young, in which the girls of God's party bore a special burden:
"They understood that they must act as God's decoys, saving the souls
of the boys for Jesus and binding the bodies of the boys in marriage.
For this was the beginning of our burning time."[13]

Baldwin's adolescent rebellion began, it seems plain, when his dawn-
ing sensuality collided with his youthful ministry. At first he rebelled
against the store-front church, then Harlem, seeking to escape at any
cost. Ultimately he came to reject the female sex, the white world, and
the Christian God. As his rebellion grew, he discovered in his gift for
language a means of liberation. Like hundreds of American writers,

---

[13] *The Fire Next Time*, p. 32.

he fled from the provinces (in his case, Harlem) to Greenwich Village and the Left Bank. There he hoped to find a haven of sexual, racial, and intellectual freedom.

He quickly discovered, however, that he had not left the Avenue behind. In Greenwich Village or its French equivalent, he peered into the abyss, the demi-monde of gay bars, street boys, and male prostitutes. This he recognized as Hell and recoiled in horror. But what alternative does he offer to promiscuity and fleeting physical encounter? He speaks in the rhetoric of commitment and responsibility, but what he has in mind is simply a homosexual version of romantic love. It is a familiar spiritual maneuver. Baldwin has built a palace on the ramparts of Hell and called it Heaven. Its proper name is Pandemonium.

In an effort to make Hell endurable, Baldwin attempts to spiritualize his sexual rebellion. Subjectively, I have no doubt, he is convinced that he has found God. Not the white God of his black father, but a darker deity who dwells in the heart of carnal mystery. One communes with this dark power through what Baldwin calls "the holy and liberating orgasm."[14] The stranger the sex partner, the better for orgasm, for it violates a stronger taboo. Partners of a different race, or the same sex, or preferably both, afford the maximum spiritual opportunities.

Baldwin imagines his new faith to be a complete break with the past, but in fact he has merely inverted the Christian orthodoxy of his youth. Properly regarded, *Another Country* will be seen as the celebration of a Black Mass. The jazzman is Baldwin's priest; the homosexual, his acolyte. The bandstand is his altar; Bessie Smith his choir. God is carnal mystery, and through orgasm, the Word is made flesh. Baldwin's ministry is as vigorous as ever. He summons to the mourners' bench all who remain, so to say, hardened in their innocence. Lose that, he proclaims, and you will be saved. To the truly unregenerate, those stubborn heterosexuals, he offers the prospect of salvation through sodomy. With this novel doctrine, the process of inversion is complete.

These contentions are best supported by a brief discussion of Baldwin's style. Two idioms were available to him from the Negro world: the consecrated and the profane. They derive respectively from the church-oriented and the jazz-oriented segments of the Negro community. To Baldwin, the church idiom signifies submission, reconciliation, brotherhood, and Platonic love. Conversely, the hipster idiom conveys rebellion, defiance, retaliation, and sexual love.

The predominant mode of *Another Country* is the hipster idiom. For Baldwin it is the language of apostasy. In rejecting the God of his youth, he inverts the consecrated language of the saints. The general

---

[14] See *Blues for Mister Charlie* (New York, Dial Press, 1964), p. 105.

effect is blasphemous: "What a pain in the ass old Jesus Christ had turned out to be, and it probably wasn't even the poor, doomed, loving, hopheaded old Jew's fault" (p. 308). Baldwin's diction is deliberately shocking; its function is to challenge limits, to transgress. In the sexual realm, it exploits the fascination of the forbidden, like a cheap film aimed at the teen-age trade. Indeed, if the style proclaims the man, we are dealing with an adolescent: who else gets his kicks from the violation of taboo?

Curiously, however, the language of the store-front church persists. For the hipster idiom is really Baldwin's second language, and in moments of high emotion he reverts to his native tongue. This occurs primarily when he tries to heighten or exalt the moment of sexual union. In the vicinity of orgasm, his diction acquires a religious intensity; his metaphors announce the presence of a new divinity: "When he entered that marvelous wound in her, *rending and tearing! rending and tearing!* was he surrendering, in joy, to the Bridegroom, Lord, and Savior?" (p. 308, emphasis in original).

This sudden shift into the church idiom betrays on Baldwin's part a deep need to spiritualize his sexual revolt. Here he describes Eric's first homosexual encounter: "What had always been *hidden* was to him, that day, *revealed*, and it did not matter that, fifteen years later, he sat in an armchair, overlooking a foreign sea, still struggling to find that *grace* which would allow him to bear that *revelation*" (p. 206, emphasis supplied). This is the language of Pandemonium: evil has become Baldwin's good. The loss of meaning which ensues is both moral and semantic, and the writer who permits it betrays both self and craft.

Another Country is not simply a bad novel, but a dead end. It is symptomatic of a severe crisis in Baldwin's life and art. The author's popular acclaim, his current role as a political celebrity, and the Broadway production of his recent play, have tended to obscure the true state of affairs. But Baldwin must suspect that his hipster phase is coming to a close. He has already devoted two novels to his sexual rebellion. If he persists, he will surely be remembered as the greatest American novelist since Jack Kerouac. The future now depends on his ability to transcend the emotional reflexes of his adolescence. So extraordinary a talent requires of him no less an effort.

JAMES T. STEWART

The Development

of the

Black

Revolutionary

Artist

James T. Stewart is a musician, painter, and critic who believes that black American artists have traditionally suffered from the imposition of white esthetic standards that do not correspond with black reality. Closely tied with the Afro-American's affirmation of his African roots, such an attitude has gained converts among black writers and intellectuals, for it challenges the entire "Western tradition" that many blacks hold responsible for their enslavement. Stewart and others, particularly those influenced by the writings of the Algerian nationalist, Frantz Fanon, find that Western tradition fraudulent and bankrupt; they see it as an anti-human set of doctrines cunningly designed to maintain the supremacy of white Europeans. This view has had an important influence on many contemporary black novelists. Stewart believes that the novelist should not have to worry about white models for his art, that he should not be striving for "lasting" fiction, since "perpetuation, as the white culture understands it, simply does not exist in the black culture." Rather, the emphasis must be on revolutionary change, and the writer must create according to the "dialectic of change."

Whether or not one agrees with Stewart (and many black writers do not), he does represent the value of a revolutionary esthetic. It would seem doubtful that black—or white—novelists are likely to suffer much from a re-examination of the value assumptions behind their creative efforts.

JAMES T. STEWART

The Development of the Black Revolutionary Artist

COSMOLOGY IS THAT BRANCH OF PHYSICS THAT STUDIES THE UNIVERSE. IT then proceeds to make certain assumptions, and from these, construct "models." If the model corresponds to reality, and certain factors are predictable, then it can be presumed to substantiate the observable phenomena in the universe. This essay is an attempt to construct a model; a particular way of looking at the world. This is necessary because existing white paradigms or models do not correspond to the realities of black existence. It is imperative that we construct models with different basic assumptions.

The dilemma of the "negro" artist is that he makes assumptions based on the wrong models. He makes assumptions based on white models. These assumptions are not only wrong, they are even antithetical to his existence. The black artist must construct models which correspond to his own reality. The models must be non-white. Our models must be consistent with a black style, our natural aesthetic styles, and our moral and spiritual styles. In doing so, we will be merely following the natural demands of our culture. These demands are suppressed in the larger (white) culture, but, nonetheless, are found in our music and in our spiritual and moral philosophy. Particularly in music, which happens to be the purest expression of the black man in America.

In Jahn Janheinz's *Muntu*, he tells us about temples made of mud that vanish in the rainy seasons and are erected elsewhere. They are never made of much sturdier material. The buildings and the statues in them are always made of mud. And when the rains come the buildings and the statues are washed away. Likewise, most of the great Japanese artists of the eighteenth and nineteenth centuries did their exquisite drawings on rice paper with black ink and spit. These were then reproduced by master engravers on fragile newssheets that were distributed to the people for next to nothing. These sheets were often used for wrapping fish. They were a people's newssheet. Very much like the sheets circulated in our bars today.

My point is this: that in both of the examples just given, there is little concept of fixity. The work is fragile, destructible; in other words, there is a total disregard for the perpetuation of the product, the picture, the statue, and the temple. Is this ignorance? According to Western culture evaluations, we are led to believe so. The white researcher, the white scholar, would have us believe that he "rescues" these "valuable" pieces. He "saves" them from their creators, those "ignorant" colored peoples who would merely destroy them. Those people who do not know their value. What an audacious presumption!

The fact is that *these* people did know their value. But the premises and values of their creation are of another order, of another cosmology, constructed in terms agreeing with their own particular models of existence. Perpetuation, as the white culture understands it, simply does not exist in the black culture. We know, all non-whites know, that man can not create *a* forever; but he can create forever. But he can only create if he creates as change. Creation is itself perpetuation and change is being.

In this dialectical apprehension of reality it is the act of creation of a work as it comes into existence that is its only being. The operation of art is dialectical. Art goes. Art is not fixed. Art can not be fixed. Art is change, like music, poetry and writing are, when conceived. They must move (swing). Not necessarily as physical properties, as music and poetry do; but intrinsically, by their very nature. But they must go spiritually, noumenally. This is what makes those mud temples in Nigeria go. Those prints in Japan. This is what makes black culture go.

All white Western art forms, up to and including those of this century, were matrixed. They all had a womb, the germinative idea out of which the work evolved, or as in the tactile forms (sculpture and painting, for instance), unifying factors that welded the work together, e.g. the plot of a play, the theme of a musical composition, and the figure. The trend in contemporary white forms is toward the elimination of the matrix, in the play "happenings," and in music, aleatory or random techniques. All of these are influenced by Eastern traditions. It is curious and sometimes amusing to see the directions that these forms take.

The music that black people in this country created was matrixed to some degree; but it was largely improvisational also, and that aspect of it was non-matrixed. And the most meaningful music being created today is non-matrixed. The music of Ornette Coleman.

The sense in which "revolutionary" is understood is that a revolutionary is against the established order, regime, or culture. The bourgeoisie calls him a revolutionary because he threatens the established way of life—things as they are. They can not accept change, though change is inevitable. The revolutionary understands change. Change is what it is all about. He is not a revolutionary to his people, to his compatriots, to his comrades. He is, instead, a brother. He is a son. She is a sister, a daughter.

The dialectical method is the best instrument we have for comprehending physical and spiritual phenomena. It is the essential nature of being, existence; it is the property of being and the "feel" of being; it is the implicit *sense* of it. This sense, black people have. And the revolutionary artist must understand this sense of reality, this philosophy of reality which exists in all non-white cultures. We need our own conventions, a convention of procedural elements, a kind of stylization, a sort of insistency which leads inevitably to a certain kind of methodology—a methodology affirmed by the spirit.

That spirit is black.

That spirit is non-white.

That spirit is patois.

That spirit is Samba.

Voodoo.

The black Baptist church in the South.

We are, in essence, the ingredients that will create the future. For this reason, we are misfits, estranged from the white cultural present. This is our position as black artists in these times. Historically and sociologically we are the rejected. Therefore, we must know that we are the building stones for the New Era. In our movement toward the future, "ineptitude" and "unfitness" will be an aspect of what we do. These are the words of the established order—the middle-class value judgments. We must turn these values in on themselves. Turn them inside out and make ineptitude and unfitness desirable, even mandatory. We must even, ultimately, be estranged from the dominant culture. This estrangement must be nurtured in order to generate and energize our black artists. This means that he can not be "successful" in any sense that has meaning in white critical evaluations. Nor can his work ever be called "good" in any context or meaning that could make sense to that traditional critique.

Revolution is fluidity. What are the criteria in times of social change? Whose criteria are they, in the first place? Are they ours or the oppressors'? If being is change, and the sense of change is the time of change —and what is, is about to end, or is over—where are the criteria?

History qualifies us to have this view. Not as some philosophical concept acting out of matter and movement—but as being. So, though the word "dialectic" is used, the meaning and sense of it more than the word, or what the word means, stand as postulated experience. Nothing can be postulated without fixing it in time—standing it still, so to speak. It can not be done. The white Westerner was on his way toward understanding this when he rejected the postulated systems of his philosophies; when he discarded methodology in favor of what has come to be called existentialism. But inevitably, he postulated existence; or at least, it was attempted. Therefore, existentialism got hung up in just the same way as the philosophical systems from which it has extricated itself.

But we need not be bothered with that. We need merely to see how it fits; how the word dialectic fits; what change means; and what fluidity, movement and revolution mean. The purpose of writing is to enforce the sense we have of the future. The purpose of writing is to enforce the sense we have of responsibility—the responsibility of understanding our roles in the shaping of a new world. After all, experience is development; and development is destruction. The great Indian thinkers had this figured out centuries ago. That is why, in the Hindu religion, the god Siva appears—Siva, the god of destruction.

All history is "tailored" to fit the needs of the particular people who write it. Thus, one of our "negro" writers failed to understand the historicity of the Nation of Islam. He failed to understand. This was because his assumptions were based on white models and on a self-conscious "objectivity." This is the plight of the "negro" man of letters, the negro intellectual who needs to demonstrate a so-called academic impartiality to the white establishment.

Now, on the other hand, a dialectical interpretation of revolutionary black development rooted in the *Western* dialectic also will not do. However, inherent in the Western dialectical approach is the idea of imperceptible and gradual quantitative change; changes which give rise to a new state. This approach has also illustrated that there are no immutable social systems or eternal principles; and that there is only the inherency in things of contradictions—of opposing tendencies. It has also illustrated that the role of the "science of history" is to help bring about a fruition of new aggregates. These were all good and canonical to the kind of dialectics that came out of Europe in the nineteenth century.

But contemporary art is rooted in a European convention. The standards whereby its products are judged are European. However, this is merely *one* convention. Black culture implies, indeed engenders, for the black artist another order, another way of looking at things. It is apparent in the music of Giuseppe Logan, for example, that the references are not white or European. But it is jazz and it is firmly rooted in the experiences of black individuals in this country. These references are found also in the work of John Coltrane, Ornette Coleman, Grachan Moncur and Milford Graves.

A revolutionary art is being expressed today. The anguish and aimlessness that attended our great artists of the 'forties and 'fifties and which drove most of them to early graves, to dissipation and dissolution, is over. Misguided by white cultural references (the models the culture set for its individuals), and the incongruity of these models with black reality, men like Bird were driven to willful self-destruction. There was no program. And the reality-model was incongruous. It was a white reality-model. If Bird had had a black reality-model, it might have been different. But though Parker knew of the new development in the black culture, even helped to ferment it, he was hung up in an incompatible situation. They were contradictions both monstrous and unbelievable. They were contradictions about the nature of black and white culture, and what that had to mean to the black individual in this society. In Bird's case, there was a dichotomy between his genius and the society. But, that he couldn't find the adequate model of being was the tragic part of the whole thing. Otherwise, things could have been more meaningful and worthwhile.

The most persistent feature of all existence is change. In other words, it is this property which is a part of everything which exists in the world. As being, the world is change. And it is this very property that the white West denies. The West denies change, defies change . . . resists change. But change is the basic nature of everything that is. Society is. Culture is. Everything that is—in society—its people and their manner of being, and the way in which they make a living. But mainly the modes of what is material, and how the material is produced. What it looks like and what it means to those who produce it and those who accept it. And this is how philosophy, art, morality, and certain other things are established. But all established things are temporary, and the nature of being is, like music, changing.

Art can not apologize out of existence the philosophical ethical position of the artist. After all, the artist is a man in society, and his social attitudes are just as relevant to his art as his aesthetic position. However, the white Western aesthetics is predicated on the idea of separating one from the other—a man's art from his actions. It is this duality that is the most distinguishable feature of Western values.

Music is a social activity. Jazz music, in particular, is a social activity, participated in by artists collectively. Within a formal context or procedure, jazz affords the participants a collective form for individual group development in a way white musical forms never did. The symphony, for instance, is a dictatorship. There is a rigidity of form and craft-practice—a virtual enslavement of the individual to the autocratic conductor. Music is a social activity in a sense that writing, painting and other arts can never be. Music is made with another. It is indulged in with others. It is the most social of the art forms except, say, architecture. But music possesses, in its essence, a property none of the other forms possesses. This property of music is its ontological procedures—the nature of which is dialectical. In other words, music possesses properties of being that come closest to the condition of life, of existence. And, in that sense, I say its procedures are ontological— which doesn't mean a thing, but that music comes closest to being. This is why music teaches. This is what music teaches.

The point of the whole thing is that we must emancipate our minds from Western values and standards. We must rid our minds of these values. Saying so will not be enough. We must try to shape the thinking of our people. We must goad our people by every means, remembering as Ossie Davis stated: that the task of the Negro (*sic*, black) writer is revolutionary by definition. He must view his role *vis-a-vis* white Western civilization, and from this starting point in his estrangement begin to make new definitions founded on his own culture—on definite black values.

PART TWO

The

Black Novelist

Speaks

W. E. B. DUBOIS

Two

Novels

In the spring of 1928 two black writers published their first novels: Claude McKay's *Home to Harlem* appeared in March; Nella Larsen's *Quicksand* came out in April. A West Indian immigrant who had come to the United States to study agriculture, McKay (1889-1948) was already acknowledged as a leader in the Harlem Renaissance. Four years earlier he had published an important book of poetry, *Harlem Shadows,* and throughout the twenties he had been associated with a number of literary magazines. *Home to Harlem* is the story of a devil-may-care black Army deserter, Jake Brown, who comes "home to Harlem" after leaving his military unit in France. Not exactly a member of the black bourgeoisie, Jake hangs around gin mills, takes drugs, drinks, successfully pursues women, and generally lives to the hilt the life of the roaring twenties. The novel is roughly ordered around Jake's search for Felice, a beautiful black cabaret girl whom he met the first night of his return to New York, but who disappeared soon after. However, McKay's interest in this plot is minimal, and the novel becomes primarily a Harlem landscape. Despite an interesting sub-plot contrasting the primitivistic Jake with a sensitive

and troubled black intellectual, Ray, and various sorties into the worlds
of black railroad workers and longshoremen, *Home to Harlem* is more
than anything else an intimate tour of Harlem after dark.

The novel quickly became a *cause célèbre*, attacked particularly by
black critics because of its explicit treatment of sex; McKay was accused of helping to perpetuate a fraudulent mythology of black sexuality. The most famous black critic in America, W. E. B. DuBois
(1868-1963), edited the NAACP's magazine, *The Crisis*, which he had
long used as a forum for the discussion of Afro-American fiction. With
the nearly simultaneous publication of McKay's and Larsen's novels,
DuBois saw his chance to both condemn McKay's Harlem fiction and
at the same time offer a constructive model of what the black novel
should be.

DuBois used the Larsen novel to prove that not only was McKay
writing doubtful fiction but also doing a disservice to the "Negro
cause." *Quicksand* is an account of the tortured life of Helga Crane,
the daughter of a Danish mother and a black gambler. One of the best
portrayals of "the tragic mulatto" theme so often treated by the black
novelist, *Quicksand* charts the racial ambivalence that can consume the
mulatto's life. Helga is educated by a white uncle, teaches at a black
college, rejects marriage with a white Danish artist, is herself rejected
by a black intellectual, and finally enters into an unsatisfactory marriage with a black minister. The novel is extremely well done, a searching psychological study of the human effects of miscegenation.

There is probably no question that *Quicksand* is a "better" novel
than *Home to Harlem*. It is better constructed, more complex, shaped
by a superior intellect. But DuBois' complaint about the "filthiness"
of *Home to Harlem* and his praise of the high art in *Quicksand* indicates a unique problem which has always confronted the black novelist
and which only indirectly has to do with sex. DuBois' review asks
implicitly, what responsibility has the black novelist for the further-
ance of Afro-American racial interests? DuBois' own novels had been
designed to dramatize bigotry and racial inequities, and he spent his
entire lifetime fighting for his race; he helped to found the NAACP,
repudiated the accomodationist policies of Booker T. Washington,
wrote pioneering sociological and economic studies of black culture,
and even in his 90's would publish fiction and history repudiating a
white racist America.

Clearly DuBois feels McKay has distorted his race, emphasized the
wrong things and dealt a blow to the cause of Negro rights. He admits
that *Home to Harlem* may have some saving virtues as fiction, but he
is certain that socially it is a disaster; thus, he raises an issue of special
importance to the black novelist in America. Writers create from

experience and the black novelist usually centers his novel around the black experience. But he is also constantly urged to think about more than his art; he is reminded that his art is by definition politcal, since it is written by a black man about black people, and therefore it can play a role in assaulting white institutions.

W. E. B. DUBOIS

Two Novels

I HAVE JUST READ THE LAST TWO NOVELS OF NEGRO AMERICA. THE ONE I liked; the other I distinctly did not. I think that Mrs. Imes, writing under the pen name of Nella Larsen, has done a fine, thoughtful and courageous piece of work in her novel. It is, on the whole, the best piece of fiction that Negro America has produced since the heyday of Chesnutt, and stands easily with Jessie Fauset's "There is Confusion," in its subtle comprehension of the curious cross currents that swirl about the black American.

Claude McKay's "Home to Harlem," on the other hand, for the most part nauseates me, and after the dirtier parts of its filth I feel distinctly like taking a bath. This does not mean that the book is wholly bad. McKay is too great a poet to make any complete failure in writing. There are bits of "Home to Harlem", beautiful and fascinating: the continued changes upon the theme of the beauty of colored skins; the portrayal of the fascination of their new yearnings for each other which Negroes are developing. The chief character, Jake, has something appealing, and the glimpses of the Haitian, Ray, have all the materials of a great piece of fiction.

But it looks as though, despite this, McKay has set out to cater for that prurient demand on the part of white folk for a portrayal in Negroes of that utter licentiousness which conventional civilization holds white folk back from enjoying—if enjoyment it can be called. That which a certain decadent section of the white American world, centered particularly in New York, longs for with fierce and unrestrained passions, it wants to see written out in black and white, and saddled on black Harlem. This demand, as voiced by a number of New York publishers, McKay has certainly satisfied, and added much for good measure. He has used every art and emphasis to paint drunkenness, fighting, lascivious sexual promiscuity and utter absence of restraint in as bold and as bright colors as he can.

If this had been done in the course of a well-conceived plot or with any artistic unity, it might have been understood if not excused. But "Home to Harlem" is padded. Whole chapters here and there are inserted with no connection to the main plot, except that they are on the same dirty subject. As a picture of Harlem life or of Negro life anywhere, it is, of course, nonsense. Untrue, not so much as on account of its facts, but on account of its emphasis and glaring colors. I am

Reprinted from *The Crisis*, XXXV (June 1928), 202, with the permission of The Crisis Publishing Co., Inc. Copyright © 1928 by *The Crisis*.

sorry that the author of "Harlem Shadows" stooped to this. I sincerely hope that he will some day rise above it and give us in fiction the strong, well-knit as well as beautiful theme, that it seems to me he might do.

Nella Larsen on the other hand has seized an interesting character and fitted her into a close yet delicately woven plot. There is no "happy ending" and yet the theme is not defeatist like the work of Peterkin and Green. Helga Crane sinks at last still master of her whimsical, unsatisfied soul. In the end she will be beaten down even to death but she never will utterly surrender to hypocrisy and convention. Helga is typical of the new, honest, young fighting Negro woman—the one on whom "race" sits negligibly and Life is always first and its wandering path is but darkened, not obliterated by the shadow of the Veil. White folk will not like this book. It is not near nasty enough for New York columnists. It is too sincere for the South and middle West. Therefore, buy it and make Mrs. Imes write many more novels.

ARNA BONTEMPS

The Negro Renaissance:

Jean Toomer

and the

Harlem Writers

of the 1920's

THERE IS NO MORE ENIGMATIC FIGURE IN AMERICAN LETTERS THAN JEAN Toomer (1894-1967). White enough to pass, the grandson of P. B. S. Pinchback, the black Lieutenant Governor of Louisiana during Reconstruction, a literary artist of unquestioned brilliance, a Quaker, and a follower of a Russian mystic, Jean Toomer has remained a mystery until recent years. His one novel, *Cane* (1923), is considered by many as the best work of fiction to come out of the Harlem Renaissance. Yet Toomer never published another novel, and although he did publish a small book of aphorisms in 1931, by the time of his death he was largely forgotten.

The Toomer mystery is now in the process of being solved because of the remarkable collection of manuscripts and correspondence that was given to the Fisk University Library after he died. In the collection are unpublished writings of all kinds, including ten full length works, and a large number of short stories, plays, critical essays, poems, and psychological treatises. Among the manuscripts are parts of an unpublished autobiography that explains much about Toomer's curious life. The collection is uneven, as one might expect, but it makes clear that Toomer's mysticism turned into a psychological didacticism that caused publishers to reject his works after *Cane.*

Following his intense literary activity during the twenties, Jean Toomer married a white novelist, Margery Bodine Latimer in 1931; she died in childbirth a year later. He eventually re-married and lived most of the latter part of his life in Doylestown, Pennsylvania, where he was very active in the Society of Friends. These outward facts do not, however, explain Jean Toomer or the crusade that consumed him.

From the early thirties on, Toomer argued in print and in private that he was not a Negro—that he was a member of the "American race." In his book of aphorisms, *Essentials,* printed privately in 1931, he wrote, "I am of no particular race, I am of the human race." Interviewed by *Time* magazine in 1932, he said:

> Americans probably do not realize it . . . but there are no racial barriers anymore, because there are so many Americans with strains of Negro, Indian, and Oriental blood. As I see America, it is like a great stomach into which are thrown the elements which make up the life blood. From this source is coming a distinct race of people. They will achieve tremendous works of art, literature, and music. They will not be white, black, or yellow—just Americans.

He believed so strongly in this conviction that he did not permit his work to be included in James Weldon Johnson's *The Book of American Negro Poetry* and he even refused to send a copy of *Essentials* to the New York Public Library's famous repository of Black Studies, the Schomburg Collection.

Although rumors were legion during his final three decades that Toomer was passing, the attitude revealed here does not exactly constitute "crossing the color line." But it does indicate the lengths to which a man can be driven by a color-conscious American society, and it suggests that the racial ambiguities of our national life can push even so talented a novelist as Jean Toomer away from the art form that manifests his genius.

It is appropriate that Arna Bontemps (1902–   ) should write about Toomer, for not only were they contemporaries, but Bontemps himself played an important part in the Harlem Renaissance—as, indeed, he has played some role in most movements within Negro literature for over 40 years; Bontemps was also for many years the Librarian at Fisk University, the repository of the Toomer papers. Coming to New York from the West Coast during the twenties, Bontemps won a number of prizes for his poetry, including one from *The*

Crisis in 1927. He has also written novels, histories, and children's literature in a long career that has always seen him ready to help young writers. Currently, he is the curator of the James Weldon Johnson collection at the Yale University Library.

ARNA BONTEMPS

The Negro Renaissance: Jean Toomer and the Harlem Writers of the 1920's

THAT STORY FROM ONE OF THE OLD COUNTRIES ABOUT THE MAN WITH the marriageable daughter comes to mind when I think of a leading literary pundit in the second decade of this century. In a land where brides were bartered it was, of course, not uncommon for subtle salesmanship to flourish. Sometimes it could become high pressured. In this old yarn the eager parent of the bride had recited so many of his daughter's excellent qualities the prospective husband began to wonder whether she had any human faults at all. "Well, yes," the father finally acknowledged. "A tiny one. She is just a little bit pregnant."

Similarly, in the Twenties the man whose comments on writing by or about Negroes were most respected was just a little bit Negro. He was William Stanley Braithwaite, literary critic for the Boston *Transcript* and editor of an annual series, "Anthologies of Magazine Verse, 1913-1929." In "Braithwaite's Anthologies," as they were commonly known, Spoon River poems by Edgar Lee Masters, chants by Vachel Lindsay, free verse by Carl Sandburg and the early works of many other important American poets were recognized and published before the authors had received general acceptance or acclaim.

But Braithwaite did not completely disassociate himself from Negroes, as he might have. Indeed, he was awarded the Spingarn medal in 1917 as "the Negro who, according to a committee appointed by the board [of the NAACP], has reached the highest achievement in his field of activity." His occasional observations on Negro writing in the decade preceding Harlem's golden era are therefore useful as prologue. In 1913, for example, Braithwaite took note of James Weldon Johnson's "Fiftieth Anniversary Ode" on the Emancipation and suggested that it represented a move by the Negro poet to disengage himself. A decade of near silence had followed Paul Laurence Dunbar's last lyrics, and Braithwaite's language created an image of the Negro poet in chains, seeking to free himself.

The reappearance of this Johnson poem in a collection called *Fifty Years and Other Poems*, in 1917—the same year that Braithwaite was awarded the Spingarn medal, incidentally—prompted Braithwaite to remark, in effect, that this could be the beginning of something big, like a new awakening among Negro writers, perhaps. But, actually, John-

Reprinted from *Anger, and Beyond*, ed. Herbert Hill (New York: Harper and Row, 1966), pp. 20-36, by permission of the publisher. Copyright © 1966 by Herbert Hill.

son's most significant poetic achievement was still a decade in the future, when his collection of folk sermons in verse was to be published as *God's Trombones* in 1927. Nevertheless, Braithwaite appears to have picked the right year for the first sign of "disengagement" or "awakening" or whatever it was. The year 1917 now stands out, where Negro poetry in the United States is concerned, as the year in which Claude McKay's poem "The Harlem Dancer" appeared in *The Seven Arts* magazine under the pen name of Eli Edwards. You may know the poem. It was in sonnet form:

> Applauding youths laughed with young prostitutes
> And watched her perfect, half-clothed body sway;
> Her voice was like the sound of blended flutes
> Blown by black players upon a picnic day.
> She sang and danced on gracefully and calm,
> The light gauze hanging loose about her form;
> To me she seemed a proudly-swaying palm
> Grown lovelier for passing through a storm.
> Upon her swarthy neck black shiny curls
> Luxuriant fell; and tossing coins in praise,
> The wine-flushed, bold-eyed boys, and even the girls,
> Devoured her shape with eager, passionate gaze;
> But looking at her falsely-smiling face,
> I knew her self was not in that strange place.

Now this I submit was the anticipation and the theme of an early outburst of creativity later described as the Negro or Harlem Renaissance. When McKay's "The Harlem Dancer" reappeared in his collection *Harlem Shadows* in 1922, along with other poems so fragrant and fresh they almost drugged the senses, things immediately began to happen. Here was poetry written from experience, differing from poetry written from books and other cultural media in somewhat the same way that real flowers differ from artificial ones. A chorus of other new voices led by Jean Toomer, Langston Hughes and Countee Cullen promptly began to make the Twenties a decade which *Time* magazine has described as Harlem's "golden age."

Interestingly, Braithwaite recognized McKay as the first voice in this new chorus, but he spoke of him as "a genius meshed in [a] dilemma." It bothered Braithwaite that McKay seemed to "waiver between the racial and the universal notes." In some of his poems, Braithwaite felt, McKay was clearly "contemplating life and nature with a wistful sympathetic passion," but in others the poet became what Braithwaite called a "strident propagandist, using his poetic gifts to clothe arrogant and defiant thoughts." Braithwaite thought this was bad. He cited McKay's "The Harlem Dancer" and his "Spring in New

Hampshire" as instances of the former, his "If We Must Die" as a shameless instance of the latter. But, ironically, a generation later it was "If We Must Die," a poem that would undoubtedly stir the blood of almost any Black Muslim, that Sir Winston Churchill quoted as climax and conclusion of his oration before the joint houses of the American Congress when he was seeking to draw this nation into the common effort in World War II. McKay had written it as the Negro American's defiant answer to lynching and mob violence in the Southern states. Churchill made it the voice of the embattled Allies as he read aloud McKay's poem "If We Must Die."

Obviously neither Churchill nor McKay had at that time considered the possibilities of nonviolence. The poem does show, however, how a short span of years and certain historical developments can alter the meaning of a literary work. It also demonstrates the risk of trying to separate too soon the local or special subject from the universal.

But if Braithwaite's attitude toward Claude McKay was ambivalent, it was certainly unequivocal with respect to the second, and in some ways the most inspiring, of the writers who made the Harlem Renaissance significant in the long-range development of the Negro writer in the United States.

"In Jean Toomer, the author of *Cane*," Braithwaite wrote in 1925, "we come upon the very first artist of the race, who with all an artist's passion and sympathy for life, its hurts, its sympathies, its desires, its joys, its defeats and strange yearnings, can write about the Negro without the surrender or compromise of the artist's vision. So objective is it, that we feel that it is a mere accident that birth or association has thrown him into contact with the life he has written about. He would write just as well, just as poignantly, just as transmutingly, about the peasants of Russia, or the peasants of Ireland, had experience brought him in touch with their existence. *Cane* is a book of gold and bronze, of dusk and flame, of ecstasy and pain, and Jean Toomer is a bright morning star of a new day of the race in literature."

Cane was published in 1923 after portions of it had first appeared in *Broom, The Crisis, Double Dealer, Liberator, Little Review, Modern Review, Nomad, Prairie* and *S 4 N*. But *Cane* and Jean Toomer, its gifted author, presented an enigma—an enigma which has, if anything, deepened in the forty-three years since its publication. Given such a problem, perhaps one may be excused for not wishing to separate the man from his work. Indeed, so separated, Toomer's writing could scarcely be understood at all, and its significance would escape us now as it has escaped so many others in the past.

In any case, *Who's Who in Colored America* listed Toomer in 1927 and gave the following vita:

> b. Dec. 26, 1894, Washington, D.C.; s. Nathan and Nina (Pinchback) Toomer; educ. Public Scho., Washington, D.C.; Dunbar, High Scho.; Univ. of Wisconsin, 1914-15; taught schools, Sparta, Ga., for four months, traveled, worked numerous occupations; auth. *Cane,* pub. Boni and Liveright, 1923; Short Stories and Literary Criticisms in various magazines; address, c/o Civic Club, 439 W. 23rd St., New York, N.Y.

Needless to say, no subsequent listing of Toomer is to be found in this or any other directory of conspicuous Negro Americans. Judging by the above, however, Toomer had always been elusive, and the interest that *Cane* awakened did nothing to change this. Several years later Toomer faded completely into white obscurity leaving behind a literary mystery almost as intriguing as the disappearance of Ambrose Bierce into Mexico in 1913.

Why did he do it? What did it mean?

Concerned with writing, as we are, we automatically turn to Toomer's book for clues. This could be difficult, because copies are scarce. *Cane's* two printings were small, and the few people who went quietly mad about the strange book were evidently unable to do much toward enlarging its audience. But among these few was pratically the whole generation of young Negro writers then just beginning to appear, and their reaction to Toomer's *Cane* marked an awakening that soon thereafter began to be called a Negro renaissance.

Cane's influence was not limited to the happy band that included Langston Hughes, Countee Cullen, Eric Walrond, Zora Neale Hurston, Wallace Thurman, Rudolph Fisher and their contemporaries of the Twenties. Subsequent writing by Negroes in the United States as well as in the West Indies and Africa has continued to reflect its mood and often its method, and, one feels, it also has influenced the writing about Negroes by others. And certainly no earlier volume of poetry or fiction or both had come close to expressing the ethos of the Negro in the Southern setting as *Cane* did.

There are many odd and provocative things about *Cane*, and not the least is its form. Reviewers who read it in 1923 were generally stumped. Poetry and prose were whipped together in a kind of frappé. Realism was mixed with what they called mysticism, and the result seemed to many of them confusing. Still, one of them could conclude that "*Cane* is an interesting, occasionally beautiful and often queer book of exploration into old country and new ways of writing." Another noted, "Toomer has not interviewed the Negro, has not asked opinions about him, has not drawn conclusions about him from his reactions to outside stimuli, but has made the much more searching, and much more self-forgetting effort of seeing life with him, through him."

Such comment was cautious, however, compared to the trumpetings of Waldo Frank in the Foreword he contributed:

> A poet has arisen among our American youth who has known how to turn the essence and materials of his Southland into the essences and materials of literature. A poet has arisen in that land who writes, not as a Southerner, not as a rebel against Southerners, not as a Negro, not as apologist or priest or critic: who writes as a *poet*. The fashioning of beauty is ever foremost in his inspiration: not forcedly but simply, and because these ultimate aspects of his world are to him more real than all its specific problems. He has made songs and lovely stories of his land. . . .
>
> The gifted Negro has been too often thwarted from becoming a poet because his world was forever forcing him to recollect that he was a Negro. The artist must lose such lesser identities in the great well of life. . . . The whole will and mind of the creator must go below the surfaces of race. And this has been an almost impossible condition for the American Negro to achieve, forced every moment of his life into a specific and superficial plane of consciousness. . . .
>
> It seems to me, therefore, that this is a first book in more ways than one. It is a harbinger of the South's literary maturity: of its emergence from the obsession put upon its minds by the unending racial crisis. . . . It marks the dawn of direct and unafraid creation. And, as the initial work of a man of twenty-seven, it is the harbinger of a literary force of whose incalculable future I believe no reader 'of this book will doubt.

It is well to keep in mind the time of these remarks. Of the novels by which T. S. Stribling is remembered, only *Birthright* had been published. Julia Peterkin had not yet published a book. DuBose Heyward's *Porgy* was still two years away. William Faulkner's first novel was three years away. His Mississippi novels were six or more years in the future. Robert Penn Warren, a student at Vanderbilt University, was just beginning his association with the Fugitive poets. His first novel was still more than a decade and a half ahead. Tennessee Williams was just nine years old.

A chronology of Negro writers is equally revealing. James Weldon Johnson had written lyrics for popular songs, some of them minstrel style, and a sort of documentary novel obscurely published under a pseudonym, but *God's Trombones* was a good four years in the offing. Countee Cullen's *Color* was two and Langston Hughes' *The Weary Blues* three years away, though both of these poets had become known to readers of the Negro magazine *Crisis* while still in their teens, and Hughes at twenty-one, the year of *Cane's* publication, could already be called a favorite.

The first fiction of the Negro Renaissance required apologies. It was not first-rate. But it was an anticipation of what was to come later. Even so, it followed *Cane* by a year or two, and Eric Walrond's *Tropic Death* did not come for three. Zora Neale Hurston's first novel was published in 1931 [sic], eight years after *Cane*. Richard Wright made his bow with *Uncle Tom's Children* in 1938, fifteen years later. *Invisible Man* by Ralph Ellison followed Toomer's *Cane* by just thirty years. James Baldwin was not born when Toomer began to publish.

Waldo Frank's use of "harbinger" as the word for *Cane* becomes both significant and ironic when we recognize the debt most of these individuals owe Toomer. Consciously or unconsciously, one after another they picked up his cue and began making the "more searching" effort to see life *with* the Negro, "through him." *Cane* heralded an awakening of artistic expression by Negroes that brought to light in less than a decade a surprising array of talents, and these in turn made way for others. An equally significant change in the writing about Negroes paralleled this awakening. Strangely, however, *Cane* was not at all the harbinger Frank seemed to imagine. Despite his promise—a promise which must impress anyone who puts this first book beside the early writings of either Faulkner or Hemingway, Toomer's contemporaries—Jean Toomer rejected his prospects and turned his back on greatness.

The book by which we remember this writer is as hard to classify as its author. At first glance it appears to consist of assorted sketches, stories and a novelette interspersed with poems. Some of the prose is poetic, and often Toomer slips from one form into the other almost imperceptibly. The novelette is constructed like a play.

His characters, always evoked with effortless strength, are as recognizable as they are unexpected in the fiction of that period. Fern is a "creamy brown" beauty so complicated men take her "but get no joy from it." Becky is a white outcast beside a Georgia road who bears two Negro children. Laymon, a preacher-teacher in the same area, "knows more than would be good for anyone other than a silent man." The name character in the novelette *Kabnis* is a languishing idealist finally redeemed from cynicism and dissipation by the discovery of underlying strength in his people.

It doesn't take long to discover that *Cane* is not without design, however. A world of black peasantry in Georgia appears in the first section. The scene changes to the Negro community of Washington, D.C., in the second. Rural Georgia comes up again in the third.

Changes in the concerns of Toomer's folk are noted as the setting moves from the Georgia pike to the bustling Negro section in the nation's capital. The change in the level of awareness that the author discloses is more subtle, but it is clearly discernible when he returns to the Georgia background.

A young poet-observer moves through the book. Drugged by beauty "perfect as dusk when the sun goes down," lifted and swayed by folk song, arrested by eyes that "desired nothing that *you* could give," silenced by "corn leaves swaying, rusty with talk," he recognized that "the Dixie Pike has grown from a goat path in Africa." A native richness is here, he concluded, and the poet embraces it with the passion of love.

This was the sensual power most critics noticed and most readers remembered about *Cane*. It was the basis for Alfred Kreymborg's remark in *Our Singing Strength* that "Jean Toomer is *one* of the finest artists among the dark people, if not *the* finest." The reviewer for the New York *Herald Tribune* had the rich imagery of *Cane* in mind when he said, "Here are the high brown and black and half-caste colored folk of the cane fields, the gin hovel and the brothel realized with a sure touch of artistry." But there remained much in the book that he could not understand or appreciate. Speaking of Toomer's "sometimes rather strident reactions to the Negro," he added that "at moments his outbursts of emotion approach the inarticulately maudlin," though he had to admit that *Cane* represented "a distinct achievement wholly unlike anything of this sort done before."

Others found "obscurity" and "mysticism" in the novelette which comprises the last third of the book. This is not surprising, for in Toomer's expressed creed "A symbol is as useful to the spirit as a tool is to the hand," and his fiction is full of them. Add to puzzling symbols an itch to find "new ways of writing" that led him to bold experimentation and one may begin to see why Toomer baffled as he pleased readers interested in writing by or about Negroes in the early Twenties.

Kreymborg spoke of Toomer as "a philosopher and a psychologist by temperament" and went on to say that "the Washington writer is now fascinated by the larger, rather than the parochial interest of the human race, and should some day compose a book in the grand manner."

Of course, Toomer didn't, or at least he has not published one up to now, and to this extent Kreymborg has failed as a prophet, but his reference to Toomer as philosopher and psychologist was certainly on the mark, and his rather large estimate of this writer's capacities was significant, considering its date. The "new criticism," as we have come to recognize it, had scarcely been heard from them, and apparently it has still not discovered Toomer, but the chances are it may yet find him challenging. He would have comforted them, I am almost sorry to say, incarnating, as he does, some of their favorite attitudes. But at the same time, he could have served as a healthy corrective for others. Whether or not he would prove less complex or less rewarding than Gertrude Stein or James Joyce, for example, remains to be determined.

Saunders Redding gave *Cane* a close reading fifteen years after its publication and saw it as an unfinished experiment, "the conclusion to which we are fearful of never knowing, for since 1923 Toomer has published practically nothing." He meant, one assumes, that Toomer had published little poetry or fiction, or anything else that seemed closely related to *Cane* or to *Cane's* author. Toomer had published provocative articles here and there as well as a small book of definitions and aphorisms during that time, and since then he has allowed two of his lectures to be published semi-privately. But Redding must be included in the small group who recognized a problem in *Cane* that has yet to be explained.

To him Toomer was a young writer "fresh from the South," who found a paramount importance in establishing "racial kinship" with Negroes in order to treat them artistically. He was impressed by Toomer's "unashamed and unrestrained" love for the race and for the soil and setting that nourished it. He saw a relationship between the writer's "hot, colorful, primitive" moods and the "naive hysteria of the spirituals," which he held in contrast to "the sophistic savagery of jazz and the blues." *Cane*, he concluded, "was a lesson in emotional release and freedom."

Chapters about Toomer were included in Paul Rosenfeld's *Men Seen* in 1925 and in Gorham B. Munson's *Destinations* in 1928, and elsewhere there are indications that Toomer continued to write and to experiment for at least a decade after the publication of *Cane*. Long stories by him appeared in the second and third volumes of the *American Caravan*. A thoughtful essay on "Race Problems and Modern Society" became part of a volume devoted to *Problems of Civilization* in Baker Brownell's series on "Man and His World." Seven years later, in the *New Caravan* of 1936, Toomer presented similar ideas in the long poem "Blue Meridian." Meanwhile, contributing a chapter to the book *America & Alfred Stieglitz* in 1934, Toomer was explicit about his own writing as well as several other matters.

The rumor that Toomer had crossed the color line began circulating when his name stopped appearing in print. But a reasonable effort to find out what it was Toomer was trying to say to us subsequently makes it hard to accept "passing" as the skeleton key to the Jean Toomer mystery. He seemed too concerned with truth to masquerade. One wants to believe that Toomer's mind came at last to reject the myth of race as it is fostered in our culture. A man of fair complexion, indistinguishable from the majority of white Americans, he had always had a free choice as to where he would take his place in a color-caste scheme. Having wandered extensively and worked at odd jobs in a variety of cities before he began contributing to little magazines, as he has stated, he could scarcely have escaped being taken at face value by strangers who had no way of knowing that the youth, who looked like Hollywood's conception of an Ivy League basketball star, but who spoke so beautifully, whose very presence was such an influence upon them, was not only a product of the Negro community but a grandson of the man whom the *Dictionary of American Biography* describes as "the typical Negro politician of the Reconstruction."

Men of this kind, such as Walter White of the NAACP or Adam Clayton Powell of the U.S. Congress, sometimes called voluntary Negroes when they elect to remain in the fold, so to speak, have in other circumstances been discovered in strange places in our society— in neo-fascist organizations in the United States, among big city bosses, on movie screens, in the student body at "Ole Miss"—but seldom if ever before in an organization working "for understanding between people." Yet Jean Toomer's first publication, following the rumors and the silence, was "An Interpretation of Friends Worship," published by the Committee on Religious Education of Friends General Conference, 1515 Cherry Street, Philadelphia, 1947. It was followed two years later by a pamphlet, "The Flavor of Man." The writing is eloquent with commitment. It reflects unhurried reading and contemplation, as was also true of his piece on "Race Problems and Modern Society." Toomer did not fail to remind his readers that certain racial attitudes could not be condoned. He certainly did not speak as a Negro bent on escaping secretly into white society. Jean Toomer, who, like his high-spirited grandfather, had exuberantly published his pride in his Negro heritage, appears to have reached a point in his thinking at which categories of this kind tend to clutter rather than classify. The stand he appears to have taken at first involved nothing more clandestine than the closing of a book or the changing of a subject.

Yet he is on record as having denied later that he was a Negro. That is a story in itself. Nevertheless, at that point, it seems, Jean Toomer stepped out of American letters. Despite the richness of his thought, his gift of expression, he ceased to be a writer and, as I have suggested, turned his back on greatness. His choice, whatever else may be said about it, reflects the human sacrifices in the field of the arts exacted by the racial myth on which so much writing in the United States is based. While he may have escaped its strictures and inconveniences in his personal life, he did not get away from the racial problem in any real sense. His dilemmas and frustrations as a writer are equally the dilemmas and frustrations of the Negro writers who have since emerged. The fact that most of them have not been provided with his invisible cloak makes little difference. He is their representative man. He stands as their prototype.

What, then, ordinarily happened to the Negro writer of Toomer's time in America after his first phase, after he had been published and taken his first steps? Encouraged by reviewers, assured that his talent was genuine, that he was not *just* a Negro writer but an American writer who happened to be a Negro, that his first book had broken new ground and that his next would be awaited with keen interest unrelated to any exotic qualities he may have shown but simply as arresting art, he was readily convinced. The "American writer" tag was especially appealing. It stuck in his mind, and when he got the bad news from the sales department, he coupled it with remarks he had heard from his publishers about a certain "resistance" in bookstores to books about "the problem." Obviously the solution for him, as an American writer, was not to write narrowly about Negroes but broadly about people.

So sooner or later he did it: a novel not intended to depict Negro life. The results may be examined: Paul Laurence Dunbar's *The Love of Landry,* Richard Wright's *Savage Holiday,* Chester B. Himes' *Cast the First Stone,* Ann Petry's *Country Place,* Zora Neale Hurston's *Seraph on the Suwanee,* James Baldwin's *Giovanni's Room,* along with Jean Toomer's *York Beach.* While the implication that books about whites are about people while those about Negroes are *not* should have provoked laughter, the young Negro writer was too excited to catch it. The discovery which followed was that the bookstore "resistance" was not removed by this switch. Moreover, he found to his dismay that friendly reviewers had in most instances become cool. In any case, none of these writers seemed sufficiently encouraged by the results to continue in the same direction. Whatever it was that blocked the Negro writer of fiction, that denied him the kind of acceptance accorded the Negro maker of music, for example, was clearly not just the color of his characters.

Southern white novelists from T. S. Stribling to Julia Peterkin to DuBose Heyward to William Faulkner to Robert Penn Warren had thronged their novels with Negroes of all descriptions without appearing to meet reader resistance or critical coolness. So now it could be seen that the crucial issue was not the choice of subject but the author's attitude toward it. With this knowledge the young Negro writers pondered and then made their decisions. Dunbar chose drink. Wright and Himes went to Paris to think it over, as did James Baldwin, at first. Toomer disappeared into Bucks County, Pennsylvania. Frank

Yerby, on the basis of a short story in *Harper's Magazine* and a manuscript novel that went the rounds without finding a publisher, took the position that "an unpublished writer, or even one published but unread, is no writer at all." He chose "entertainment" over "literature," and worked his way out of the segregated area of letters in the costume of a riverboat gambler. His book *The Foxes of Harrow* about the Mississippi riverboat gambler became the first successful non-Negro novel by a Negro American writer.

A curious historical irony is suggested. The memoirs of George H. Devol, published in 1887 under the title *Forty Years a Gambler on the Mississippi*, relates the following about a cabin boy called Pinch:

> I raised him and trained him. I took him out of a steamboat barber shop. I instructed him in the mysteries of card-playing, and he was an apt pupil. . . .

Devol recalled with much amusement a night they left New Orleans on the steamer *Doubloon*:

> There was a strong team of us—Tom Brown, Holly Chappell, and the boy Pinch. We sent Pinch and staked him to open a game of chuck-aluck with the Negro passengers on deck, while we opened up monte in the cabin. The run of luck that evening was something grand to behold. I do not think there was a solitary man on the boat that did not drop around in the course of the evening and lose his bundle. When about thirty miles from New Orleans a heavy fog overtook us, and it was our purpose to get off and walk about six miles to Kennersville, where we could take the cars to the city.
>
> Pinchback got our valises together, and a start was made. A drizzling rain was falling, and the darkness was so great that one could not see his hand before his face. Each of us grabbed a valise except Pinch, who carried along the faro tools. The walking was so slippery that we were in the mud about every ten steps, and poor Pinch he groaned under the load that he carried. At last he broke out:
>
> "Tell you what it is, Master Devol, I'll be dumbed if this aint rough on Pinch. Ise going to do better than this toting along old faro tools."
>
> "What's that, Pinch? What you going to do?"
>
> "Ise going to get into that good old Legislature and I'll make Rome howl if I get there."
>
> Of course I thought at the time that this was all bravado and brag; but the boy was in earnest, and sure enough he got into the Legislature, became Lieutenant Governor, and by the death of the Governor he slipped into the gubernatorial chair, and at last crawled into the United States Senate.

Without necessarily accepting the gambler Devol as an authority on Reconstruction history we may still take his account as substantially factual. P. B. S. Pinchback himself often referred to his career on the river. He was still a prominent public figure when these memoirs were published. He could have denied them had he wished. That Frank Yerby, who became a teacher in a Negro college in Louisiana after his graduation from Fisk University, should center the story of *The Foxes of Harrow* around a Mississippi riverboat gambler is not an odd coincidence. But that Jean Toomer should be the grandson of Pinchback and one of the two people to accompany his body back to New Orleans for burial in 1921 suggests another historical irony.

The behavior pattern known sociologically as "passing for white," then, has its literary equivalent, and the question it raises is whether or not this is proper in the arts. The writer's desire to widen his audience by overcoming what has been called resistance to racial material is certainly understandable, but sooner or later the Negro novelist realizes that what he has encountered, as often critical as popular, is more subtle than that. What annoys some readers of fiction, it seems, is not so much that characters in a book are Negro or white or both as the *attitude of the writer* toward these characters. Does he accept the status quo with respect to the races? If so, any character or racial situation can be taken in stride, not excluding miscegenation. But rejection of traditional status, however reflected, tends to alienate these readers.

On the other hand, the Negro reader has little taste for any art in which the racial attitudes of the past are condoned or taken for granted. Since this is what he has come to expect in the fiction in which he sees himself, he too has developed resistance. His is a wider resistance to the whole world of the contemporary novel. To him literature means poetry, by and large. He knows Phillis Wheatley and Paul Laurence Dunbar far better than he knows any prose writers of the past. James Weldon Johnson and Countee Cullen are familiar and honored names. There is seldom a sermon in a Negro church, a commencement, a banquet, a program in which one of these or a contemporary poet like Hughes or Margaret Walker or Gwendolyn Brooks is not quoted. But the Negro novelists, aside from Richard Wright, possibly are lumped with the whole questionable lot in the mind of this reader. When he is not offended by the image of himself that modern fiction has projected, he is at least embarrassed.

The Negro writer, like the white writer of the South, is a product of the Southern condition. Whether he wills it or not, he reflects the tensions and cross-purposes of that environment. Just as the myth of the old South weakens under close examination, the myth of literature divorced from what have been called sociological considerations dissolves in a bright light.

The fictional world on which most of us first opened our eyes, where the Negro is concerned, is epitomized by a remark made by a character in William Faulkner's *Sartoris*. "What us niggers want ter be free fer, anyhow?" asks old Uncle Simon. "Ain't we got es many white folks now es we kin suppo't?"

The elusiveness of Jean Toomer in the face of complexities like these can well stand for the elusiveness of Negro writers from Charles W. Chesnutt to Frank Yerby. What Toomer was trying to indicate to us by the course he took still intrigues, but I suspect he realizes by now that there is no further need to *signify*. The secrets are out. As the song says, "There's no hiding place down here."

RICHARD WRIGHT

How

"Bigger"

Was

Born

As a foreword to one of the early 1940 editions of *Native Son*, Richard Wright included a long and detailed account of how the character of Bigger Thomas grew out of his experience and finally found expression in a novel. A fascinating description of the esthetic process, Wright's essay has never been reprinted in full in a collection of this sort. The essay exhibits a proletarian bias that one would expect from Wright's Communist Party membership at the time, and in some ways it echoes the popular front clichés that would mar the second half of *Native Son*. But Wright's account of Bigger's growth in his own imagination clearly transcends political issues and becomes a stark account of the special triumphs and agonies that characterize the creative effort of the black novelist. The process Wright describes is unique and yet typical: unique because the experience and genius of Richard Wright alone could produce *Native Son*; typical because Wright's struggle to create a meaningful fiction typifies the special problems and concerns of the black American novelist. It also reminds us of the impossibly complex and yet simple task of all novelists: the fusion of technique and experience into a fictional construct that affirms the possibilities of the human imagination.

RICHARD WRIGHT

How "Bigger" Was Born

I AM NOT SO PRETENTIOUS AS TO IMAGINE THAT IT IS POSSIBLE FOR ME TO account completely for my own book, *Native Son*. But I am going to try to account for as much of it as I can, the sources of it, the material that went into it, and my own years' long changing attitude toward that material.

In a fundamental sense, an imaginative novel represents the merging of two extremes; it is an intensely intimate expression on the part of a consciousness couched in terms of the most objective and commonly known events. It is at once something private and public by its very nature and texture. Confounding the author who is trying to lay his cards on the table is the dogging knowledge that his imagination is a kind of community medium of exchange: what he has read, felt, thought, seen, and remembered is translated into extensions as impersonal as a worn dollar bill.

The more closely the author thinks of why he wrote, the more he comes to regard his imagination as a kind of self-generating cement which glued his facts together, and his emotions as a kind of dark and obscure designer of those facts. Always there is something that is just beyond the tip of the tongue that could explain it all. Usually, he ends up by discussing something far afield, an act which incites skepticism and suspicion in those anxious for a straight-out explanation.

Yet the author is eager to explain. But the moment he makes the attempt his words falter, for he is confronted and defied by the inexplicable array of his own emotions. Emotions are subjective and he can communicate them only when he clothes them in objective guise; and how can he ever be so arrogant as to know when he is dressing up the right emotion in the right Sunday suit? He is always left with the uneasy notion that maybe *any* objective drapery is as good as *any* other for any emotion.

And the moment he does dress up an emotion, his mind is confronted with the riddle of that "dressed up" emotion, and he is left peering with eager dismay back into the dim reaches of his own incommunicable life. Reluctantly, he comes to the conclusion that to

Acknowledgment is made to *The Saturday Review of Literature* for permission to reproduce those parts of this article which appeared in the issue of June 1, 1940. The entire article, as Mr. Wright wrote it, is here published for the first time. *[The preceding acknowledgment is in the* Native Son *appearance.]*

account for his book is to account for his life, and he knows that that is impossible. Yet, some curious, wayward motive urges him to supply the answer, for there is the feeling that his dignity as a living being is challenged by something within him that is not understood.

So, at the outset, I say frankly that there are phases of *Native Son* which I shall make no attempt to account for. There are meanings in my book of which I was not aware until they literally spilled out upon the paper. I shall sketch the outline of how I *consciously* came into possession of the materials that went into *Native Son*, but there will be many things I shall omit, not because I want to, but simply because I don't know them.

The birth of Bigger Thomas goes back to my childhood, and there was not just one Bigger, but many of them, more than I could count and more than you suspect. But let me start with the first Bigger, whom I shall call Bigger No. 1.

When I was a bareheaded, barefoot kid in Jackson, Mississippi, there was a boy who terrorized me and all of the boys I played with. If we were playing games, he would saunter up and snatch from us our balls, bats, spinning tops, and marbles. We would stand around pouting, sniffling, trying to keep back our tears, begging for our playthings. But Bigger would refuse. We never demanded that he give them back; we were afraid, and Bigger was bad. We had seen him clout boys when he was angry and we did not want to run that risk. We never recovered our toys unless we flattered him and made him feel that he was superior to us. Then, perhaps, if he felt like it, he condescended, threw them at us and then gave each of us a swift kick in the bargain, just to make us feel his utter contempt.

That was the way Bigger No. 1 lived. His life was a continuous challenge to others. At all times he *took* his way, right or wrong, and those who contradicted him had him to fight. And never was he happier than when he had someone cornered and at his mercy; it seemed that the deepest meaning of his squalid life was in him at such times.

I don't know what the fate of Bigger No. 1 was. His swaggering personality is swallowed up somewhere in the amnesia of my childhood. But I suspect that his end was violent. Anyway, he left a marked impression upon me; maybe it was because I longed secretly to be like him and was afraid. I don't know.

If I had known only one Bigger I would not have written *Native Son*. Let me call the next one Bigger No. 2; he was about seventeen and tougher than the first Bigger. Since I, too, had grown older, I was a little less afraid of him. And the hardness of this Bigger No. 2 was not directed toward me or the other Negroes, but toward the whites who ruled the South. He bought clothes and food on credit and would not pay for them. He lived in the dingy shacks of the white landlords and refused to pay rent. Of course, he had no money, but neither did we. We did without the necessities of life and starved ourselves, but he never would. When we asked him why he acted as he did, he would tell us (as though we were little children in a kindergarten) that the white folks had everything and he had nothing. Further, he would tell us that we were fools not to get what we wanted while we were alive in this world. We would listen and silently agree. We longed to believe and act as he did, but we were afraid. We were Southern Negroes and we were hungry and we wanted to live, but we were more willing to tighten our belts than risk conflict. Bigger No. 2 wanted to live and he did; he was in prison the last time I heard from him.

There was Bigger No. 3, whom the white folks called a "bad nigger." He carried his life in his hands in a literal fashion. I once worked as a ticket-taker in a Negro movie house (all movie houses in Dixie are Jim Crow; there are movies for whites and movies for blacks), and many times Bigger No. 3 came to the door and gave my arm a hard pinch and walked into the theater. Resentfully and silently, I'd nurse my bruised arm. Presently, the proprietor would come over and ask how things were going. I'd point into the darkened theater and say: "Bigger's in there." "Did he pay?" the proprietor would ask. "No, sir," I'd answer. The proprietor would pull down the corners of his lips and speak through his teeth: "We'll kill that goddamn nigger one of these days." And the episode would end right there. But later on Bigger No. 3 was killed during the days of Prohibition: while delivering liquor to a customer he was shot through the back by a white cop.

And then there was Bigger No. 4, whose only law was death. The Jim Crow laws of the South were not for him. But as he laughed and cursed and broke them, he knew that some day he'd have to pay for his freedom. His rebellious spirit made him violate all the taboos and consequently he always oscillated between moods of intense elation and depression. He was never happier than when he had outwitted some foolish custom, and he was never more melancholy than when brooding over the impossibility of his ever being free. He had no job, for he regarded digging ditches for fifty cents a day as slavery. "I can't live on that," he would say. Ofttimes I'd find him reading a book; he would stop and in a joking, wistful, and cynical manner ape the antics of the white folks. Generally, he'd end his mimicry in a depressed state and say: "The white folks won't let us do nothing." Bigger No. 4 was sent to the asylum for the insane.

Then there was Bigger No. 5, who always rode the Jim Crow streetcars without paying and sat wherever he pleased. I remember one morning his getting into a streetcar (all streetcars in Dixie are

divided into two sections: one section is for whites and is labeled—FOR
WHITES; the other section is for Negroes and is labeled—FOR
COLORED) and sitting in the white section. The conductor went to
him and said: "Come on, nigger. Move over where you belong. Can't
you read?" Bigger answered: "Naw, I can't read." The conductor flared
up: "Get out of that seat!" Bigger took out his knife, opened it, held
it nonchalantly in his hand, and replied: "Make me." The conductor
turned red, blinked, clenched his fists, and walked away, stammering:
"The goddamn scum of the earth!" A small angry conference of white
men took place in the front of the car and the Negroes sitting in the
Jim Crow section overheard: "That's that Bigger Thomas nigger and
you'd better leave 'im alone." The Negroes experienced an intense flash
of pride and the streetcar moved on its journey without incident. I
don't know what happened to Bigger No. 5. But I can guess.

The Bigger Thomases were the only Negroes I know of who consistently violated the Jim Crow laws of the South and got away with it,
at least for a sweet brief spell. Eventually, the whites who restricted
their lives made them pay a terrible price. They were shot, hanged,
maimed, lynched, and generally hounded until they were either dead
or their spirits broken.

There were many variations to this behavioristic pattern. Later on
I encountered other Bigger Thomases who did not react to the locked-in
Black Belts with this same extremity and violence. But before I use
Bigger Thomas as a springboard for the examination of milder types,
I'd better indicate more precisely the nature of the environment that
produced these men, or the reader will be left with the impression that
they were essentially and organically bad.

In Dixie there are two worlds, the white world and the black world,
and they are physically separated. There are white schools and black
schools, white churches and black churches, white businesses and black
businesses, white graveyards and black graveyards, and, for all I know,
a white God and a black God. . . .

This separation was accomplished after the Civil War by the terror
of the Ku Klux Klan, which swept the newly freed Negro through
arson, pillage, and death out of the United States Senate, the House of
Representatives, the many state legislatures, and out of the public,
social, and economic life of the South. The motive for this assault was
simple and urgent. The imperialistic tug of history had torn the Negro
from his African home and had placed him ironically upon the most
fertile plantation areas of the South; and, when the Negro was freed,
he outnumbered the whites in many of these fertile areas. Hence, a
fierce and bitter struggle took place to keep the ballot from the Negro,
for had he had a chance to vote, he would have automatically con-

trolled the richest lands of the South and with them the social, political, and economic destiny of a third of the Republic. Though the South is politically a part of America, the problem that faced her was peculiar and the struggle between the whites and the blacks after the Civil War was in essence a struggle for power, ranging over thirteen states and involving the lives of tens of millions of people.

But keeping the ballot from the Negro was not enough to hold him in check; disfranchisement had to be supplemented by a whole panoply of rules, taboos, and penalties designed not only to insure peace (complete submission), but to guarantee that no real threat would ever arise. Had the Negro lived upon a common territory, separate from the bulk of the white population, this program of oppression might not have assumed such a brutal and violent form. But this war took place between people who were neighbors, whose homes adjoined, whose farms had common boundaries. Guns and disfranchisement, therefore, were not enough to make the black neighbor keep his distance. The white neighbor decided to limit the amount of education his black neighbor could receive; decided to keep him off the police force and out of the local national guards; to segregate him residentially; to Jim Crow him in public places; to restrict his participation in the professions and jobs; and to build up a vast, dense ideology of racial superiority that would justify any act of violence taken against him to defend white dominance; and further, to condition him to hope for little and to receive that little without rebelling.

But, because the blacks were so *close* to the very civilization which sought to keep them out, because they could not *help* but react in some way to its incentives and prizes, and because the very tissue of their consciousness received its tone and timbre from the strivings of that dominant civilization, oppression spawned among them a myriad variety of reactions, reaching from outright blind rebellion to a sweet, other-worldly submissiveness.

In the main, this delicately balanced state of affairs has not greatly altered since the Civil War, save in those parts of the South which have been industrialized or urbanized. So volatile and tense are these relations that if a Negro rebels against rule and taboo, he is lynched and the reason for the lynching is usually called "rape," that catchword which has garnered such vile connotations that it can raise a mob anywhere in the South pretty quickly, even today.

Now for the variations in the Bigger Thomas pattern. Some of the Negroes living under these conditions got religion, felt that Jesus would redeem the void of living, felt that the more bitter life was in the present the happier it would be in the hereafter. Others, clinging still to that brief glimpse of post-Civil War freedom, employed a thousand

ruses and stratagems of struggle to win their rights. Still others projected their hurts and longings into more naïve and mundane forms—
blues, jazz, swing—and, without intellectual guidance, tried to build up
a compensatory nourishment for themselves. Many labored under hot
suns and then killed the restless ache with alcohol. Then there were
those who strove for an education, and when they got it, enjoyed the
financial fruits of it in the style of their bourgeois oppressors. Usually
they went hand in hand with the powerful whites and helped to keep
their groaning brothers in line, for that was the safest course of action.
Those who did this called themselves "leaders." To give you an idea of
how completely these "leaders" worked with those who oppressed, I
can tell you that I lived the first seventeen years of my life in the South
without so much as hearing of or seeing one act of rebellion from *any*
Negro, save the Bigger Thomases.

But why did Bigger revolt? No explanation based upon a hard and
fast rule of conduct can be given. But there were always two factors
psychologically dominant in his personality. First, through some quirk
of circumstance, he had become estranged from the religion and the
folk culture of his race. Second, he was trying to react to and answer
the call of the dominant civilization whose glitter came to him through
the newspapers, magazines, radios, movies, and the mere imposing
sight and sound of daily American life. In many respects his emergence
as a distinct type was inevitable.

As I grew older, I became familiar with the Bigger Thomas conditioning and its numerous shadings no matter where I saw it in Negro
life. It was not, as I have already said, as blatant or extreme as in the
originals; but it was there, nevertheless, like an undeveloped negative.

Sometimes, in areas far removed from Mississippi, I'd hear a Negro
say: "I wish I didn't have to live this way. I feel like I want to burst."
Then the anger would pass; he would go back to his job and try to eke
out a few pennies to support his wife and children.

Sometimes I'd hear a Negro say: "God, I wish I had a flag and a
country of my own." But that mood would soon vanish and he would
go his way placidly enough.

Sometimes I'd hear a Negro ex-soldier say: "What in hell did I fight
in the war for? They segregated me even when I was offering my life
for my country." But he, too, like the others, would soon forget, would
become caught up in the tense grind of struggling for bread.

I've even heard Negroes, in moments of anger and bitterness, praise
what Japan is doing in China, not because they believed in oppression
(being objects of oppression themselves), but because they would
suddenly sense how empty their lives were when looking at the dark
faces of Japanese generals in the rotogravure supplements of the Sun-

day newspapers. They would dream of what it would be like to live in a country where they could forget their color and play a responsible role in the vital processes of the nation's life.

I've even heard Negroes say that maybe Hitler and Mussolini are all right; that maybe Stalin is all right. They did not say this out of any intellectual comprehension of the forces at work in the world, but because they felt that these men "did things," a phrase which is charged with more meaning than the mere words imply. There was in the back of their minds, when they said this, a wild and intense longing (wild and intense because it was suppressed!) to belong, to be identified, to feel that they were alive as other people were, to be caught up forgetfully and exultingly in the swing of events, to feel the clean, deep, organic satisfaction of doing a job in common with others.

It was not until I went to live in Chicago that I first thought seriously of writing of Bigger Thomas. Two items of my experience combined to make me aware of Bigger as a meaningful and prophetic symbol. First, being free of the daily pressure of the Dixie environment, I was able to come into possession of my own feelings. Second, my contact with the labor movement and its ideology made me see Bigger clearly and feel what he meant.

I made the discovery that Bigger Thomas was not black all the time; he was white, too, and there were literally millions of him, everywhere. The extension of my sense of the personality of Bigger was the pivot of my life; it altered the complexion of my existence. I became conscious, at first dimly, and then later on with increasing clarity and conviction, of a vast, muddied pool of human life in America. It was as though I had put on a pair of spectacles whose power was that of an x-ray enabling me to see deeper into the lives of men. Whenever I picked up a newspaper, I'd no longer feel that I was reading of the doings of whites alone (Negroes are rarely mentioned in the press unless they've committed some crime!), but of a complex struggle for life going on in my country, a struggle in which I was involved. I sensed, too, that the Southern scheme of oppression was but an appendage of a far vaster and in many respects more ruthless and impersonal commodity-profit machine.

Trade-union struggles and issues began to grow meaningful to me. The flow of goods across the seas, buoying and depressing the wages of men, held a fascination. The pronouncements of foreign governments, their policies, plans, and acts were calculated and weighed in relation to the lives of people about me. I was literally overwhelmed when, in reading the works of Russian revolutionists, I came across descriptions of the "holiday energies of the masses," "the locomotives of history," "the conditions prerequisite for revolution," and so forth. I approached all of these new revelations in the light of Bigger Thomas, his hopes, fears, and despairs; and I began to feel far-flung kinships, and sense, with fright and abashment, the possibilities of *alliances* between the American Negro and other people possessing a kindred consciousness.

As my mind extended in this general and abstract manner, it was fed with even more vivid and concrete examples of the lives of Bigger Thomas. The urban environment of Chicago, affording a more stimulating life, made the Negro Bigger Thomases react more violently than even in the South. More than ever I began to see and understand the environmental factors which made for this extreme conduct. It was not that Chicago segregated Negroes more than the South, but that Chicago had more to offer, that Chicago's physical aspect—noisy, crowded, filled with the sense of power and fulfillment—did so much more to dazzle the mind with a taunting sense of possible achievement that the segregation it did impose brought forth from Bigger a reaction more obstreperous than in the South.

So the concrete picture and the abstract linkages of relationships fed each other, each making the other more meaningful and affording my emotions an opportunity to react to them with success and understanding. The process was like a swinging pendulum, each to and fro motion throwing up its tiny bit of meaning and significance, each stroke helping to develop the dim negative which had been implanted in my mind in the South.

During this period the shadings and nuances which were filling in Bigger's picture came, not so much from Negro life, as from the lives of whites I met and grew to know. I began to sense that they had their own kind of Bigger Thomas behavioristic pattern which grew out of a more subtle and broader frustration. The waves of recurring crime, the silly fads and crazes, the quicksilver changes in public taste, the hysteria and fears—all of these had long been mysteries to me. But now I looked back of them and felt the pinch and pressure of the environment that gave them their pitch and peculiar kind of being. I began to feel with my mind the inner tensions of the people I met. I don't mean to say that I think that environment *makes* consciousness (I suppose God makes that, if there is a God), but I do say that I felt and still feel that the environment supplies the instrumentalities through which the organism expresses itself, and if that environment is warped or tranquil, the mode and manner of behavior will be affected toward deadlocking tensions or orderly fulfillment and satisfaction.

Let me give examples of how I began to develop the dim negative of Bigger. I met white writers who talked of their responses, who told me how whites reacted to this lurid American scene. And, as they talked, I'd translate what they said in terms of Bigger's life. But what was more important still, I read their novels. Here, for the first time, I found ways and techniques of gauging meaningfully the effects of American civilization upon the personalities of people. I took these techniques, these ways of seeing and feeling, and twisted them, bent them, adapted them, until they became *my* ways of apprehending the locked-in life of the Black Belt areas. This association with white writers was the life preserver of my hope to depict Negro life in fiction, for my race possessed no fictional works dealing with such problems, had no background in such sharp and critical testing of experience, no novels that went with a deep and fearless will down to the dark roots of life.

Here are examples of how I culled information relating to Bigger from my reading:

There is in me a memory of reading an interesting pamphlet telling of the friendship of Gorky and Lenin in exile. The booklet told of how Lenin and Gorky were walking down a London street. Lenin turned to Gorky and, pointing, said: "Here is *their* Big Ben." "There is *their* Westminster Abbey." "There is *their* library." And at once, while reading that passage, my mind stopped, teased, challenged with the effort to remember, to associate widely disparate but meaningful experiences in my life. For a moment nothing would come, but I remained convinced that I had heard the meaning of those words sometime, somewhere before. Then, with a sudden glow of satisfaction of having gained a little more knowledge about the world in which I lived, I'd end up by saying: "That's Bigger. That's the Bigger Thomas reaction."

In both instances the deep sense of exclusion was identical. The feeling of looking at things with a painful and unwarrantable nakedness was an experience, I learned, that transcended national and racial boundaries. It was this intolerable sense of feeling and understanding so much, and yet living on a plane of social reality where the look of a world which one did not make or own struck one with a blinding objectivity and tangibility, that made me grasp the revolutionary impulse in my life and the lives of those about me and far away.

I remember reading a passage in a book dealing with old Russia which said: "We must be ready to make endless sacrifices if we are to be able to overthrow the Czar." And again I'd say to myself: "I've heard that somewhere, sometime before." And again I'd hear Bigger Thomas, far away and long ago, telling some white man who was trying to impose upon him: "I'll kill you and go to hell and pay for it." While living in America I heard from far away Russia the bitter accents of tragic calculation of how much human life and suffering it would cost a man to live as a man in a world that denied him the right to live with dignity. Actions and feelings of men ten thousand miles from home helped me to understand the moods and impulses of those walking the streets of Chicago and Dixie.

I am not saying that I heard any talk of revolution in the South when I was a kid there. But I did hear the lispings, the whispers, the mutters which some day, under one stimulus or another, will surely grow into open revolt unless the conditions which produce Bigger Thomases are changed.

In 1932 another source of information was dramatically opened up to me and I saw data of a surprising nature that helped to clarify the personality of Bigger. From the moment that Hitler took power in Germany and began to oppress the Jews, I tried to keep track of what was happening. And on innumerable occasions I was startled to detect, either from the side of the Fascists or from the side of the oppressed, reactions, moods, phrases, attitudes that reminded me strongly of Bigger, that helped to bring out more clearly the shadowy outlines of the negative that lay in the back of my mind.

I read every account of the Fascist movement in Germany I could lay my hands on, and from page to page I encountered and recognized familiar emotional patterns. What struck me with particular force was the Nazi preoccupation with the construction of a society in which there would exist among all people (*German* people, of course!) *one* solidarity of ideals, *one* continuous circulation of fundamental beliefs, notions, and assumptions. I am not now speaking of the popular idea of regimenting people's thought; I'm speaking of the implicit, almost unconscious, or pre-conscious, assumptions and ideals upon which whole nations and races act and live. And while reading these Nazi pages I'd be reminded of the Negro preacher in the South telling of a life beyond this world, a life in which the color of men's skins would not matter, a life in which each man would know what was deep down in the hearts of his fellow man. And I could hear Bigger Thomas standing on a street corner in America expressing his agonizing doubts and chronic suspicions, thus: "I ain't going to trust nobody. Everything is a racket and everybody is out to get what he can for himself. Maybe if we had a true leader, we could do something." And I'd know that I was still on the track of learning about Bigger, still in the midst of the modern struggle for solidarity among men.

When the Nazis spoke of the necessity of a highly ritualized and symbolized life, I could hear Bigger Thomas on Chicago's South Side saying: "Man, what we need is a leader like Marcus Garvey. We need a nation, a flag, an army of our own. We colored folks ought to orga- nize into groups and have generals, captains, lieutenants, and so forth. We ought to take Africa and have a national home." I'd know, while listening to these childish words, that a white man would smile derisively at them. But I could not smile, for I knew the truth of those simple words from the facts of my own life. The deep hunger in those childish ideas was like a flash of lightning illuminating the whole dark inner landscape of Bigger's mind. Those words told me that the civilization which had given birth to Bigger contained no spiritual sustenance, had created no culture which could hold and claim his allegiance and faith, had sensitized him and had left him stranded, a free agent to roam the streets of our cities, a hot and whirling vortex of undisciplined and unchannelized impulses. The results of these observations made me feel more than ever estranged from the civilization in which I lived, and more than ever resolved toward the task of creating with words a scheme of images and symbols whose direction could enlist the sympathies, loyalties, and yearnings of the millions of Bigger Thomases in every land and race. . . .

But more than anything else, as a writer, I was fascinated by the similarity of the emotional tensions of Bigger in America and Bigger in Nazi Germany and Bigger in old Russia. All Bigger Thomases, white and black, felt tense, afraid, nervous, hysterical, and restless. From far away Nazi Germany and old Russia had come to me items of knowledge that told me that certain modern experiences were creating types of personalities whose existence ignored racial and national lines of demarcation, that these personalities carried with them a more universal drama-element than anything I'd ever encountered before; that these personalities were mainly imposed upon men and women living in a world whose fundamental assumptions could no longer be taken for granted: a world ridden with national and class strife; a world whose metaphysical meanings had vanished; a world in which God no longer existed as a daily focal point of men's lives; a world in which men could no longer retain their faith in an ultimate hereafter. It was a highly geared world whose nature was conflict and action, a world whose limited area and vision imperiously urged men to satisfy their organisms, a world that existed on a plane of animal sensation alone.

It was a world in which millions of men lived and behaved like drunkards, taking a stiff drink of hard life to lift them up for a thrilling moment, to give them a quivering sense of wild exultation and fulfillment that soon faded and let them down. Eagerly they took another drink, wanting to avoid the dull, flat look of things, then still another, this time stronger, and then they felt that their lives had meaning. Speaking figuratively, they were soon chronic alcoholics, men who lived by violence, through extreme action and sensation, through drowning daily in a perpetual nervous agitation.

From these items I drew my first political conclusions about Bigger: I felt that Bigger, an American product, a native son of this land, carried within him the potentialities of either Communism or Fascism. I don't mean to say that the Negro boy I depicted in *Native Son* is either a Communist or a Fascist. He is not either. But he is product of a dislocated society; he is a dispossessed and disinherited man; he is all of this, and he lives amid the greatest possible plenty on earth and he is looking and feeling for a way out. Whether he'll follow some gaudy, hysterical leader who'll promise rashly to fill the void in him, or whether he'll come to an understanding with the millions of his kindred fellow workers under trade-union or revolutionary guidance depends upon the future drift of events in America. But, granting the emotional state, the tensity, the fear, the hate, the impatience, the sense of exclusion, the ache for violent action, the emotional and cultural hunger, Bigger Thomas, conditioned as his organism is, will not become an ardent, or even a lukewarm, supporter of the *status quo*.

The difference between Bigger's tensity and the German variety is that Bigger's, due to America's educational restrictions on the bulk of her Negro population, is in a nascent state, not yet articulate. And the difference between Bigger's longing for self-identification and the Russian principle of self-determination is that Bigger's, due to the effects of American oppression, which has not allowed for the forming of deep ideas of solidarity among Negroes, is still in a state of individual anger and hatred. Here, I felt, was *drama!* Who will be the first to touch off these Bigger Thomases in America, white and black?

For a long time I toyed with the idea of writing a novel in which a Negro Bigger Thomas would loom as a symbolic figure of American life, a figure who would hold within him the prophecy of our future. I felt strongly that he held within him, in a measure which perhaps no other contemporary type did, the outlines of action and feeling which we would encounter on a vast scale in the days to come. Just as one sees when one walks into a medical research laboratory jars of alcohol containing abnormally large or distorted portions of the human body, just so did I see and feel that the conditions of life under which Negroes are forced to live in America contain the embryonic emotional prefigurations of how a large part of the body politic would react under stress.

So, with this much knowledge of myself and the world gained and known, why should I not try to work out on paper the problem of what will happen to Bigger? Why should I not, like a scientist in a laboratory, use my imagination and invent test-tube situations, place Bigger in them, and, following the guidance of my own hopes and fears, what I had learned and remembered, work out in fictional form an emotional statement and resolution of this problem?

But several things militated against my starting to work. Like Bigger himself, I felt a mental censor—product of the fears which a Negro feels from living in America—standing over me, draped in white, warning me not to write. This censor's warnings were translated into my own thought processes thus: "What will white people think if I draw the picture of such a Negro boy? Will they not at once say: 'See, didn't we tell you all along that niggers are like that? Now, look, one of their own kind has come along and drawn the picture for us!' " I felt that if I drew the picture of Bigger truthfully, there would be many reactionary whites who would try to make of him something I did not intend. And yet, and this was what made it difficult, I knew that I could not write of Bigger convincingly if I did not depict him as he *was*: that is, resentful toward whites, sullen, angry, ignorant, emotionally unstable, depressed and unaccountably elated at times, and unable even, because of his own lack of inner organization which American oppression has fostered in him, to unite with the members of his own race. And would not whites misread Bigger and, doubting his authenticity, say: "This man is preaching hate against the whole white race"?

The more I thought of it the more I became convinced that if I did not write of Bigger as I saw and felt him, if I did not try to make him a living personality and at the same time a symbol of all the larger things I felt and saw in him, I'd be reacting as Bigger himself reacted: that is, I'd be acting out of *fear* if I let what I thought whites would say constrict and paralyze me.

As I contemplated Bigger and what he meant, I said to myself: "I must write this novel, not only for others to read, but to free *myself* of this sense of shame and fear." In fact, the novel, as time passed, grew upon me to the extent that it became a necessity to write it; the writing of it turned into a way of living for me.

Another thought kept me from writing. What would my own white and black comrades in the Communist party say? This thought was the most bewildering of all. Politics is a hard and narrow game; its policies represent the aggregate desires and aspirations of millions of people. Its goals are rigid and simply drawn, and the minds of the majority of politicians are set, congealed in terms of daily tactical maneuvers. How could I create such complex and wide schemes of associational thought and feeling, such filigreed webs of dreams and politics, without being mistaken for a "smuggler of reaction," "an ideological confusionist," or "an individualistic and dangerous element"? Though my heart is with the collectivist and proletarian ideal, I solved this problem by assuring myself that honest politics and honest feeling in imaginative representation ought to be able to meet on common healthy ground without fear, suspicion, and quarreling. Further, and more importantly, I steeled myself by coming to the conclusion that whether politicians accepted or rejected Bigger did not really matter; my task, as I felt it, was to free myself of this burden of impressions and feelings, recast them into the image of Bigger and make him *true*. Lastly, I felt that a right more immediately deeper than that of politics or race was at stake; that is, a *human* right, the right of a man to think and feel honestly. And especially did this personal and human right bear hard upon me, for temperamentally I am inclined to satisfy the claims of my own ideals rather than the expectations of others. It was this obscure need that had pulled me into the labor movement in the beginning and by exercising it I was but fulfilling what I felt to be the laws of my own growth.

There was another constricting thought that kept me from work. It deals with my own race. I asked myself: "What will Negro doctors, lawyers, dentists, bankers, school teachers, social workers and business men, think of me if I draw such a picture of Bigger?" I knew from long and painful experience that the Negro middle and professional classes were the people of my own race who were more than others ashamed of Bigger and what he meant. Having narrowly escaped the Bigger Thomas reaction pattern themselves—indeed, still retaining traces of it within the confines of their own timid personalities—they would not relish being publicly reminded of the lowly, shameful depths of life above which they enjoyed their bourgeois lives. Never did they want people, especially *white* people, to think that their lives were so much touched by anything so dark and brutal as Bigger.

Their attitude toward life and art can be summed up in a single paragraph: "But, Mr. Wright, there are so many of us who are *not* like Bigger? Why don't you portray in your fiction the *best* traits of our race, something that will show the white people what we have done in *spite* of oppression? Don't represent anger and bitterness. Smile when a white person comes to you. Never let him feel that you are so small that what he has done to crush you has made you hate him! Oh, above all, save your *pride*!"

But Bigger won over all these claims; he won because I felt that I was hunting on the trail of more exciting and thrilling game. What Bigger meant had claimed me because I felt with all of my being that he was more important than what any person, white or black, would say or try to make of him, more important than any political analysis designed to explain or deny him, more important, even, than my own sense of fear, shame, and diffidence.

But Bigger was still not down upon paper. For a long time I had been writing of him in my mind, but I had yet to put him into an image, a breathing symbol draped out in the guise of the only form of life my native land had allowed me to know intimately, that is, the ghetto life of the American Negro. But the basic reason for my hesitancy was that another and far more complex problem had risen to plague me. Bigger, as I saw and felt him, was a snarl of many realities; he had in him many levels of life.

First, there was his personal and private life, that intimate existence that is so difficult to snare and nail down in fiction, that elusive core of being, that individual data of consciousness which in every man and woman is like that in no other. I had to deal with Bigger's dreams, his fleeting, momentary sensations, his yearning, visions, his deep emotional responses.

Then I was confronted with that part of him that was dual in aspect, dim, wavering, that part of him which is so much a part of *all* Negroes and *all* whites that I realized that I could put it down upon paper only by feeling out its meaning first within the confines of my own life. Bigger was attracted and repelled by the American scene. He was an American, because he was a native son; but he was also a Negro nationalist in a vague sense because he was not allowed to live as an American. Such was his way of life and mine; neither Bigger nor I resided fully in either camp.

Of this dual aspect of Bigger's social consciousness, I placed the nationalistic side first, not because I agreed with Bigger's wild and intense hatred of white people, but because his hate had placed him, like a wild animal at bay, in a position where he was most symbolic and explainable. In other words, his nationalist complex was for me a concept through which I could grasp more of the total meaning of his life than I could in any other way. I tried to approach Bigger's *snarled* and *confused* nationalist feelings with *conscious* and *informed* ones of my own. Yet, Bigger was not nationalist enough to feel the need of religion or the folk culture of his own people. What made Bigger's social consciousness most complex was the fact that he was hovering unwanted between two worlds—between powerful America and his own stunted place in life—and I took upon myself the task of trying to make the reader feel this No Man's Land. The most that I could say of Bigger was that he felt the *need* for a whole life and *acted* out of that need; that was all.

Above and beyond all this, there was that American part of Bigger which is the heritage of us all, that part of him which we get from our seeing and hearing, from school, from the hopes and dreams of our friends; that part of him which the common people of America never talk of but take for granted. Among millions of people the deepest convictions of life are never discussed openly; they are felt, implied, hinted at tacitly and obliquely in their hopes and fears. We live by an idealism that makes us believe that the Constitution is a good docu-

ment of government, that the Bill of Rights is a good legal and humane
principle to safeguard our civil liberties, that every man and woman
should have the opportunity to realize himself, to seek his own individual fate and goal, his own peculiar and untranslatable destiny. I
don't say that Bigger knew this in the terms in which I'm speaking of
it; I don't say that any such thought ever entered his head. His emotional and intellectual life was never that articulate. But he knew it
emotionally, intuitively, for his emotions and his desires were developed, and he caught it, as most of us do, from the mental and emotional climate of our time. Bigger had all of this in him, damned up,
buried, implied, and I had to develop it in fictional form.

There was still another level of Bigger's life that I felt bound to
account for and render, a level as elusive to discuss as it was to grasp
in writing. Here again, I had to fall back upon my own feelings as a
guide, for Bigger did not offer in his life any articulate verbal explana-
tions. There seems to hover somewhere in that dark part of all our
lives, in some more than in others, an objectless, timeless, spaceless
element of primal fear and dread, stemming, perhaps, from our birth
(depending upon whether one's outlook upon personality is Freudian
or non-Freudian!), a fear and dread which exercises an impelling influence upon our lives all out of proportion to its obscurity. And,
accompanying this *first fear*, is, for the want of a better name, a reflex
urge toward ecstasy, complete submission, and trust. The springs of
religion are here, and also the origins of rebellion. And in a boy like
Bigger, young, unschooled, whose subjective life was clothed in the
tattered rags of American "culture," this primitive fear and ecstasy
were naked, exposed, unprotected by religion or a framework of government or a scheme of society whose final faiths would gain his love
and trust; unprotected by trade or profession, faith or belief; opened
to every trivial blast of daily or hourly circumstance.

There was yet another level of reality in Bigger's life: the impliedly
political. I've already mentioned that Bigger had in him impulses
which I had felt were present in the vast upheavals of Russia and
Germany. Well, somehow, I had to make these political impulses felt
by the reader in terms of Bigger's daily actions, keeping in mind as I
did so the probable danger of my being branded as a propagandist by
those who would not like the subject matter.

Then there was Bigger's relationship with white America, both North
and South, which I had to depict, which I had to make known once
again, alas; a relationship whose effects are carried by every Negro,
like scars, somewhere in his body and mind.

I had also to show what oppression had done to Bigger's relationships with his own people, how it had split him off from them, how it

had baffled him; how oppression seems to hinder and stifle in the victim those very qualities of character which are so essential for an effective struggle against the oppressor.

Then there was the fabulous city in which Bigger lived, an indescribable city, huge, roaring, dirty, noisy, raw, stark, brutal; a city of extremes: torrid summers and sub-zero winters, white people and black people, the English language and strange tongues, foreign born and native born, scabby poverty and gaudy luxury, high idealism and hard cynicism! A city so young that, in thinking of its short history, one's mind, as it travels backward in time, is stopped abruptly by the barren stretches of wind-swept prairie! But a city old enough to have caught within the homes of its long, straight streets the symbols and images of man's age-old destiny, of truths as old as the mountains and seas, of dramas as abiding as the soul of man itself! A city which has become the pivot of the Eastern, Western, Northern, and Southern poles of the nation. But a city whose black smoke clouds shut out the sunshine for seven months of the year; a city in which, on a fine balmy May morning, one can sniff the stench of the stockyards; a city where people have grown so used to gangs and murders and graft that they have honestly forgotten that government can have a pretense of decency!

With all of this thought out, Bigger was still unwritten. Two events, however, came into my life and accelerated the process, made me sit down and actually start work on the typewriter, and just stop the writing of Bigger in my mind as I walked the streets.

The first event was my getting a job in the South Side Boys' Club, an institution which tried to reclaim the thousands of Negro Bigger Thomases from the dives and the alleys of the Black Belt. Here, on a vast scale, I had an opportunity to observe Bigger in all of his moods, actions, haunts. Here I felt for the first time that the rich folk who were paying my wages did not really give a good goddamn about Bigger, that their kindness was prompted at bottom by a selfish motive. They were paying me to distract Bigger with ping-pong, checkers, swimming, marbles, and baseball in order that he might not roam the streets and harm the valuable white property which adjoined the Black Belt. I am not condemning boys' clubs and ping-pong as such; but these little stopgaps were utterly inadequate to fill up the centuries-long chasm of emptiness which American civilization had created in these Biggers. I felt that I was doing a kind of dressed-up police work, and I hated it.

I would work hard with these Biggers, and when it would come time for me to go home I'd say to myself, under my breath so that no one could hear: "Go to it, boys! Prove to the bastards that gave you these games that life is stronger than ping-pong. . . . Show them that full-blooded life is harder and hotter than they suspect, even though that life is draped in a black skin which at heart they despise. . . ."

They did. The police blotters of Chicago are testimony to how *much* they did. That was the only way I could contain myself for doing a job I hated; for a moment I'd allow myself, vicariously, to feel as Bigger felt—not much, just a little, just a *little*—but, still, there it was.

The second event that spurred me to write of Bigger was more personal and subtle. I had written a book of short stories which was published under the title of *Uncle Tom's Children*. When the reviews of that book began to appear, I realized that I had made an awfully naïve mistake. I found that I had written a book which even bankers' daughters could read and weep over and feel good about. I swore to myself that if I ever wrote another book, no one would weep over it; that it would be so hard and deep that they would have to face it without the consolation of tears. It was this that made me get to work in dead earnest.

Now, until this moment I did not stop to think very much about the plot of *Native Son*. The reason I did not is because I was not for one moment ever worried about it. I had spent years learning about Bigger, what had made him, what he meant; so, when the time came for writing, *what had made him and what he meant* constituted my plot. But the far-flung items of his life had to be couched in imaginative terms, terms known and acceptable to a common body of readers, terms which would, in the course of the story, manipulate the deepest held notions and convictions of their lives. That came easy. The moment I began to write, the plot fell out, so to speak. I'm not trying to oversimplify or make the process seem oversubtle. At bottom, what happened is very easy to explain.

Any Negro who has lived in the North or the South knows that times without number he has heard of some Negro boy being picked up on the streets and carted off to jail and charged with "rape." This thing happens so often that to my mind it had become a representative symbol of the Negro's uncertain position in America. Never for a second was I in doubt as to what kind of social reality or dramatic situation I'd put Bigger in, what kind of test-tube life I'd set up to evoke his deepest reactions. Life had made the plot over and over again, to the extent that I knew it by heart. So frequently do these acts recur that when I was halfway through the first draft of *Native Son* a case paralleling Bigger's flared forth in the newspapers of Chicago. (Many of the newspaper items and some of the incidents in *Native Son* are but fictionalized versions of the Robert Nixon case and rewrites of news stories from the *Chicago Tribune*.) Indeed, scarcely was *Native Son* off the press before Supreme Court Justice Hugo L. Black gave the nation a long and vivid account of the American police methods of handling Negro boys.

Let me describe this stereotyped situation: A crime wave is sweeping a city and citizens are clamoring for police action. Squad cars cruise the Black Belt and grab the first Negro boy who seems to be unattached and homeless. He is held for perhaps a week without charge or bail, without the privilege of communicating with anyone, including his own relatives. After a few days this boy "confesses" anything that he is asked to confess, any crime that handily happens to be unsolved and on the calendar. Why does he confess? After the boy has been grilled night and day, hanged up by his thumbs, dangled by his feet out of twenty-story windows, and beaten (in places that leave no scars—cops have found a way to do that), he signs the papers before him, papers which are usually accompanied by a verbal promise to the boy that he will not go to the electric chair. Of course, he ends up by being executed or sentenced for life. If you think I'm telling tall tales, get chummy with some white cop who works in a Black Belt district and ask him for the lowdown.

When a black boy is carted off to jail in such a fashion, it is almost impossible to do anything for him. Even well-disposed Negro lawyers find it difficult to defend him, for the boy will plead guilty one day and then not guilty the next, according to the degree of pressure and persuasion that is brought to bear upon his frightened personality from one side or the other. Even the boy's own family is scared to death; sometimes fear of police intimidation makes them hesitate to acknowledge that the boy is a blood relation of theirs.

Such has been America's attitude toward these boys that if one is picked up and confronted in a police cell with ten white cops, he is intimidated almost to the point of confessing anything. So far removed are these practices from what the average American citizen encounters in his daily life that it takes a huge act of his imagination to believe that it is true; yet, this same average citizen, with his kindness, his American sportsmanship and good will, would probably act with the mob if a self-respecting Negro family moved into his apartment building to escape the Black Belt and its terrors and limitations. . . .

Now, after all of this, when I sat down to the typewriter, I could not work; I could not think of a good opening scene for the book. I had definitely in mind the kind of emotion I wanted to evoke in the reader in that first scene, but I could not think of the type of concrete event that would convey the motif of the entire scheme of the book, that would sound, in varied form, the note that was to be resounded throughout its length, that would introduce to the reader just what kind of an organism Bigger's was and the environment that was bearing hourly upon it. Twenty or thirty times I tried and failed; then I argued that if I could not write the opening scene, I'd start with the scene that followed. I did. The actual writing of the book began with the scene in the pool room.

Now, for the writing. During the years in which I had met all of those Bigger Thomases, those varieties of Bigger Thomases, I had not consciously gathered material to write of them; I had not kept a note-book record of their sayings and doings. Their actions had simply made impressions upon my sensibilities as I lived from day to day, impressions which crystallized and coagulated into clusters and configurations of memory, attitudes, moods, ideas. And these subjective states, in turn, were automatically stored away somewhere in me. I was not even aware of the process. But, excited over the book which I had set myself to write, under the stress of emotion, these things came surging up, tangled, fused, knotted, entertaining me by the sheer variety and potency of their meaning and suggestiveness.

With the whole theme in mind, in an attitude almost akin to prayer, I gave myself up to the story. In an effort to capture some phase of Bigger's life that would not come to me readily, I'd jot down as much of it as I could. Then I'd read it over and over, adding each time a word, a phrase, a sentence until I felt that I had caught all the shadings of reality I felt dimly were there. With each of these rereadings and rewritings it seemed that I'd gather in facts and facets that tried to run away. It was an act of concentration, of trying to hold within one's center of attention all of that bewildering array of facts which science, politics, experience, memory, and imagination were urging upon me. And then, while writing, a new and thrilling relationship would spring up under the drive of emotion, coalescing and telescoping alien facts into a known and felt truth. That was the deep fun of the job: to feel within my body that I was pushing out to new areas of feeling, strange landmarks of emotion, tramping upon foreign soil, compounding new relationships of perceptions, making new and—until that very split second of time!—unheard-of and unfelt effects with words. It had a buoying and tonic impact upon me; my senses would strain and seek for more and more of such relationships; my temperature would rise as I worked. That is writing as I feel it, a kind of significant living.

The first draft of the novel was written in four months, straight through, and ran to some 576 pages. Just as a man rises in the mornings to dig ditches for his bread, so I'd work daily. I'd think of some abstract principle of Bigger's conduct and at once my mind would turn it into some act I'd seen Bigger perform, some act which I hoped would be familiar enough to the American reader to gain his credence. But in the writing of scene after scene I was guided by but one criterion: to tell the truth as I saw it and felt it. That is, to objectify in words some insight derived from my living in the form of action, scene, and dialogue. If a scene seemed improbable to me, I'd not tear it up, but ask myself: "Does it reveal enough of what I feel to stand in spite of its unreality?" If I felt it did, it stood. If I felt that it did not, I ripped it out. The degree of morality in my writing depended upon the degree of felt life and truth I could put down upon the printed page. For example, there is a scene in *Native Son* where Bigger stands in a cell with a Negro preacher, Jan, Max, the State's Attorney, Mr. Dalton, Mrs. Dalton, Bigger's mother, his brother, his sister, Al, Gus, and Jack. While writing that scene, I knew that it was unlikely that so many people would ever be allowed to come into a murderer's cell. But I wanted those people in that cell to elicit a certain important emotional response from Bigger. And so the scene stood. I felt that what I wanted that scene to say to the reader was *more important than its surface reality or plausibility.*

Always, as I wrote, I was both reader and writer, both the conceiver of the action and the appreciator of it. I tried to write so that, in the same instant of time, the objective and subjective aspects of Bigger's life would be caught in a focus of prose. And always I tried to *render, depict,* not merely to tell the story. If a thing was cold, I tried to make the reader *feel* cold, and not just tell about it. In writing in this fashion, sometimes I'd find it necessary to use a stream of consciousness technique, then rise to an interior monologue, descend to a direct rendering of a dream state, then to a matter-of-fact depiction of what Bigger was saying, doing, and feeling. Then I'd find it impossible to say what I wanted to say without stepping in and speaking outright on my own; but when doing this I always made an effort to retain the mood of the story, explaining everything only in terms of Bigger's life and, if possible, in the rhythms of Bigger's thought (even though the words would be mine). Again, at other times, in the guise of the lawyer's speech and the newspaper items, or in terms of what Bigger would overhear or see from afar, I'd give what others were saying and thinking of him. But always, from the start to the finish, it was Bigger's story, Bigger's fear, Bigger's flight, and Bigger's fate that I tried to depict. I wrote with the conviction in mind (I don't know if this is right or wrong; I only know that I'm temperamentally inclined to feel this way) that the main burden of all serious fiction consists almost wholly of character-destiny and the items, social, political, and personal, of that character-destiny.

As I wrote I followed, almost unconsciously, many principles of the novel which my reading of the novels of other writers had made me feel were necessary for the building of a well-constructed book. For the most part the novel is rendered in the present; I wanted the reader to feel that Bigger's story was happening *now*, like a play upon the stage or a movie unfolding upon the screen. Action follows action, as in a prize fight. Wherever possible, I told of Bigger's life in close-up, slow-motion, giving the feel of the grain in the passing of time. I had long had the feeling that this was the best way to "enclose" the reader's mind in a new world, to blot out all reality except that which I was giving him.

Then again, as much as I could, I restricted the novel to what Bigger saw and felt, to the limits of his feeling and thoughts, even when I was conveying *more* than that to the reader. I had the notion that such a manner of rendering made for a sharper effect, a more pointed sense of the character, his peculiar type of being and consciousness. Throughout there is but one point of view: Bigger's. This, too, I felt, made for a richer illusion of reality.

I kept out of the story as much as possible, for I wanted the reader to feel that there was nothing between him and Bigger; that the story was a special *première* given in his own private theater.

I kept the scenes long, made as much happen within a short space of time as possible; all of which, I felt, made for greater density and richness of effect.

In a like manner I tried to keep a unified sense of background throughout the story; the background would change, of course, but I tried to keep before the eyes of the reader at all times the forces and elements against which Bigger was striving.

And, because I had limited myself to rendering only what Bigger saw and felt, I gave no more reality to the other characters than that which Bigger himself saw.

This, honestly, is all I can account for in the book. If I attempted to account for scenes and characters, to tell why certain scenes were written in certain ways, I'd be stretching facts in order to be pleasantly intelligible. All else in the book came from my feelings reacting upon the material, and any honest reader knows as much about the rest of what is in the book as I do; that is, if, as he reads, he is willing to let his emotions and imagination become as influenced by the materials as I did. As I wrote, for some reason or other, one image, symbol, character, scene, mood, feeling evoked its opposite, its parallel, its complimentary, and its ironic counterpart. Why? I don't know. My emotions and imagination just like to work that way. One can account for just so much of life, and then no more. At least, not yet.

With the first draft down, I found that I could not end the book satisfactorily. In the first draft I had Bigger going smack to the electric chair; but I felt that two murders were enough for one novel. I cut the final scene and went back to worry about the beginning. I had no luck. The book was one-half finished, with the opening and closing scenes unwritten. Then, one night, in desperation—I hope that I'm not disclosing the hidden secrets of my craft!—I sneaked out and got a bottle. With the help of it, I began to remember many things which I could not remember before. One of them was that Chicago was overrun with rats. I recalled that I'd seen many rats on the streets, that I'd heard and read of Negro children being bitten by rats in their beds. At first I rejected the idea of Bigger battling a rat in his room; I was afraid that the rat would "hog" the scene. But the rat would not leave me; he presented himself in many attractive guises. So, cautioning myself to allow the rat scene to disclose *only* Bigger, his family, their little room, and their relationships, I let the rat walk in, and he did his stuff.

Many of the scenes were torn out as I reworked the book. The mere rereading of what I'd written made me think of the possibility of developing themes which had been only hinted at in the first draft. For example, the entire guilt theme that runs through *Native Son* was woven in *after* the first draft was written.

At last I found out how to end the book; I ended it just as I had begun it, showing Bigger living dangerously, taking his life into his hands, accepting what life had made him. The lawyer, Max, was placed in Bigger's cell at the end of the novel to register the moral—or what *I* felt was the moral—horror of Negro life in the United States.

The writing of *Native Son* was to me an exciting, enthralling, and even a romantic experience. With what I've learned in the writing of this book, with all of its blemishes, imperfections, with all of its unrealized potentialities, I am launching out upon another novel, this time about the status of women in modern American society. This book, too, goes back to my childhood just as Bigger went, for, while I was storing away impressions of Bigger, I was storing away impressions of many other things that made me think and wonder. Some experience will ignite somewhere deep down in me the smoldering embers of new fires and I'll be off again to write yet another novel. It is good to live when one feels that such as that will happen to one. Life becomes sufficient unto life; the rewards of living are found in living.

I don't know if *Native Son* is a good book or a bad book. And I don't know if the book I'm working on now will be a good book or a bad book. And I really don't care. The mere writing of it will be more fun and a deeper satisfaction than any praise or blame from anybody.

I feel that I'm lucky to be alive to write novels today, when the whole world is caught in the pangs of war and change. Early American writers, Henry James and Nathaniel Hawthorne, complained bitterly about the bleakness and flatness of the American scene. But I think that if they were alive, they'd feel at home in modern America. True, we have no great church in America; our national traditions are still of such a sort that we are not wont to brag of them; and we have no army that's above the level of mercenary fighters; we have no group acceptable to the whole of our country upholding certain humane values; we have no rich symbols, no colorful rituals. We have only a money-grubbing, industrial civilization. But we do have in the Negro the embodiment of a past tragic enough to appease the spiritual hunger of even a James; and we have in the oppression of the Negro a shadow athwart our national life dense and heavy enough to satisfy even the gloomy broodings of a Hawthorne. And if Poe were alive, he would not have to invent horror; horror would invent him.

RICHARD WRIGHT
New York, March 7, 1940

J. SAUNDERS REDDING

The

Negro Writer—

Shadow

and

Substance

J. SAUNDERS REDDING (1906–   ) HAS WRITTEN A NOVEL, *A Stranger and Alone* (1950); a book of personal essays, *On Being Negro in America* (1951); studies of black American history, *They Came in Chains* (1950), *The Lonesome Road* (1958); and a pioneering study of American Negro poetry, *To Make A Poet Black* (1938). A graduate of Brown University, he has taught at Morehouse College, Southern University, and Hampton Institute, has served as Director of Research and Publications at the National Endowment for the Humanities, and is presently a professor of American Studies at George Washington University.

In 1950 Redding published this short essay in a special literary issue of *Phylon*, Atlanta University's "Review of Race and Culture." In it he attacks the crucial problem of "audience," the unique difficulty of a black author trying to successfully write about black experience in a world of white publishers interested in fiction that appeals to white readers. How does one affirm simple human values in writing that is inevitably met with preconceived expectations? Does the artist court the anticipated reaction, or does he remain true to his own ideas despite the rebuffs and rejection slips? Does he address his work to a white audience so it will sell?

The answers to such questions necessarily must be self-evident, even though writers do not always act as though they were. What Redding saw at mid-century, however, was the beginning of a new health in American society which would presumably free the black writer from the cult of publisher's and reader's preconceptions. It is perhaps safe to assert that what he saw beginning has contributed to the remarkable vitality of contemporary Afro-American art—a vitality that is accepted uneasily by many arbiters of the dominant culture.

J. SAUNDERS REDDING

The Negro Writer—Shadow and Substance

SEASON IT AS YOU WILL, THE THOUGHT THAT THE NEGRO AMERICAN IS different from other people, and especially from other Americans, is still unpalatable to most Negroes. But a rather inexorable logic both explains the aversion (for of course Negro "differentness" was and is largely responsible for the social ills that beset him) and supports the notion. The Negro is different. An iron ring of historical circumstances has made him so. Slavery, organized terrorism, discrimination, prejudice—the point need not be labored.

But the differentness has little depth. It goes only so far as the superficies, as lineament rather than character. It does not reach down into the biology. It does not thrust deep into the idioplasm, into the matrix of emotion. It transforms nothing fundamental. It does not make the Negro a monster. That he has long borne a monstrous reputation (and that individuals in the race have lived up to it) would be entirely beside the point were it not for the patent fact that this imputation set artificial bounds to the Negro's thinking about himself and to the thinking of whites about him. And this itself would be of no consequence except that it led the Negro, as creator, into the *cul de sac* of insincerity and dishonesty and, as audience, into the aversion mentioned above.

It has been until very recently a vicious circle. The aversion has had the result of leaving the Negro writer with an audience only disingenuously his; an audience which he has had to trick, to bait, to lure. I take it that these terms carry the very strongest connotations of improbity and hypocrisy. In the very earliest and in some later days it was the lure of imitativeness. Take Wheatley and Watkins and Whitfield and Braithwaite, and James Weldon Johnson when he wrote for the *Century*. In Dunbar's day it was the lure of dialect and the contrived comic, and Dunbar is a self-confessed dissembler. In the Twenties and Thirties it was the lure of the naughty peep-show, the sensational and gross, and the most financially successful and the most often commented-upon Negro writers, Claude McKay and Wallace Thurman, were hucksters of filth. Only now and then did Negro writers working in Negro material deal sincerely and/or profoundly with Negro life. When they did, or tried to, they were rejected. Sutton Griggs and Charles Chesnutt. The first novel that James Weldon Johnson wrote and could never find a publisher for. The novel, *The Autobiography*

Reprinted from *Phylon*, XI (Fourth Quarter 1950), 371-73, by permission of the publisher and the author. Copyright © 1950 by *Phylon*.

of An Ex-Coloured Man, which he wrote and published first at his own expense in 1912.

But I think that the day of all this is past or fast passing. The social and intellectual and spiritual climate of Roosevelt's New Deal and of the world's second war was exactly tempered to produce a change in the outlook of the American Negro. This change is reflected in his writing over the last fifteen years. (It is also reflected, but less importantly, in writing by whites about Negroes). And I think that the ethnocentric compulsions to racial chauvinism and racial escape and cultural and empirical denial are weakened and that the American Negro writer's progress is toward realistic idealism and a sort of scientific humanism, and these, I think, are the highest goals of most of the world's creative effort.

But let me not simply bandy these terms about. By progress toward realistic idealism and scientific humanism, I mean the engagement of the imagination, the intellect, the passions and the will in transforming the real—say, a people or a social philosophy—into something no less real but more rewarding and fulfilling. Out of the obscure and sometimes not fully realized potentials, which the creative mind recognizes intuitively and which are based in realities, spiritual and emotional as well as physical, the realistic idealist seeks to establish desired actualities. Realistic idealism is Dewey's pragmatism, Gilson's Catholicism, and Finkelstein and Koestler's Judaism translated in terms of art rather than of social philosophy.

There is inevitably some relation between a people's daily exertion to live and what they hope to make of life; some relation between effort and ideal. There is proof of this in every great social or moral movement, and sometimes in economic movements, like the late lamented technocracy—all of which owe their origins to a congruity between what is—the real, and what could be—the ideal.

It is true that this congruity is sometimes destroyed by fanaticism, or cynicism, or the use of the wrong means to attain the desired end, and then the real and the ideal become separated and grow into conflict. Because of the resurgence of the Klan spirit, because of the political cynicism of the period 1900 through Hoover, because of the corruption of justice, because of a thousand daily sneers at a despised people's dream of equality, the separation and conflict between the real and the ideal was happening to the Negro. Then the New Deal and World War Two put a stop to it.

Do not question how. It was because of the very nature of the prinicples of Roosevelt's revolution, and it was because of the creed for the establishment of which the whole English-speaking world declared itself to be fighting. And so the Negro, but more especially the

Negro writer, found himself being slowly liberated from racial chains by the very impulses which he had been reviled for feeling. With his liberation he could begin to see himself as in no fundamental way different and particular. He could begin to explain himself and his motives and his character in terms of conditioning forces common to all humanity. Virtue, let us say, he could begin to see now was not ludicrous because a Negro possesed it. Treason was no more monstrous—and no less so—because it was committed by a Negro; adultery no more sinful; lying no more reprehensible; cowardice no more shameful. He began to see that the values were human, not racial. And he began to prove this by testing them in creatures of his own imagination who were not Negro.

But at the same time he began to see this, he saw also, I think and hope, that within his special observation and within his special category of race-experience there is still a mine of creative material, and that this material, no longer artificially bounded by fear and shame, is full of lessons and of truth for the world.

WILLIAM GARDNER SMITH

The

Negro Writer—

Pitfalls

and

Compensations

Like Saunders Redding, William Gardner Smith (1927–   ) contributed to the special 1950 *Phylon* issue entitled "The Negro in Literature: The Current Scene." Smith had just published his second novel, *Anger at Innocence,* an account of an unusual love affair between two inhabitants of a South Philadelphia slum. He had been widely praised for his first novel, *Last of the Conquerors* (1948), written about the Negro occupation forces in Germany after World War II, and describing the supreme irony in the absence of German racial prejudice toward black American troops. Since then, Smith has published two other novels. *South Street* (1954) is a vivid portrayal of the Philadelphia ghetto and the types of racial conflicts which surround and permeate it. The book is also a sensitive account of the trials of intermarriage and the difficulties likely to afflict such a union. *Stone Face* (1963) is set in Paris and centers upon the black hero's discovery that prejudice is world wide, even though it is not always directed toward Negroes. The hero learns that in France Algerians and North African Arabs are treated like he was in America, a revelation which changes his life.

A journalist who now lives and works in Europe, Smith grew up in Philadelphia, graduated from Temple University and was a reporter for the Afro-American newspaper, *The Pittsburg Courier*. His essay in the *Phylon* issue represents an important statement by a young black writer (Smith was 23 at the time) about the difficulties of his craft, but it is especially important in its emphasis on the international politics involved in the black writer's experience. From Richard Wright to Eldridge Cleaver many black writers have looked for a political and economic system which appears to offer a viable alternative to American capitalism, and as a result some black novelists are often referred to as "revolutionary." It should also be emphasized, however, that frequently the only thing revolutionary being suggested is the application of American constitutional principles to life in the United States, the assumption being that the system would change radically if such principles were applied.

WILLIAM GARDNER SMITH

The Negro Writer—Pitfalls and Compensations

THIS IS, AS EVERYONE RECOGNIZES BY NOW, A WORLD OF RELATIVITY. WE measure the rights of individuals against the rights of the society; the rights of the artist against the rights of his public; the right of free speech against the right of the individual to protection from slander. Degrees of good and evil are measured against other degrees of good and evil.

This apprehension of infinite relativity is, I think, instructive in considering the position of the Negro writer—I speak particularly of the novelist—in American society. For a moment, disregard the mechanical pros and cons, debits and credits—whether it is easier or more difficult, for a Negro writer to have his work published; consider the purely esthetic question: What handicaps, and what advantages, does the American writer possess by virtue of being a Negro?

Because the handicaps are better known, and perhaps easier to understand, I will consider them first. The Negro writer is, first of all, invariably bitter. There are degrees of this bitterness, ranging from the anger of Richard Wright and the undercurrent of contempt for the white world in Chester Himes to the cruel satire exhibited by George Schuyler in his semi-classic *Black No More*. A writer is a man of sensitivity; otherwise, he would not be a writer. The sensitivities of the Negro writer react, therefore, more strongly against the ignorance, prejudice and discrimination of American society than do those of the average Negro in America.

There are all forms and varieties of this inevitable strain of bitterness in the Negro writer. Sometimes it results in militancy; sometimes in contempt for race and self; sometimes in hatred for the whole of American society, with blindness for the good things contained therein. It is often hard for the Negro writer to resist polemicizing. He is driven often to write a tract, rather than a work of art. So conscious is he of the pervading evil of race prejudice that he feels duty-bound to assault it at every turn, injecting opinion into alleged narration and inserting his philosophy into the mouths of his characters.

Writing of Negroes, the novelist has difficulty with his characterizations. His people usually become walking, talking propaganda, rather than completely rounded individuals. The Negro writer hesitates, perhaps unconsciously, to temper the goodness of his Negro characters with the dialectical "evil." Fearful of re-enforcing stereotypes in the

Reprinted from *Phylon*, XI (Fourth Quarter 1950), 297-303, by permission of the publisher. Copyright © 1950 by *Phylon*.

white reader's mind, he often goes to the other extreme, idealizing his characters, making them flat rather than many-sided. Or, conscious of the pitfalls listed above, and anxious to prove that he is not idealizing his Negro characters, the writer goes to the other extreme—in the name of naturalism—and paints the American Negro as an exaggerated Bigger Thomas, with all the stereotyped characteristics emphasized three times over. To strike a compromise—and, incidentally, the truth— is possibly the most difficult feat for a Negro writer. Proof of this is the fact that I have not read one Negro novel which has truthfully represented the many-sided character of the Negro in American society today. Chester Himes, perhaps, has come closer than any other Negro author to such a representation.

It seems that it is difficult for the Negro writer to add to his weighty diatribes the leaven of humor. Writing is an art; the writer works upon the emotions of his reader. Every sentence, every cadence, every description, every scene, produces an emotional response in this reader. Consciously did Shakespeare lead his audiences through one powerful emotion after another to achieve the final, powerful effect of the death of Desdemona at the hands of Othello; consciously did Marlowe lead to the final descent into hell of Faust. In each of these journeys through dramatic experience there were rises and falls; there were moments of stern conflict and moments of relative relaxation; there were moments of tears and moments of relieving laughter.

Too often, however, in Negro novels do we witness the dull procession of crime after crime against the Negro, without relief in humor or otherwise. These monotonous repetitions of offenses against the Negro serve only to bore the reader in time; and in so doing, they defeat the very purpose of the writer, for they become ineffective. One might even say that the chronicles of offenses constitute truth; however, they do not constitute art. And art is the concern of any novelist.

Novels which last through all time are concerned with universal themes. Dostoievski's great Raskolnikov is all of us in the aftermath of great crime; Tolstoi describes the universal ruling class in time of national crisis. The Negro writer is under tremendous pressure to write about the topical and the transient—the plight of the Negro in American society today. It may be that the greatest of such novels will last because of their historical interest. It may even be that one or two will last because the writer has managed to infuse into his work some universal elements—as Dickens did, even when writing about the social conditions in the England of his day. But most Negro writers do not inject the universal element. They write only about the here and the now. Thus, their novels come and they go: in ten years, they are forgotten.

At this point, let me emphasize that the drive of the Negro writer to write about purely topical themes is of fantastic strength, and difficult for the non-Negro to appreciate. Starving and land-hungry Chinese want food and land: they are not much concerned about such abstractions as the rights of free speech, habeas corpus, the ballot, etc. When day to day problems press upon the individual, they become, in his mind, paramount. This sense of the immediate problem confronts the Negro writer. But it is significant to note that we do not today consider highly that literature which arose in protest against, say, the system of Feudalism, or even, in the United States, slavery.

But there are compensations for these difficulties confronting the Negro writer. They are great compensations.

Writing is concerned with people, with society and with ethics. Great writing is concerned with the individual in the group or tribe; obedience to or deviation from the laws of that tribe, and the consequences. Usually, by the very process of selection, omission and arrangement of his material, the author implies a judgment—approval or rejection of the laws of the society, be they in legal, ethical or religious form. Basic to such writing, obviously, is some understanding of both the society and the people in it.

To grasp social and individual truth, it is my opinion that the novelist must maintain emotional contact with the basic people of his society. At first glance, this appears a simple thing; but, in reality, it is difficult. Consider the material circumstances of the "successful" writer. He becomes a celebrity. He makes money. Usually, he begins to move in the sphere of people like himself—authors, artists, critics, etc. He purchases a home on Long Island. He no longer uses the subway; for now he has an automobile. He lectures; he speaks at luncheons; he autographs books; he attends cocktail parties; he discusses style, form, and problems of psychology with friends in a rather esoteric circle; and he writes. In a word, he moves, to some degree, into an ivory tower; he becomes, in a fashion, detached from the mainstream of American life.

In times of stability this detachment is often not too harmful: for the moral code remains what it was at the moment of the writer's detachment and, despite its rarification in his new environment, still may serve as the wellspring for vital work. In moments of social crisis, however, the established moral code comes into violent conflict with the desires of the people of society. Thus, immediately prior to the French Revolution, the ethics of Feudalism, though still officially recognized, actually were outdated and in conflict with the democratic tendencies of the people; and thus, today, the individualistic and basically selfish ethic of Capitalism, while still officially proclaimed, is in reality contrary to the socialist tendency which has spread over the world, and even made itself felt in America through Roosevelt's New Deal and Truman's election on a Fair Deal program.

The writer who is detached from society does not perceive this contradiction; and thus is missing from his writing some element of social truth. He is behind the times; he is holding onto a shell. Part of the greatness of Tolstoi is that he perceived the ethical, i.e., social, conflict, and accurately recorded it.

The Negro writer cannot achieve—at least, not as easily as the white American writer—this social detachment, however much he might desire it. The very national prejudice he so despises compels him to remember his social roots, perceive the social reality; in a word, compels him to keep his feet on the ground. He cannot register at the Mayflower Hotel. He cannot loll on the Miami Beach. He cannot ignore disfranchisement, epithets, educational and employment discrimination, mob violence. He is bound by unbreakable cords to the Negro social group. And so his writing, however poor artistically, must almost invariably contain some elements of social truth.

The Negro writer is endowed by his environment with relative emotional depth. What does a writer write about? We have said: people, and their problems, conflicts, etc. But—what problems, what conflicts? Pick up any popular American magazine or book and you will find out —the problem of whether John D., a thoroughly empty individual, should leave his wife Mary C., a thoroughly empty individual, to marry Jane B., a thoroughly empty individual. To this problem are devoted hundreds of pages; hundreds of thousands of words. And in the end the reader of intelligence must ask the question: So what?

Emotional depth, perception of real problems and real conflicts, is extremely rare in American literature—as it is in American society generally. Instead of issues of significance, our fiction (our serious fiction) is overladen with such trite themes as that of Tennessee Williams' *The Roman Spring of Mrs. Stone*. America's is a superficial civilization: it is soda-pop land, the civilization of television sets and silk stockings and murder mysteries and contempt for art and poetry. It is difficult, out of such environment, to bring forth works with the emotional force of, say, *Crime and Punishment.*

Here again the Negro writer's social experience is, despite its bitterness, also an artistic boon. To live continually with prejudice based on the accident of skin color is no superficial experience; and neither is the reaction produced by such constant exposure superficial. There is a depth and intensity to the emotions of Negroes—as demonstrated in "Negro music"—which is largely lacking in white Americans. How often has the Negro maid or housecleaner come home to laugh at her white mistress' great concern about the color of a hat, the shape of a shoe, keeping up with the next-door Joneses? How often have Negroes, on the job, laughed in amazement at the inane trivialities which occupy the thoughts of their white fellow workers. And this laughter is logical. The Europeans would understand it. For, what man or woman who has seen a lynching, or been close to the furnaces of Dachau, or been rebuffed and rejected because of his skin color, can really seriously concern himself with the insipid and shallow love affair between Susie Bell and Jerry?

Thus, the Negro writer, if he does not make the tragic error of trying to imitate his white counterparts, has in his possession the priceless "gift" of thematic intuition. Provided he permits his writing to swell truthfully from his deepest emotional reaches, he will treat problems of real significance, which can strike a cord in the heart of basic humanity. He will be able to convey suffering without romanticizing; he will be able to describe happiness which is not merely on the surface; he will be able to search out and concretize the hopes and ambitions which are the basic stuff of human existence. And he will, in Hemingway's words, be able to do this "without cheating." For the basic fact about humanity in our age is that it suffers; and only he who suffers with it can truthfully convey its aches and pains, and thwarted desires.

And now, speaking only of this period in which now we live, I should like to point out one last advantage which I feel accrues to the writer by virtue of being a Negro. It concerns the international power struggle.

We live, it appears, in an age of struggle between the American brand of Capitalism and the Russian brand of Communism. This is the obvious struggle; and most of the individuals in the world seem to feel that one must choose between one or the other. But is this, really, the root struggle? Or is mankind, the great majority of it, not actually groping for a rational social order, free from the tensions of economic and political crisis, free from war and from dictatorship, in which the individual will be permitted to live according to an ethic all sensible and truly just men can subscribe to?

For a moment, leave the last question. Consider the writer in the American scene, in this day and age. Picture him as being young and filled with ideals; consider him intelligent, sensitive and understanding. Ask the question: Can he approve of American society as it exists today?

I say, on the basis of experience and of individual reaction, no! The young writer will notice many good things, worthy of retention, in the America of today. He will approve of free speech (now being seriously curtailed); he will approve the idea of a free press (even though becoming a monopoly because of the economics involved); he will believe in free artistic expression, realizing that only through freedom can real art survive. But can he approve of the dog-eat-dog existence we glorify by the name of Free Enterprise?—an existence which distorts the personality, turns avarice into virtue and permits the strong to run roughshod over the weak, profiteering on human misery? Can he approve chronic depressions and endless wars? Can he approve racial and religious prejudice?

The young writer of ideas and ideals, I say, must instantly be repelled by the ugly aspects of American society. The history of our literature will bear this out—at a swift glance, I think of Emily Dickinson, Thoreau, Emerson, Hawthorne, Dos Passos, Faulkner, Henry James, Melville and, recently, Norman Mailer. And, being repelled, the writer seeks a substitute, something which offers hope of cure. Today, at first glance, the only alternative seems to be Russian Communism.

To list the important American writers who have turned from American Capitalism to Communism since the latter part of the nineteenth century would take up more space than this article is permitted. Suffice it to say that nearly every naturalistic writer in America has made this turn. Our young writer of intelligence and ideals, then, makes this turn. He embraces Communism of the Russian brand. And, immediately, he begins to feel uncomfortable.

For he discovers, in the folds of Russian Communism, the evils of dictatorship. He learns about purge trials; and is handed fantastic lies, which insult his intelligence, to justify them. He learns of the stifling of literature, art and music in the Soviet Union. He learns that Hitler is one day evil, the next day (following a pact with the Soviet Union) good, and the next day evil again. He discovers that Roosevelt is today a warmonger, tomorrow a true democrat and peoples' friend, whose "grand design" the Communist Party, U.S.A., seeks only to imitate. He learns that Tito, only yesterday a Communist hero only a little lower than Stalin, has in reality been a spy and a Fascist since 1936. He learns that a book which is "good" today becomes "bad," "bourgeois" and "decadent" tomorrow when the Party Line changes.

In panic does our idealistic and intelligent writer flee from alliance with the Communist Party. And at this point, the advantage of the Negro writer is discovered. For, having become disillusioned with the Soviet dictatorship, where does the white writer turn for political truth? Back to Capitalism, in ninety-nine out of a hundred cases; back to the very decaying system which lately he had left, a system he now calls "Democracy," "Freedom" and "Western Culture." He repeats the performance of John Dos Passos and, more recently and more strikingly (though in another field) Henry Wallace. The things he formerly found unbearable in Capitalism—he now ignores. Prejudice, depressions, imperialism, political chicanery, support of dictators, dog-eat-dog, strong-kill-the-weak philosophy—these things no longer exist. Black becomes white again. And the creative artist is dead! For he is blind.

The Negro writer, too, makes this retreat from Communism—for he, too, is opposed to lies, deceit, dictatorship and the other evils of the Soviet regime. But—and this is the significant point—the Negro writer does not, in most cases, come back to bow at the feet of Capitalism. He cannot, as can the white writer, close his eyes to the evils of the system under which he lives. Seeing the Negro ghetto, feeling the prejudice, his relatives and friends experiencing unemployment, injustice, police brutality, segregation in the South, white supremacy—seeing these things, the Negro writer cannot suddenly kiss the hand which slaps him. Looking at China, at Indo China and at Africa, he cannot avoid the realization that these are people of color, struggling, as he is struggling, for dignity. Again, prejudice has forced him to perceive the real, the ticking world.

Denied many freedoms, robbed of many rights, the Negro—and the Negro writer—rejects those aspects of both American Capitalism and Russian Communism which trample on freedoms and rights. Repelled now by both contending systems, the Negro writer of strength and courage stands firmly as a champion of the basic human issues—dignity, relative security, freedom and the end of savagery between one human being and another. And in this stand he is supported by the mass of human beings the world over.

So add it up. The handicaps are great. Many Negro writers—the majority, I should say, so far—have been unable to overcome them. The work of others is impaired by them. But if the handicaps can be overcome, the advantages remain. And, as I said before, they are great advantages. Because I believe that an increasing number of Negro writers will be able to overcome the disadvantages inherent in their social situation, I predict that a disproportionate percentage of the outstanding writers of the next decade will be Negroes.

RALPH ELLISON

The

Art

of

Fiction:

An Interview

In the spring of 1953, *The Paris Review*, a literary journal edited by Americans in Europe, published its first issue. Included in that number was an interview with the English novelist, E. M. Forster, the first in a long and famous series of interviews with noted authors that has appeared in the magazine ever since, and in which have been recorded some of the most important statements about writing uttered in the twentieth century.

In the spring of 1955 Ralph Ellison was traveling in Europe and consented to be interviewed by Alfred Chester and Vilma Howard for *The Paris Review* series. Ellison's interview has assumed an importance commensurate with interviews with Faulkner and Hemingway which also have appeared in the magazine. It is a basic statement of Ellison's esthetic and stresses his belief in the universality of successful literature—whether written by black or white, whether written about Negroes or Caucasians. Ellison believes that black writers can't "afford to indulge" in the false issue of pleading black humanity, and he claims his position within that modern tradition of the American novel from Twain through Faulkner. The interview also reminds us that there cannot be "double standards" of quality for literature (even though both white and black critics have often acted as though there were), but that there is a double standard of experience in America—white and black—which often requires the black novelist to express the universal values of his vision in a different manner from his white counterpart, despite the universality of man that both struggle to describe.

RALPH ELLISON

The Art of Fiction: An Interview

ELLISON: Let me say right now that my book is not an autobiographical work.

INTERVIEWERS: You weren't thrown out of school like the boy in your novel?

ELLISON: No. Though, like him, I went from one job to another.

INTERVIEWERS: Why did you give up music and begin writing?

ELLISON: I didn't give up music, but I became interested in writing through incessant reading. In 1935 I discovered Eliot's *The Waste Land* which moved and intrigued me but defied my powers of analysis —such as they were—and I wondered why I had never read anything of equal intensity and sensibility by an American Negro writer. Later on, in New York, I read a poem by Richard Wright, who, as luck would have it, came to town the next week. He was editing a magazine called *New Challenge* and asked me to try a book review of E. Waters Turpin's *These Low Grounds*. On the basis of this review Wright suggested that I try a short story, which I did. I tried to use my knowledge of riding freight trains. He liked the story well enough to accept it and it got as far as the galley proofs when it was bumped from the issue because there was too much material. Just after that the magazine failed.

INTERVIEWERS: But you went on writing—

ELLISON: With difficulty, because this was the Recession of 1937. I went to Dayton, Ohio, where my brother and I hunted and sold game to earn a living. At night I practiced writing and studied Joyce, Dostoevski, Stein, and Hemingway. Especially Hemingway; I read him to learn his sentence structure and how to organize a story. I guess many young writers were doing this, but I also used his description of hunting when I went into the fields the next day. I had been hunting since I was eleven, but no one had broken down the process of wing-shooting for me, and it was from reading Hemingway that I learned to lead a bird. When he describes something in print, believe him; believe him even when he describes the process of art in terms of baseball or boxing; he's been there.

INTERVIEWERS: Were you affected by the social realism of the period?

ELLISON: I was seeking to learn and social realism was a highly regarded theory, though I didn't think too much of the so-called

Reprinted from *Writers at Work: The Paris Review Interviews, Second Series* (New York: The Viking Press, 1963), pp. 320-34. Copyright © 1963 by *The Paris Review, Inc.* All rights reserved. Reprinted by permission of The Viking Press, Inc.

proletarian fiction even when I was most impressed by Marxism. I was intrigued by Malraux, who at that time was being claimed by the Communists. I noticed, however, that whenever the heroes of *Man's Fate* regarded their condition during moments of heightened self-consciousness, their thinking was something other than Marxist. Actually they were more profoundly intellectual than their real-life counterparts. Of course, Malraux was more of a humanist than most of the Marxist writers of that period—and also much more of an artist. He was the artist-revolutionary rather than a politician when he wrote *Man's Fate*, and the book lives not because of a political position embraced at the time but because of its larger concern with the tragic struggle of humanity. Most of the social realists of the period were concerned less with tragedy than with injustice. I wasn't, and am not, *primarily* concerned with injustice, but with art.

INTERVIEWERS: Then you consider your novel a purely literary work as opposed to one in the tradition of social protest.

ELLISON: Now, mind, I recognize no dichotomy between art and protest. Dostoevski's *Notes from Underground* is, among other things, a protest against the limitations of nineteenth-century rationalism; *Don Quixote, Man's Fate, Oedipus Rex, The Trial*—all these embody protest, even against the limitation of human life itself. If social protest is antithetical to art, what then shall we make of Goya, Dickens, and Twain? One hears a lot of complaints about the so-called "protest novel," especially when written by Negroes; but it seems to me that the critics could more accurately complain about the lack of craftsmanship and the provincialism which is typical of such works.

INTERVIEWERS: But isn't it going to be difficult for the Negro writer to escape provincialism when his literature is concerned with a minority?

ELLISON: All novels are about certain minorities: the individual is a minority. The universal in the novel—and isn't that what we're all clamoring for these days?—is reached only through the depiction of the specific man in a specific circumstance.

INTERVIEWERS: But still, how is the Negro writer, in terms of what is expected of him by critics and readers, going to escape his particular need for social protest and reach the "universal" you speak of?

ELLISON: If the Negro, or any other writer, is going to do what is expected of him, he's lost the battle before he takes the field. I suspect that all the agony that goes into writing is borne precisely because the writer longs for acceptance—but it must be acceptance on his own terms. Perhaps, though, this thing cuts both ways: the Negro novelist draws his blackness too tightly around him when he sits down to write—that's what the anti-protest critics believe—but perhaps the white reader draws his whiteness around himself when he sits down to read. He doesn't want to identify himself with Negro characters in terms of our immediate racial and social situation, though on the deeper human level identification can become compelling when the situation is revealed artistically. The white reader doesn't want to get too close, not even in an imaginary re-creation of society. Negro writers have felt this, and it has led to much of our failure.

Too many books by Negro writers are addressed to a white audience. By doing this the authors run the risk of limiting themselves to the audience's presumptions of what a Negro is or should be; the tendency is to become involved in polemics, to plead the Negro's humanity. You know, many white people question that humanity, but I don't think that Negroes can afford to indulge in such a false issue. For us the question should be, what are the specific *forms* of that humanity, and what in our background is worth preserving or abandoning. The clue to this can be found in folklore, which offers the first drawings of any group's character. It preserves mainly those situations which have repeated themselves again and again in the history of any given group. It describes those rites, manners, customs, and so forth, which insure the good life, or destroy it; and it describes those boundaries of feeling, thought, and action which that particular group has found to be the limitation of the human condition. It projects this wisdom in symbols which express the group's will to survive; it embodies those values by which the group lives and dies. These drawings may be crude but they are nonetheless profound in that they represent the group's attempt to humanize the world. It's no accident that great literature, the product of individual artists, is erected upon this humble base. The hero of Dostoevski's *Notes from Underground* and the hero of Gogol's "The Overcoat" appear in their rudimentary forms far back in Russian folklore. French literature has never ceased exploring the nature of the Frenchman. Or take Picasso—

INTERVIEWERS: How does Picasso fit into all this?

ELLISON: Why, he's the greatest wrestler with forms and techniques of them all. Just the same, he's never abandoned the old symbolic forms of Spanish art: the guitar, the bull, daggers, women, shawls, veils, mirrors. Such symbols serve a dual function: they allow the artist to speak of complex experiences and to annihilate time with simple lines and curves; and they allow the viewer an orientation, both emotional and associative, which goes so deep that a total culture may resound in a simple rhythm, an image. It has been said that Escudero could recapitulate the history and spirit of the Spanish dance with a simple arabesque of his fingers.

INTERVIEWERS: But these are examples from homogeneous cultures. How representative of the American nation would you say Negro folklore is?

ELLISON: The history of the American Negro is a most intimate part of American history. Through the very process of slavery came the building of the United States. Negro folklore, evolving within a larger culture which regarded it as inferior, was an especially courageous expression. It announced the Negro's willingness to trust his own experience, his own sensibilities as to the definition of reality, rather than allow his masters to define these crucial matters for him. His experience is that of America and the West, and is as rich a body of experience as one would find anywhere. We can view it narrowly as something exotic, folksy, or "low-down," or we may identify ourselves with it and recognize it as an important segment of the larger American experience —not lying at the bottom of it, but intertwined, diffused in its very texture. I can't take this lightly or be impressed by those who cannot see its importance; it is important to *me*. One ironic witness to the beauty and the universality of this art is the fact that the descendants of the very men who enslaved us can now sing the spirituals and find in the singing an exaltation of their own humanity. Just take a look at some of the slave songs, blues, folk ballads; their possibilities for the writer are infinitely suggestive. Some of them have named human situations so well that a whole corps of writers could not exhaust their universality. For instance, here's an old slave verse:

Ole Aunt Dinah, she's just like me
She work so hard she want to be free
But ole Aunt Dinah's gittin' kinda ole
She's afraid to go to Canada on account of the cold.

Ole Uncle Jack, now he's a mighty "good nigger"
You tell him that you want to be free for a fac'
Next thing you know they done stripped the skin off your back.

Now ole Uncle Ned, he want to be free
He found his way north by the moss on the tree
He cross that river floating in a tub
The patateroller* give him a mighty close rub.

It's crude, but in it you have three universal attitudes toward the problem of freedom. You can refine it and sketch in the psychological subtleties and historical and philosophical allusions, action and whatnot, but I don't think its basic definition can be exhausted. Perhaps some genius could do as much with it as Mann has done with the Joseph story.

---

* Patroller.

INTERVIEWERS: Can you give us an example of the use of folklore in your own novel?

ELLISON: Well, there are certain themes, symbols, and images which are based on folk material. For example, there is the old saying among Negroes: If you're black, stay back; if you're brown, stick around; if you're white, you're right. And there is the joke Negroes tell on themselves about their being so black they can't be seen in the dark. In my book this sort of thing was merged with the meanings which blackness and light have long had in Western mythology: evil and goodness, ignorance and knowledge, and so on. In my novel the narrator's development is one through blackness to light; that is, from ignorance to enlightenment: invisibility to visibility. He leaves the South and goes North; this, as you will notice in reading Negro folk tales, is always the road to freedom—the movement upward. You have the same thing again when he leaves his underground cave for the open.

It took me a long time to learn how to adapt such examples of myth into my work—also ritual. The use of ritual is equally a vital part of the creative process. I learned a few things from Eliot, Joyce and Hemingway, but not how to adapt them. When I started writing, I knew that in both *The Waste Land* and *Ulysses* ancient myth and ritual were used to give form and significance to the material; but it took me a few years to realize that the myths and rites which we find functioning in our everyday lives could be used in the same way. In my first attempt at a novel—which I was unable to complete—I began by trying to manipulate the simple structural unities of *beginning, middle,* and *end,* but when I attempted to deal with the psychological strata—the images, symbols, and emotional configurations—of the experience at hand, I discovered that the unities were simply cool points of stability on which one could suspend the narrative line—but beneath the surface of apparently rational human relationships there seethed a chaos before which I was helpless. People rationalize what they shun or are incapable of dealing with; these superstitions and their rationalizations become ritual as they govern behavior. The rituals become social forms, and it is one of the functions of the artist to recognize them and raise them to the level of art.

I don't know whether I'm getting this over or not. Let's put it this way: Take the "Battle Royal" passage in my novel, where the boys are blindfolded and forced to fight each other for the amusement of the white observers. This is a vital part of behavior pattern in the South, which both Negroes and whites thoughtlessly accept. It is a ritual in preservation of caste lines, a keeping of taboo to appease the gods and ward off bad luck. It is also the initiation ritual to which all greenhorns are subjected. This passage states what Negroes will see I did not have to invent; the patterns were already there in society so that all I had to do was present them in a broader context of meaning. In any society there are mnay rituals of situation which, for the most part, go unquestioned. They can be simple or elaborate, but they are the connective tissue between the work of art and the audience.

INTERVIEWERS: Do you think a reader unacquainted with this folklore can properly understand your work?

ELLISON: Yes, I think so. It's like jazz; there's no inherent problem which prohibits understanding but the assumptions brought to it. We don't all dig Shakespeare uniformly, or even "Little Red Riding Hood." The understanding of art depends finally upon one's willingness to extend one's humanity and one's knowledge of human life. I noticed, incidentally, that the Germans, having no special caste assumptions concerning American Negroes, dealt with my work simply as a novel. I think the Americans will come to view it that way in twenty years—if it's around that long.

INTERVIEWERS: Don't you think it will be?

ELLISON: I doubt it. It's not an important novel. I failed of eloquence and many of the immediate issues are rapidly fading away. If it does last, it will be simply because there are things going on in its depth that are of more permanent interest than on its surface. I hope so, anyway.

INTERVIEWERS: Have the critics given you any constructive help in your writing, or changed in any way your aims in fiction?

ELLISON: No, except that I have a better idea of how the critics react, of what they see and fail to see, of how their sense of life differs with mine and mine with theirs. In some instances they were nice for the wrong reasons. In the U.S.—and I don't want this to sound like an apology for my own failures—some reviewers did not see what was before them because of this nonsense about protest.

INTERVIEWERS: Did the critics change your view of yourself as a writer?

ELLISON: I can't say that they did. I've been seeing by my own candle too long for that. The critics did give me a sharper sense of a larger audience, yes; and some convinced me that they were willing to judge me in terms of my writing rather than in terms of my racial identity. But there is one widely syndicated critical bankrupt who made liberal noises during the thirties and has been frightened ever since. He attacked my book as a "literary race riot." By and large, the critics and readers gave me an affirmed sense of my identity as a writer. You might know this within yourself, but to have it affirmed by others is of utmost importance. Writing is, after all, a form of communication.

INTERVIEWERS: When did you begin *Invisible Man?*

ELLISON: In the summer of 1945. I had returned from the sea, ill, with advice to get some rest. Part of my illness was due, no doubt, to the fact that I had not been able to write a novel for which I'd received a Rosenwald Fellowship the previous winter. So on a farm in Vermont where I was reading *The Hero* by Lord Ragland and speculating on the nature of Negro leadership in the U.S., I wrote the first paragraph of *Invisible Man,* and was soon involved in the struggle of creating the novel.

INTERVIEWERS: How long did it take you to write it?

ELLISON: Five years with one year out for a short novel which was unsatisfactory, ill-conceived, and never submitted for publication.

INTERVIEWERS: Did you have everything thought out before you began to write *Invisible Man?*

ELLISON: The symbols and their connections were known to me. I began it with a chart of the three-part division. It was a conceptual frame with most of the ideas and some incidents indicated. The three parts represent the narrator's movement from, using Kenneth Burke's terms, purpose to passion to perception. These three major sections are built up of smaller units of three which mark the course of the action and which depend for their development upon what I hoped was a consistent and developing motivation. However, you'll note that the maximum insight on the hero's part isn't reached until the final section. After all, it's a novel about innocence and human error, a struggle through illusion to reality. Each section begins with a sheet of paper; each piece of paper is exchanged for another and contains a definition of his identity, or the social role he is to play as defined for him by others. But all say essentially the same thing: "Keep this nigger boy running." Before he could have some voice in his own destiny he had to discard these old identities and illusions; his enlightenment couldn't come until then. Once he recognizes the hole of darkness into which these papers put him, he has to burn them. That's the plan and the intention; whether I achieved this is something else.

INTERVIEWERS: Would you say that the search for identity is primarily an American theme?

ELLISON: It is *the* American theme. The nature of our society is such that we are prevented from knowing who we are. It is still a young society, and this is an integral part of its development.

INTERVIEWERS: A common criticism of "first novels" is that the central incident is either omitted or weak. *Invisible Man* seems to suffer here;

shouldn't we have been present at the scenes which are the dividing lines in the book—namely, when. the Brotherhood organization moves the narrator downtown, then back uptown?

ELLISON: I think you missed the point. The major flaw in the hero's character is his unquestioning willingness to do what is required of him by others as a way to success, and this was the specific form of his "innocence." He goes where he is told to go; he does what he is told to do; he does not even choose his Brotherhood name. It is chosen for him and he accepts it. He has accepted party discipline and thus cannot be present at the scene since it is not the will of the Brotherhood leaders. What is important is not the scene but his failure to question their decision. There is also the fact that no single person can be everywhere at once, nor can a single consciousness be aware of all the nuances of a large social action. What happens uptown while he is downtown is part of his darkness, both symbolic and actual. No; I don't feel that any vital scenes have been left out.

INTERVIEWERS: Why did you find it necessary to shift styles throughout the book; particularly in the Prologue and Epilogue?

ELLISON: The Prologue was written afterwards, really—in terms of a shift in the hero's point of view. I wanted to throw the reader off balance—make him accept certain non-naturalistic effects. It was really a memoir written underground, and I wanted a foreshadowing through which I hoped the reader would view the actions which took place in the main body of the book. For another thing, the styles of life presented are different. In the South, where he was trying to fit into a traditional pattern and where his sense of certainty had not yet been challenged, I felt a more naturalistic treatment was adequate. The college trustee's speech to the students is really an echo of a certain kind of Southern rhetoric and I enjoyed trying to re-create it. As the hero passes from the South to the North, from the relatively stable to the swiftly changing, his sense of certainty is lost and the style becomes expressionistic. Later on during his fall from grace in the Brotherhood it becomes somewhat surrealistic. The styles try to express both his state of consciousness and the state of society. The Epilogue was necessary to complete the action begun when he set out to write his memoirs.

INTERVIEWERS: After four hundred pages you still felt the Epilogue was necessary?

ELLISON: Yes. Look at it this way. The book is a series of reversals. It is the portrait of the artist as a rabble-rouser, thus the various mediums of expression. In the Epilogue the hero discovers what he had not discovered throughout the book: you have to make your own decisions; you have to think for yourself. The hero comes up from underground because the act of writing and thinking necessitated it. He could not stay down there.

INTERVIEWERS: You say that the book is "a series of reversals." It seemed to us that this was a weakness, that it was built on a series of provocative situations which were canceled by the calling up of conventional emotions.

ELLISON: I don't quite see what you mean.

INTERVIEWERS: Well, for one thing, you begin with a provocative situation of the American Negro's status in society. The responsibility for this is that of the white American citizen; that's where the guilt lies. Then you cancel it by introducing the Communist Party, or the Brotherhood, so that the reader tends to say to himself, "Ah, they're the guilty ones. They're the ones who mistreat him; not us."

ELLISON: I think that's a case of misreading. And I didn't identify the Brotherhood as the C.P., but since you do I'll remind you that they too are white. The hero's invisibility is not a matter of being seen, but a refusal to run the risk of his own humanity, which involves guilt. This is not an attack upon white society! It is what the hero refuses to do in each section which leads to further action. He must assert and achieve his own humanity; he cannot run with the pack and do this— this is the reason for all the reversals. The Epilogue is the most final reversal of all; therefore it is a necessary statement.

INTERVIEWERS: And the love affairs—or almost love-affairs—

ELLISON: [*Laughing*] I'm glad you put it that way. The point is that when thrown into a situation which he thinks he wants, the hero is sometimes thrown at a loss; he doesn't know how to act. After he had made this speech about the Place of the Woman in Our Society, for example, and was approached by one of the women in the audience; he thought she wanted to talk about the Brotherhood and found that she wanted to talk about brother-*and-sisterhood*. Look, didn't you find the book at all *funny?* I felt that such a man as this character would have been incapable of a love affair; it would have been inconsistent with his personality.

INTERVIEWERS: Do you have any difficulty controlling your characters? E. M. Forster says that he sometimes finds a character running away with him.

ELLISON: No, because I find that a sense of the ritual understructure of the fiction helps to guide the creation of characters. Action is the thing. We are what we do and do not do. The problem for me is to get from A to B to C. My anxiety about transitions greatly prolonged the writing of my book. The naturalists stick to case histories and sociology and are willing to compete with the camera and the tape recorder. I despise concreteness in writing, but when reality is deranged in fiction, one must worry about the seams.

INTERVIEWERS: Do you have difficulty turning real characters into fiction?

ELLISON: Real characters are just a limitation. It's like turning your own life into fiction: you have to be hindered by chronology and fact. A number of the characters just jumped out, like Rinehart and Ras.

INTERVIEWERS: Isn't Ras based on Marcus Garvey?*

ELLISON: No. In 1950 my wife and I were staying at a vacation spot where we met some white liberals who thought the best way to be friendly was to tell us what it was like to be Negro. I got mad at hearing this from people who otherwise seemed very intelligent. I had already sketched Ras, but the passion of his statement came out after I went upstairs that night feeling that we needed to have this thing out once and for all and get it done with; then we could go on living like people and individuals. No conscious reference to Garvey is intended.

INTERVIEWERS: What about Rinehart? Is he related to Rinehart in the blues tradition, or Django Rheinhardt, the jazz musician?

ELLISON: There is a peculiar set of circumstances connected with my choice of that name. My old Oklahoma friend, Jimmy Rushing, the blues singer, used to sing one with a refrain that went:

> Rinehart, Rinehart,
> It's so lonesome up here
> On Beacon Hill,

which haunted me, and as I was thinking of a character who was a master of disguise, of coincidence, this name with its suggestion of inner and outer came to my mind. Later I learned that it was a call used by Harvard students when they prepared to riot, a call to chaos. Which is very interesting, because it is not long after Rinehart appears in my novel that the riot breaks out in Harlem. Rinehart is my name for the personification of chaos. He is also intended to represent America and change. He has lived so long with chaos that he knows how to manipulate it. It is the old theme of *The Confidence Man*. He is a figure in a country with no solid past or stable class lines; therefore he is able to move about easily from one to the other. . . .

You know, I'm still thinking of your question about the use of Negro experience as material for fiction. One function of serious literature is to deal with the moral core of a given society. Well, in the United States the Negro and his status have always stood for that moral con-

---

* Marcus Garvey: Negro nationalist and founder of a "Back to Africa" movement in the United States during the early 1900s.

cern. He symbolizes among other things the human and social possibility of equality. This is the moral question raised in our two great nineteenth-century novels, *Moby Dick* and *Huckleberry Finn.* The very center of Twain's book revolves finally around the boy's relations with Nigger Jim and the question of what Huck should do about getting Jim free after the two scoundrels had sold him. There is a magic here worth conjuring, and that reaches to the very nerve of the American consciousness—so why should I abandon it? Our so-called race problem has now lined up with the world problems of colonialism and the struggle of the West to gain the allegiance of the remaining non-white people who have thus far remained outside the Communist sphere; thus its possibilities for art have increased rather than lessened. Looking at the novelist as manipulator and depicter of moral problems, I ask myself how much of the achievement of democratic ideals in the U.S. has been affected by the steady pressure of Negroes and those whites who were sensitive to the implications of our condition; and I know that without that pressure the position of our country before the world would be much more serious than it is even now. Here is part of the social dynamics of a great society. Perhaps the discomfort about protest in books by Negro authors comes because since the nineteenth century American literature has avoided profound moral searching. It was too painful and besides there were specific problems of language and form to which the writers could address themselves. They did wonderful things, but perhaps they left the real problems untouched. There are exceptions, of course, like Faulkner who has been working the great moral theme all along, taking it up where Mark Twain put it down.

I feel that with my decision to devote myself to the novel I took on one of the responsibilities inherited by those who practice the craft in the U.S.: that of describing for all that fragment of the huge diverse American experience which I know best, and which offers me the possibility of contributing not only to the growth of the literature but to the shaping of the culture as I should like it to be. The American novel is in this sense a conquest of the frontier; as it describes our experience, it creates it.

JAMES BALDWIN

Everybody's

Protest

Novel

IN 1949 JAMES BALDWIN PUBLISHED THIS ESSAY IN *Zero*, A SMALL literary magazine printed in Paris. It was the first shot fired in what became a bitter and pathetic war of wills between Baldwin and the man who had given him aid and comfort in his struggle to become a writer, Richard Wright. Although Baldwin only mentioned Wright's novel in his last two paragraphs, Wright took the "anti-protest" argument of the essay as a personal affront. He accused Baldwin of betraying him as well as all American Negroes by repudiating the idea of protest literature. Bluntly, Wright maintained that "art for art's sake" was "crap," that "*all* literature is protest." Baldwin has written about this quarrel at some length, and his statements (in *Nobody Knows My Name*) about its significance are interesting and important. They pertain to Baldwin's own quest for a viable art, help to define the much discussed Wright-Baldwin relationship and drive to the center of the argument about what form a black writer's protest should take.

Perhaps all these matters are summarized in Baldwin's frank admission that "Richard was right to be hurt, I was wrong to have hurt him. He saw clearly enough, far more clearly than I had dared to allow myself to see, what I had done: I had used his work as a kind of springboard into my own. His work was a road-block in my road, the sphinx really, whose riddles I had to answer before I could become myself."*

* Quoted from James Baldwin, *Nobody Knows My Name* (New York, 1961) by permission of the publisher, The Dial Press, Inc.

JAMES BALDWIN

Everybody's Protest Novel

IN *Uncle Tom's Cabin,* THAT CORNERSTONE OF AMERICAN SOCIAL PROtest fiction, St. Clare, the kindly master, remarks to his coldly disapproving Yankee cousin, Miss Ophelia, that, so far as he is able to tell, the blacks have been turned over to the devil for the benefit of the whites in this world—however, he adds thoughtfully, it may turn out in the next. Miss Ophelia's reaction is, at least, vehemently right-minded: "This is perfectly horrible!" she exclaims. "You ought to be ashamed of yourselves!"

Miss Ophelia, as we may suppose, was speaking for the author; her exclamation is the moral, neatly framed, and incontestable like those improving mottoes sometimes found hanging on the walls of furnished rooms. And, like these mottoes, before which one invariably flinches, recognizing an insupportable, almost an indecent glibness, she and St. Clare are terribly in earnest. Neither of them questions the medieval morality from which their dialogue springs: black, white, the devil, the next world—posing its alternatives between heaven and the flames—were realities for them as, of course, they were for their creator. They spurned and were terrified of the darkness, striving mightily for the light; and considered from this aspect, Miss Ophelia's exclamation, like Mrs. Stowe's novel, achieves a bright, almost a lurid significance, like the light from a fire which consumes a witch. This is the more striking as one considers the novels of Negro oppression written in our own, more enlightened day, all of which say only: "This is perfectly horrible! You ought to be ashamed of yourselves!" (Let us ignore, for the moment, those novels of oppression written by Negroes, which add only a raging, near-paranoiac postscript to this statement and actually reinforce, as I hope to make clear later, the principles which activate the oppression they decry.)

Uncle Tom's Cabin is a very bad novel, having, in its self-righteous, virtuous sentimentality, much in common with *Little Women.* Sentimentality, the ostentatious parading of excessive and spurious emotion, is the mark of dishonesty, the inability to feel; the wet eyes of the sentimentalist betray his aversion to experience, his fear of life, his arid heart; and it is always, therefore, the signal of secret and violent inhumanity, the mask of cruelty. *Uncle Tom's Cabin*—like its multitudinous, hard-boiled descendants—is a catalogue of violence. This is explained by the nature of Mrs. Stowe's subject matter, her laudable determination to flinch from nothing in presenting the complete picture; an explanation which falters only if we pause to ask whether or not her picture is indeed complete; and what constriction or failure of perception forced her to so depend on the description of brutality—unmotivated, senseless—and to leave unanswered and unnoticed the only important question: what it was, after all, that moved her people to such deeds.

But this, let us say, was beyond Mrs. Stowe's powers; she was not so much a novelist as an impassioned pamphleteer; her book was not intended to do anything more than prove that slavery was wrong; was, in fact, perfectly horrible. This makes material for a pamphlet but it is hardly enough for a novel; and the only question left to ask is why we are bound still within the same constriction. How is it that we are so loath to make a further journey than that made by Mrs. Stowe, to discover and reveal something a little closer to the truth?

But that battered word, truth, having made its appearance here, confronts one immediately with a series of riddles and has, moreover, since so many gospels are preached, the unfortunate tendency to make one belligerent. Let us say, then, that truth, as used here, is meant to imply a devotion to the human being, his freedom and fulfillment; freedom which cannot be legislated, fulfillment which cannot be charted. This is the prime concern, the frame of reference; it is not to be confused with a devotion to Humanity which is too easily equated with a devotion to a Cause; and Causes, as we know, are notoriously bloodthirsty. We have, as it seems to me, in this most mechanical and interlocking of civilizations, attempted to lop this creature down to the status of a time-saving invention. He is not, after all, merely a member of a Society or a Group or a deplorable conundrum to be explained by Science. He is—and how old-fashioned the words sound!—something more than that, something resolutely indefinable, unpredictable. In overlooking, denying, evading his complexity —which is nothing more than the disquieting complexity of ourselves— we are diminished and we perish; only within this web of ambiguity, paradox, this hunger, danger, darkness, can we find at once ourselves and the power that will free us from ourselves. It is this power of revelation which is the business of the novelist, this journey toward a more vast reality which must take precedence over all other claims. What is today parroted as his Responsibility—which seems to mean that he must make formal declaration that he is involved in, and affected by, the lives of other people and to say something improving about this somewhat self-evident fact—is, when he believes it, his corruption and our loss; moreover, it is rooted in, interlocked with and intensifies this same mechanization. Both *Gentleman's Agreement* and *The Postman Always Rings Twice* exemplify this terror of the human being, the determination to cut him down to size. And in *Uncle Tom's Cabin* we may find foreshadowing of both: the formula created by the necessity to find a lie more palatable than the truth has been handed down and memorized and persists yet with a terrible power.

It is interesting to consider one more aspect of Mrs. Stowe's novel, the method she used to solve the problem of writing about a black man at all. Apart from her lively procession of field hands, house niggers, Chloe, Topsy, etc.—who are the stock, lovable figures presenting no problem—she has only three other Negroes in the book. These are the important ones and two of them may be dismissed immediately, since we have only the author's word that they are Negro and they are, in all other respects, as white as she can make them. The two are George and Eliza, a married couple with a wholly adorable child— whose quaintness, incidentally, and whose charm, rather put one in mind of a darky bootblack doing a buck and wing to the clatter of condescending coins. Eliza is a beautiful, pious hybrid, light enough to pass—the heroine of *Quality* might, indeed, be her reincarnation— differing from the genteel mistress who has overseered her education only in the respect that she is a servant. George is darker, but makes up for it by being a mechanical genius, and is, moreover, sufficiently un-Negroid to pass through town, a fugitive from his master, disguised as a Spanish gentleman, attracting no attention whatever beyond admiration. They are a race apart from Topsy. It transpires by the end of the novel, through one of those energetic, last-minute convolutions of the plot, that Eliza has some connection with French gentility. The figure from whom the novel takes its name, Uncle Tom, who is a figure of controversy yet, is jet-black, wooly-haired, illiterate; and he is phenomenally forbearing. He has to be; he is black; only through this forbearance can he survive or triumph. (*Cf.* Faulkner's preface to *The Sound and the Fury*: These others were not Compsons. They were black:—They endured.) His triumph is metaphysical, unearthly; since he is black, born without the light, it is only through humility, the incessant mortification of the flesh, that he can enter into communion with God or man. The virtuous rage of Mrs. Stowe is motivated by nothing so temporal as a concern for the relationship of men to one another—or, even, as she would have claimed, by a concern for their relationship to God—but merely by a panic of being hurled into the flames, of being caught in traffic with the devil. She embraced this merciless doctrine with all her heart, bargaining shamelessly before the throne of grace: God and salvation becoming her personal property, purchased with the coin of her virtue. Here, black equates with evil and white with grace; if, being mindful of the necessity of good works, she could not cast out the blacks—a wretched, huddled mass, apparently, claiming like an obsession, her inner eye—she could not embrace them either without purifying them of sin. She must cover their intimidating nakedness, robe them in white, the garments of salvation; only thus could she herself be delivered from ever-present sin, only thus could she bury, as St. Paul demanded, "the carnal man, the man of the flesh." Tom, therefore, her only black man, has been robbed of his humanity and divested of his sex. It is the price for that darkness with which he has been branded.

Uncle Tom's Cabin, then is activated by what might be called a theological terror, the terror of damnation; and the spirit that breathes in this book, hot, self-righteous, fearful, is not different from that spirit of medieval times which sought to exorcize evil by burning witches; and is not different from that terror which activates a lynch mob. One need not, indeed, search for examples so historic or so gaudy; this is a warfare waged daily in the heart, a warfare so vast, so relentless and so powerful that the interracial handshake or the interracial marriage can be as crucifying as the public hanging or the secret rape. This panic motivates our cruelty, this fear of the dark makes it impossible that our lives shall be other than superficial; this, interlocked with and feeding our glittering, mechanical, inescapable civilization which has put to death our freedom.

This, notwithstanding that the avowed aim of the American protest novel is to bring greater freedom to the oppressed. They are forgiven, on the strength of these good intentions, whatever violence they do to language, whatever excessive demands they make of credibility. It is, indeed, considered the sign of a frivolity so intense as to approach decadence to suggest that these books are both badly written and wildly improbable. One is told to put first things first, the good of society coming before niceties of style or characterization. Even if this were incontestable—for what exactly is the "good" of society?—it argues an insuperable confusion, since literature and sociology are not one and the same; it is impossible to discuss them as if they were. Our passion for categorization, life neatly fitted into pegs, has led to an unforeseen, paradoxical distress; confusion, a breakdown of meaning. Those categories which were meant to define and control the world for us have boomeranged us into chaos; in which limbo we whirl, clutching the straws of our definitions. The "protest" novel, so far from being disturbing, is an accepted and comforting aspect of the American scene, ramifying that framework we believe to be so necessary. Whatever unsettling questions are raised are evanescent, titillating; remote, for this has nothing to do with us, it is safely ensconced in the social arena, where, indeed, it has nothing to do with anyone, so that finally we receive a very definite thrill of virtue from the fact that we are reading such a book at all. This report from the pit reassures us of its reality and its darkness and of our own salvation; and "As long as such books are being published," an American liberal once said to me, "everything will be all right."

But unless one's ideal of society is a race of neatly analyzed, hard-working ciphers, one can hardly claim for the protest novels the lofty purpose they claim for themselves or share the present optimism concerning them. They emerge for what they are: a mirror of our confusion, dishonesty, panic, trapped and immobilized in the sunlit prison of the American dream. They are fantasies, connecting nowhere with reality, sentimental; in exactly the same sense that such movies as *The Best Years of Our Lives* or the works of Mr. James M. Cain are fantasies. Beneath the dazzling pyrotechnics of these current operas one may still discern, as the controlling force, the intense theological preoccupations of Mrs. Stowe, the sick vacuities of *The Rover Boys*. Finally, the aim of the protest novel becomes something very closely resembling the zeal of those alabaster missionaries to Africa to cover the nakedness of the natives, to hurry them into the pallid arms of Jesus and thence into slavery. The aim has now become to reduce all Americans to the compulsive, bloodless dimensions of a guy named Joe.

It is the peculiar triumph of society—and its loss—that it is able to convince those people to whom it has given inferior status of the reality of this decree; it has the force and the weapons to translate its dictum into fact, so that the allegedly inferior are actually made so, insofar as the societal realities are concerned. This is a more hidden phenomenon now than it was in the days of serfdom, but it is no less implacable. Now, as then, we find ourselves bound, first without, then within, by the nature of our categorization. And escape is not effected through a bitter railing against this trap; it is as though this very striving were the only motion needed to spring the trap upon us. We take our shape, it is true, within and against that cage of reality bequeathed us at our birth; and yet it is precisely through our dependence on this reality that we are most endlessly betrayed. Society is held together by our need; we bind it together with legend, myth, coercion, fearing that without it we will be hurled into that void, within which, like the earth before the Word was spoken, the foundations of society are hidden. From this void—ourselves—it is the function of society to protect us; but it is only this void, our unknown selves, demanding, forever, a new act of creation, which can save us—"from the evil that is in the world." With the same motion, at the same time,

it is this toward which we endlessly struggle and from which, endlessly, we struggle to escape.

It must be remembered that the oppressed and the oppressor are
bound together within the same society; they accept the same criteria,
they share the same beliefs, they both alike depend on the same
reality. Within this cage it is romantic, more, meaningless, to speak of
a "new" society as the desire of the oppressed, for that shivering
dependence on the props of reality which he shares with the *Herren-
volk* makes a truly "new" society impossible to conceive. What is meant
by a new society is one in which inequalities will disappear, in which
vengeance will be exacted; either there will be no oppressed at all, or
the oppressed and the oppressor will change places. But, finally, as it
seems to me, what the rejected desire is, is an elevation of status,
acceptance within the present community. Thus, the African, exile,
pagan, hurried off the auction block and into the fields, fell on his
knees before that God in Whom he must now believe; who had made
him, but not in His image. This tableau, this impossibility, is the
heritage of the Negro in America: *Wash me,* cried the slave to his
Maker, *and I shall be whiter, whiter than snow!* For black is the color
of evil; only the robes of the saved are white. It is this cry, impalacable
on the air and in the skull, that he must live with. Beneath the widely
published catalogue of brutality—bringing to mind, somehow, an image,
a memory of church-bells burdening the air—is this reality which, in
the same nightmare notion, he both flees and rushes to embrace. In
America, now, this country devoted to the death of the paradox—which
may, therefore, be put to death by one—his lot is as ambiguous as a
tableau by Kafka. To flee or not, to move or not, it is all the same; his
doom is written on his forehead, it is carried in his heart. In *Native
Son,* Bigger Thomas stands on a Chicago street corner watching air-
planes flown by white men racing against the sun and "Goddamn" he
says, the bitterness bubbling up like blood, remembering a million
indignities, the terrible, rat-infested house, the humiliation of home-
relief, the intense, aimless, ugly bickering hating it; hatred smoulders
through these pages like sulphur fire. All of Bigger's life is controlled,
defined by his hatred and his fear. And later, his fear drives him to
murder and his hatred to rape; he dies, having come, through this
violence, we are told, for the first time, to a kind of life, having for the
first time redeemed his manhood. Below the surface of this novel there
lies, as it seems to me, a continuation, a complement of that monstrous
legend it was written to destroy. Bigger is Uncle Tom's descendant,
flesh of his flesh, so exactly opposite a portrait that, when the books
are placed together, it seems that the contemporary Negro novelist

and the dead New England woman are locked together in a deadly, timeless battle; the one uttering merciless exhortations, the other shouting curses. And, indeed, within this web of lust and fury, black and white can only thrust and counter-thrust, long for each other's slow, exquisite death; death by torture, acid, knives and burning; the thrust, the counter-thrust, the longing making the heavier that cloud which blinds and suffocates them both, so that they go down into the pit together. Thus has the cage betrayed us all, this moment, our life, turned to nothing through our terrible attempts to insure it. For Bigger's tragedy is not that he is cold or black or hungry, not even that he is American, black; but that he has accepted a theology that denies him life, that he admits the possibility of his being sub-human and feels constrained, therefore, to battle for his humanity according to those brutal criteria bequeathed him at his birth. But our humanity is our burden, our life; we need not battle for it; we need only to do what is infinitely more difficult—that is, accept it. The failure of the protest novel lies in its rejection of life, the human being, the denial of his beauty, dread, power, in its insistence that it is his categorization alone which is real and which cannot be transcended.

JOHN A. WILLIAMS

The

Literary

Ghetto

JOHN A. WILLIAMS (1925–   ) HAS WRITTEN FIVE NOVELS AS WELL AS
poetry, short stories, and non-fiction. Raised in Syracuse, New York,
he served in the Navy in World War II and was educated at Syracuse
University. His early novels, especially *The Angry Ones* (1960), were
little known, but *The Man Who Cried I Am* (1967) became a best-
seller, exposing Williams to a broad section of the reading public for
the first time. This novel also represented a sort of climax in Williams'
growth as a novelist. His earlier novels, such as *Sissie* (1963) and
Night Song (1961), were powerful if sometimes uneven accounts of
the black experience, told with skill and insight. *Night Song* describes
the agony of a black jazz musician who can no longer create the same
music; *Sissie* is the story of a black matriarch who irrevocably shapes
her family through the force of her uncompromising will.

    The Man Who Cried I Am, the story of a famous black writer's
struggles and triumphs in the face of his impending death, sensationally
describes the United States government's "final solution" to America's
racial problems. It is an achievement of a high order; it scathingly exposes the New York and European *literati*, and in its revelation of

international conspiracy and intrigue suggests the atmosphere of paranoia that is all too characteristic of contemporary society.

In this essay, a contribution to a 1963 *Saturday Review* Symposium also participated in by LeRoi Jones and Langston Hughes, Williams displays his consuming interest in the creation of fictional characters and makes clear special difficulties that critical ignorance (especially by the book reviewer) poses for the black novelist. He also discusses something else in this short essay that is only infrequently mentioned by black novelists: the creation of Negro characters by white novelists. Williams' plea to the white novelist is in essence the plea of black America to all those who would represent it in any way: "when you do me, do me *right*."

JOHN A. WILLIAMS

The Literary Ghetto

ALMOST WITHOUT FAIL, A NOVEL WRITTEN BY A NEGRO IS SAID TO BE ONE of anger, hatred, rage or protest. Sometimes modifiers are used: "beautiful" anger, "black" hatred, "painful" rage, "exquisite" protest. These little tickets deprive that novel of any ability it may have to voice its concern for all humankind, not only Negroes.

After the labeling, and sometimes with it, comes the grouping, the lumping together of reviews of books by Negro authors. *Sissie*, my new novel, was officially published March 26; it has had four reviews like this already, three with James Baldwin's *The Fire Next Time* and one with John Killens's *And Then We Heard the Thunder*. I was hard pressed to discover who was being reviewed—Baldwin, Killens, or me. I had the same difficulty when I encountered reviews written only about *Sissie*, but whose leads almost invariably began with some reference to Baldwin.

Negro writers are nearly always compared to one another, rather than to white writers. This, like labeling and grouping, tends to limit severely the expansion of the talents of Negro writers and confine them to a literary ghetto from which only one Negro name at a time may emerge. Today it is unmistakably James Baldwin; no Negro writing in America today can escape his shadow. He replaced Richard Wright, who, in turn, may have replaced Langston Hughes.

Editors, too, have been guilty of labeling, comparing, and grouping. "Negro stuff is selling well!" I heard an editor say. So publishers have hastened to sign up Negro writers whose best qualification often enough, was that they were Negro. Publishing has had its homosexual phase, which dies hard; its gray flannel-advertising phase, its war phase, its Jewish phase. It is now in its Negro phase. To illustrate shifting trends, six years ago an editor whose house is now the hottest because of its Negro talent, said, in essence, in a note to my agent (which was passed on to me—a sign of how grim the business of selling "Negro" books was) that it would be wiser if I were to set aside the obviously personal experiences of being Negro. Financially at least, the change in his point of view has been good for him.

The current trend toward more publishing of books by Negro authors, brought about by national considerations, has been beneficial to black writers. Nevertheless, much comparison of their work still exists in the editorial offices. This comes from my files; it is part of a report,

Reprinted from *Saturday Review*, XLVI (April 20, 1963), 21, 40, by permission of the author and publisher. Copyright © 1963 by *Saturday Review*, Inc.

dated seven years ago, on a book that I have since published elsewhere: "Mr. Williams is in the vein of Chester Himes, and to my mind achieves a similar power."

Excluding riding the trend, the other attitudes—labeling, grouping, and comparing—provide the biggest block to the expansion by Negro writers of themes and techniques (cared for so little by reviewers today). Perhaps that is the reason for the existence of these attitudes. They are automatic and no one thinks about them much except Negro writers. Either consciously or unconsciously, this kind of bigotry tells more about the reviewer than it does about the book he's reviewing.

A more specific example: In a recent article a writer discussed James Baldwin and me; we were said to be in midstream and about to drown. In our attitudes, I guess. The man did a thorough job, having researched magazines and brought what I had written in some of them to bear upon his subject, my novel *Night Song*. I was impressed. The white woman in the novel, Della, is a social worker who, after her day at the office, comes to the coffee house owned by her lover to help out. But, in view of the crisp way the writer handled his article, I could only conclude that he saw Della merely as a *waitress* because her lover was Negro.

The relationship between mixed couples is always more graciously accepted by the reviewers when related by a white author than by a Negro. Jack Kerouac's one-dimensional Negro girl and her white lover, John Updike's quiet, fleeting references to the same combination, and Robert Gover's hilarious team of Kitten and James Cartwright Holland are a few examples. But would *One Hundred Dollar Misunderstanding* have been quite so well received had Kitten been a Negro social worker instead of a whore, and the inability of man and woman, black and white, to communicate been put on an altogether different symbolic level?

I wish white writers would stop pretending they just can't reach Negroes. I want Philip Roth's little Negro boy in the Newark Public Library to be real, not a symbol of God only knows what, besides guilt. I want Pete Washington in Dennis Lynds's new novel *Uptown Downtown*, to stop sitting around with his little Italian Catholic girl bemoaning to the point of being a bore the racial situation in America.

For I can smell the *illusion* of concern as quickly as I can smell a phony and from the same distance. When you do me, do me *right*. Then some of the barriers to the expansion of America's Negro writing talent may fall.

ELDRIDGE CLEAVER

Notes

on a

Native

Son

ELDRIDGE CLEAVER (1935–   ) HAS BECOME A PERSONAL SYMBOL OF the politics of the black revolution of the 1960's. The Minister of Information of The Black Panther Party, an ex-convict, a self-taught writer and self-made intellect, Cleaver has eloquently given expression to the sentiments of the modern, urban, angry, black American. His collection of essays, *Soul on Ice,* from which this essay is taken, is a forceful account of his own journey from a life of crime to one of revolutionary politics, the pilgrimage from a maximum security cell to the political platform as a candidate for the presidency of the United States under the banner of the Peace and Freedom Party, a coalition of The Black Panthers and white radicals.

Cleaver is a much misunderstood writer, and the intensity of emotion involved in responses to his work is not altogether dissimilar from the exacerbation of opinion generated by James Baldwin. Cleaver himself responds emotionally to Baldwin's fiction, not simply because, as a black man, he can react "with an additional dimension of his being to the articulated experience of another black—in spite of the universality of human experience," but also because Baldwin seems to represent a political and social ethic antithetical to many of Cleaver's hard-won ideas. It is probably impossible to tell, amidst the trouble and tragedy that characterize black-white relations in contemporary America, whose political vision is more valid. Cleaver's thoughtful yet emotional reaction to Baldwin, however, illustrates the same sort of assumption that was implicit in W. E. B. DuBois' review of McKay's *Home to Harlem* —namely, that the black novelist, no matter what the nature of his art, is seldom very far removed from the socio-political issues that agonize his black countrymen.

ELDRIDGE CLEAVER

Notes on a Native Son

AFTER READING A COUPLE OF JAMES BALDWIN'S BOOKS, I BEGAN EXPERI-
encing that continuous delight one feels upon discovering a fascinating,
brilliant talent on the scene, a talent capable of penetrating so profoundly into one's own little world that one knows oneself to have been
unalterably changed and *liberated*, liberated from the frustrating grasp
of whatever devils happen to possess one. Being a Negro, I have found
this to be a rare and infrequent experience, for few of my black
brothers and sisters here in America have achieved the power, which
James Baldwin calls his revenge, which outlasts kingdoms: the power
of doing whatever cats like Baldwin do when combining the alphabet
with the volatile elements of his soul. (And, like it or not, a black man,
unless he has become irretrievably "white-minded," responds with an
additional dimension of his being to the articulated experience of
another black—in spite of the universality of human experience.)

I, as I imagine many others did and still do, lusted for anything that
Baldwin had written. It would have been a gas for me to sit on a
pillow beneath the womb of Baldwin's typewriter and catch each newborn page as it entered this world of ours. I was delighted that Baldwin, with those great big eyes of his, which one thought to be fixedly
focused on the macrocosm, could also pierce the microcosm. And although he was so full of sound, he was not a noisy writer like Ralph
Ellison. He placed so much of my own experience, which I thought I
had understood, into new perspective.

Gradually, however, I began to feel uncomfortable about something
in Baldwin. I was disturbed upon becoming aware of an aversion in
my heart to part of the song he sang. Why this was so, I was unable
at first to say. Then I read *Another Country*, and I knew why my love
for Baldwin's vision had become ambivalent.

Long before, I had become a student of Norman Mailer's *The White
Negro*, which seemed to me to be prophetic and penetrating in its
understanding of the psychology involved in the accelerating confrontation of black and white in America. I was therefore personally insulted
by Baldwin's flippant, schoolmarmish dismissal of *The White Negro*.
Baldwin committed a literary crime by his arrogant repudiation of one
of the few gravely important expressions of our time. *The White Negro*
may contain an excess of esoteric verbal husk, but one can forgive

Mailer for that because of the solid kernel of truth he gave us. After all, it is the baby we want and not the blood of afterbirth. Mailer described, in that incisive essay, the first important chinks in the "mountain of white supremacy"—important because it shows the depth of ferment, on a personal level, in the white world. People are feverishly, and at great psychic and social expense, seeking *fundamental and irrevocable liberation*—and, what is more important, *are succeeding in escaping*—from the big white lies that compose the monolithic myth of White Supremacy/Black Inferiority, in a desperate attempt on the part of a new generation of white Americans to enter into the cosmopolitan egalitarian spirit of the twentieth century. But let us examine the reasoning that lies behind Baldwin's attack on Mailer.

There is in James Baldwin's work the most grueling, agonizing, total hatred of the blacks, particularly of himself, and the most shameful, fanatical, fawning, sycophantic love of the whites that one can find in the writings of any black American writer of note in our time. This is an appalling contradiction and the implications of it are vast.

A rereading of *Nobody Knows My Name* cannot help but convince the most avid of Baldwin's admirers of the hatred for blacks permeating his writings. In the essay "Princes and Powers," Baldwin's antipathy toward the black race is shockingly clear. The essay is Baldwin's interpretation of the Conference of Black Writers and Artists which met in Paris in September 1956. The portrait of Baldwin that comes through his words is that of a mind in unrelenting opposition to the efforts of solemn, dedicated black men who have undertaken the enormous task of rejuvenating and reclaiming the shattered psyches and culture of the black people, a people scattered over the continents of the world and the islands of the seas, where they exist in the mud of the floor of the foul dungeon into which the world has been transformed by the whites.

In his report of the conference, Baldwin, the reluctant black, dragging his feet at every step, could only ridicule the vision and efforts of these great men and heap scorn upon them, reserving his compliments —all of them left-handed—for the speakers at the conference who were themselves rejected and booed by the other conferees because of their reactionary, sycophantic views. Baldwin felt called upon to pop his cap pistol in a duel with Aimé Césaire, the big gun from Martinique. Indirectly, Baldwin was defending his first love—the white man. But the revulsion which Baldwin felt for the blacks at this conference, who were glorying in their blackness, seeking and showing their pride in Negritude and the African Personality, drives him to self-revealing sortie after sortie, so obvious in "Princes and Powers." Each successive sortie, however, becomes more expensive than the last one, because to score each time he has to go a little farther out on the limb, and it takes him a little longer each time to hustle back to the cover and camouflage of the perfumed smoke screen of his prose. Now and then we catch a glimpse of his little jive ass—his big eyes peering back over his shoulder in the mischievous retreat of a child sneak-thief from a cookie jar.

In the autobiographical notes of *Notes of a Native Son*, Baldwin is frank to confess that, in growing into his version of manhood in Harlem, he discovered that, since his African heritage had been wiped out and was not accessible to him, he would appropriate the white man's heritage and make it his own. This terrible reality, central to the psychic stance of all American Negroes, revealed to Baldwin that he hated and feared white people. Then he says: "This did not mean that I loved black people; on the contrary, I despised them, possibly because they failed to produce Rembrandt." The psychic distance between love and hate could be the mechanical difference between a smile and a sneer, or it could be the journey of a nervous impulse from the depths of one's brain to the tip of one's toe. But this impulse in its path through North American nerves may, if it is honest, find the passage disputed: may find the leap from the fiber of hate to that of love too taxing on its meager store of energy—and so the long trip back may never be completed, may end in a reconnaissance, a compromise, and then a lie.

Self-hatred takes many forms; sometimes it can be detected by no one, not by the keenest observer, not by the self-hater himself, not by his most intimate friends. Ethnic self-hate is even more difficult to detect. But in American Negroes, this ethnic self-hatred often takes the bizarre form of a racial death-wish, with many and elusive manifestations. Ironically, it provides much of the impetus behind the motivations of integration. And the attempt to suppress or deny such drives in one's psyche leads many American Negroes to become ostentatious separationists, Black Muslims, and back-to-Africa advocates. It is no wonder that Elijah Muhammad could conceive of the process of controlling evolution whereby the white race was brought into being. According to Elijah, about 6300 years ago all the people of the earth were Original Blacks. Secluded on the island of Patmos, a mad black scientist by the name of Yacub set up the machinery for grafting whites out of blacks through the operation of a birth-control system. The population of this island of Patmos was 59,999 and whenever a couple on this island wanted to get married they were only allowed to do so if there was a difference in their color, so that by mating black with those in the population of a brownish color and brown with brown—but never black with black—all traces of the black were eventually

eliminated; the process was repeated until all the brown was eliminated, leaving only men of the red race; the red was bleached out,
leaving only yellow; then the yellow was bleached out, and only white
was left. Thus Yacub, who was long since dead, because this whole
process took hundreds of years, had finally succeeding in creating the
white devil with the blue eyes of death.

This myth of the creation of the white race, called "Yacub's History,"
is an inversion of the racial death-wish of American Negroes. Yacub's
plan is still being followed by many Negroes today. Quite simply, many
Negroes believe, as the principle of assimilation into white America
implies, that the race problem in America cannot be settled until all
traces of the black race are eliminated. Toward this end, many Negroes loathe the very idea of two very dark Negroes mating. The
children, they say, will come out ugly. What they mean is that the children are sure to be black, and this is not desirable. From the widespread use of cosmetics to bleach the black out of one's skin and other
concoctions to take Africa out of one's hair, to the extreme, resorted to
by more Negroes than one might wish to believe, of undergoing nose-
thinning and lip-clipping operations, the racial death-wish of American
Negroes—Yacub's goal—takes its terrible toll. What has been happening
for the past four hundred years is that the white man, through his
access to black women, has been pumping his blood and genes into
the blacks, has been diluting the blood and genes of the blacks—i.e.,
has been fulfilling Yacub's plan and accelerating the Negroes' racial
death-wish.

The case of James Baldwin aside for a moment, it seems that many
Negro homosexuals, acquiescing in this racial death-wish, are outraged
and frustrated because in their sickness they are unable to have a baby
by a white man. The cross they have to bear is that, already bending
over and touching their toes for the white man, the fruit of their
miscegenation is not the little half-white offspring of their dreams but
an increase in the unwinding of their nerves—though they redouble
their efforts and intake of the white man's sperm.

In this land of dichotomies and disunited opposites, those truly
concerned with the resurrection of black Americans have had eternally
to deal with black intellectuals who have become their own opposites,
taking on all of the behavior patterns of their enemy, vices and virtues,
in an effort to aspire to alien standards in all respects. The gulf between an audacious, bootlicking Uncle Tom and an intellectual buck-
dancer is filled only with sophistication and style. On second thought,
Uncle Tom comes off much cleaner here because usually he is just
trying to survive, choosing to pretend to be something other than his
true self in order to please the white man and thus receive favors.

Whereas the intellectual sycophant does not pretend to be other than he actually is, but hates what he is and seeks to redefine himself in the image of his white idols. He becomes a white man in a black body. A self-willed, automated slave, he becomes the white man's most valuable tool in oppressing other blacks.

The black homosexual, when his twist has a racial nexus, is an extreme embodiment of this contradiction. The white man has deprived him of his masculinity, castrated him in the center of his burning skull, and when he submits to this change and takes the white man for his lover as well as Big Daddy, he focuses on "whiteness" all the love in his pent up soul and turns the razor edge of hatred against "blackness"—upon himself, what he is, and all those who look like him, remind him of himself. He may even hate the darkness of night.

The racial death-wish is manifested as the driving force in James Baldwin. His hatred for blacks, even as he pleads what he conceives as their cause, makes him the apotheosis of the dilemma in the ethos of the black bourgeoisie who have completely rejected their African heritage, consider the loss irrevocable, and refuse to look again in that direction. This is the root of Baldwin's violent repudiation of Mailer's *The White Negro*.

To understand what is at stake here, and to understand it in terms of the life of this nation, is to know the central fact that the relationship between black and white in America is a power equation, a power struggle, and that this power struggle is not only manifested in the aggregate (civil rights, black nationalism, etc.) but also in the interpersonal relationships, actions, and reactions between blacks and whites where taken into account. When those "two lean cats," Baldwin and Mailer, met in a French living room, it was precisely this power equation that was at work.

It is fascinating to read (in *Nobody Knows My Name*) in what terms this power equation was manifested in Baldwin's immediate reaction to that meeting: "And here we were, suddenly, circling around each other. We liked each other at once, but each was frightened that the other would pull rank. He could have pulled rank on me because he was more famous and *had more money* and also *because he was white*; but I could have pulled rank on him precisely because I was black and knew more about that periphery he so helplessly maligns in *The White Negro* than he could ever hope to know." [Italics added.]

Pulling rank, it would seem, is a very dangerous business, especially when the troops have mutinied and the basis of one's authority, or rank, is devoid of that interdictive power and has become suspect. One would think that for Baldwin, of all people, these hues of black and white were no longer armed with the power to intimidate and if one thought this, one would be exceedingly wrong: for behind the structure of the thought of Baldwin's quoted above, there lurks the imp of Baldwin's unwinding, of his tension between love and hate—love of the white and hate of the black. And when we dig into this tension we will find that when those "two lean cats" crossed tracks in that French living room, one was a Pussy Cat, the other a Tiger. Baldwin's purr was transmitted magnificently in *The Fire Next Time*. But his work is the fruit of a tree with a poison root. Such succulent fruit, such a painful tree, what a malignant root!

It is ironic, but fascinating for what it reveals about the ferment in the North American soul in our time, that Norman Mailer, the white boy, and James Baldwin, the black boy, encountered each other in the eye of a social storm, traveling in opposite directions; the white boy, with knowledge of white Negroes, was traveling toward a confrontation with the black, with Africa; while the black boy, with a white mind, was on his way to Europe. Baldwin's nose, like the North-seeking needle on a compass, is forever pointed toward his adopted fatherland, Europe, his by intellectual osmosis and in Africa's stead. What he says of Aimé Césaire, one of the greatest black writers of the twentieth century, and intending it as an ironic rebuke, that "he had penetrated into the heart of the great wilderness which was Europe and stolen the sacred fire . . . which . . . was . . . the assurance of his power," seems only too clearly to speak more about Peter than it does about Paul. What Baldwin seems to forget is that Césaire explains that fire, whether sacred or profane, burns. In Baldwin's case, though the fire could not burn the black off his face, it certainly did burn it out of his heart.

I am not interested in denying anything to Baldwin. I, like the entire nation, owe a great debt to him. But throughout the range of his work, from *Go Tell It on the Mountain*, through *Notes of a Native Son*, *Nobody Knows My Name*, *Another Country*, to *The Fire Next Time*, all of which I treasure, there is a decisive quirk in Baldwin's vision which corresponds to his relationship to black people and to masculinity. It was this same quirk, in my opinion, that compelled Baldwin to slander Rufus Scott in *Another Country*, venerate André Gide, repudiate *The White Negro*, and drive the blade of Brutus into the corpse of Richard Wright. As Baldwin has said in *Nobody Knows My Name*. "I think that I know something about the American masculinity which most men of my generation do not know because they have not been menaced by it in the way I have been." O.K., Sugar, but isn't it true that Rufus Scott, the weak, craven-hearted ghost of *Another Country*, bears the same relation to Bigger Thomas of *Native Son*, the black rebel of the ghetto and a man, as you yourself bore to the fallen giant, Richard Wright, a rebel and a man?

Somewhere in one of his books, Richard Wright describes an encounter between a ghost and several young Negroes. The young Negroes rejected the homosexual, and this was Wright alluding to a classic, if cruel, example of a ubiquitous phenomenon in the black ghettos of America: the practice by Negro youths of going "punk-hunting." This practice of seeking out homosexuals on the prowl, rolling them, beating them up, seemingly just to satisfy some savage impulse to inflict pain on the specific target selected, the "social outcast," seems to me to be not unrelated, in terms of the psychological mechanisms involved, to the ritualistic lynchings and castrations inflicted on Southern blacks by Southern whites. This was, as I recall, one of Wright's few comments on the subject of homosexuality.

I think it can safely be said that the men in Wright's books, albeit shackled with a form of impotence, were strongly heterosexual. Their heterosexuality was implied rather than laboriously stated or emphasized; it was taken for granted, as we all take men until something occurs to make us know otherwise. And Bigger Thomas, Wright's greatest creation, was a man in violent, though inept, rebellion against the stifling, murderous, totalitarian white world. There was no trace in Bigger of a Martin Luther King-type self-effacing love for his oppressors. For example, Bigger would have been completely baffled, as most Negroes are today, at Baldwin's advice to his nephew (*The First Next Time*), concerning white people: "You must accept them *and accept them with love*. For these innocent people have no other hope." [Italics added.]

Rufus Scott, a pathetic wretch who indulged in the white man's pastime of committing suicide, who let a white bisexual homosexual fuck him in his ass, and who took a Southern Jezebel for his woman, with all that these tortured relationships imply, was the epitome of a black eunuch who has completely submitted to the white man. Yes, Rufus was a psychological freedom rider, turning the ultimate cheek, murmuring like a ghost, *"You took the best so why not take the rest,"* which has absolutely nothing to do with the way Negroes have managed to survive here in the hells of North America! This all becomes very clear from what we learn of Erich, the arch-ghost of *Another Country*, of the depths of his alienation from his body and the source of his need: "And it had taken him almost until this very moment, on the eve of his departure, to begin to recognize that part of Rufus' great power over him had to do with the past which Erich had buried in some deep, dark place; was connected with himself, in Alabama, *when I wasn't nothing but a child*; with the cold white people and the warm black people, warm at least for him. . . ."

So, too, who cannot wonder at the source of such audacious madness as moved Baldwin to make this startling remark about Richard Wright, in his ignoble essay "Alas, Poor Richard": "In my own relations with him, I was always exasperated by his notions of society, politics, and history, for they seemed to me utterly fanciful. I never believed that he had any real sense of how a society is put together."

Richard Wright is dead and Baldwin is alive and with us. Baldwin says that Richard Wright held notions that were utterly fanciful, and Baldwin is an honorable man.

> *"O judgment; thou art fled to*
> *brutish beasts,*
> *And men have lost their reason!"*

Wright has no need, as Caesar did, of an outraged Antony to plead his cause: his life and his work are his shield against the mellow thrust of Brutus' blade. The good that he did, unlike Caesar's, will not be interred with his bones. It is, on the contrary, only the living who can be harmed by Brutus.

Baldwin says that in Wright's writings violence sits enthroned where sex should be. If this is so, then it is only because in the North American reality hate holds sway in love's true province. And it is only through a rank perversion that the artist, whose duty is to tell us the truth, can turn the two-dollar trick of wedding violence to love and sex to hate—if, to achieve this end, one has basely to transmute rebellion into lamblike submission—"*You took the best,*" sniveled Rufus, "*so why not take the rest?*" Richard Wright was not ghost enough to achieve this cruel distortion. With him, sex, being not a spectator sport or a panacea but the sacred vehicle of life and love, is itself sacred. And the America which Wright knew and which *is*, is not the Garden of Eden but its opposite. Baldwin, embodying in his art the self-flagellating policy of Martin Luther King, and giving out falsely the news that the Day of the Ghost has arrived, pulled it off in *Another Country*.

Of all black American novelists, and indeed of all American novelists of any hue, Richard Wright reigns supreme for his profound political, economic, and social reference. Wright had the ability, like Dreiser, of harnessing the gigantic, overwhelming environmental forces and focusing them, with pinpoint sharpness, on individuals and their acts as they are caught up in the whirlwind of the savage, anarchistic sweep of life, love, death, and hate, pain, hope, pleasure, and despair across the face of a nation and the world. But, ah! "O masters," it is Baldwin's work which is so void of a political, economic, or even a social reference. His characters all seem to be fucking and sucking in a vacuum. Baldwin has a superb touch when he speaks of human beings, when he is inside of them—especially his homosexuals—but he flounders when he looks beyond the skin; whereas Wright's forte, it seems to me, was in reflecting the intricate mechanisms of a social organization, its functioning as a unit.

Baldwin's essay on Richard Wright reveals that he despised—not Richard Wright, but his masculinity. He cannot confront the stud in others—except that he must either submit to it or destroy it. And he was not about to bow to a *black* man. Wright understood and lived the truth of what Norman Mailer meant when he said ". . . for being a man is the continuing battle of one's life, and one loses a bit of manhood with every stale compromise to the authority of any power in which one does not believe." Baldwin, compromised beyond getting back by the white man's *power*, which is real and which has nothing to do with *authority*, but to which Baldwin has ultimately succumbed psychologically, is totally unable to extricate himself from that horrible pain. It is the scourge of his art, because the only way out for him is psychologically to embrace Africa, the land of his fathers, which he utterly refuses to do. He has instead resorted to a despicable underground guerrilla war, waged on paper, against black masculinity, playing out the racial death-wish of Yacub, reaching, I think, a point where Mailer hits the spot: "Driven into defiance, it is natural if regrettable, that many homosexuals go to the direction of assuming that there is something intrinsically superior in homosexuality, and carried far enough it is a viewpoint which is as stultifying, as ridiculous, and as anti-human as the heterosexual's prejudice."

I, for one, do not think homosexuality is the latest advance over heterosexuality on the scale of human evolution. Homosexuality is a sickness, just as are baby-rape or wanting to become the head of General Motors.

A grave danger faces this nation, of which we are as yet unaware. And it is precisely this danger which Baldwin's work conceals; indeed, leads us away from. We are engaged in the deepest, the most fundamental revolution and reconstruction which men have ever been called upon to make in their lives, and which they absolutely cannot escape or avoid except at the peril of the very continued existence of human life on this planet. The time of the sham is over, and the cheek of the suffering saint must no longer be turned twice to the brute. The titillation of the guilt complexes of bored white liberals leads to doom. The grotesque hideousness of what is happening to us is reflected in this remark by Murray Kempton, quoted in *The Realist*: "When I was a boy Stepin Fetchit was the only Negro actor who worked regularly in the movies. . . . The fashion changes, but I sometimes think that Malcolm X and, to a degree even James Baldwin, are *our* Stepin Fetchits."

Yes, the fashion does change. "Will the machinegunners please step forward," said LeRoi Jones in a poem. "The machine gun on the corner," wrote Richard Wright, "is the symbol of the twentieth century." The embryonic spirit of kamikaze, real and alive, grows each day in the black man's heart and there are dreams of Nat Turner's legacy. The ghost of John Brown is creeping through suburbia. And I wonder if James Chaney said, as Andrew Goodman and Michael Schwerner stood helplessly watching, as the grizzly dogs crushed his bones with savage blows of chains—did poor James say, after Rufus Scott—"*You took the best, so why not take the rest?*" Or did he turn to his white brothers, seeing their plight, and say, after Baldwin, "That's your problem, baby!"

I say, after Mailer, "There's a shit-storm coming."

SELECTED BIBLIOGRAPHY

Primary Works

JAMES BALDWIN

Go Tell It On The Mountain. New York: Alfred A. Knopf, Inc., 1953.

Notes of a Native Son. Boston: Beacon Press, 1955.

Giovanni's Room. New York: Dial Press, 1956.

Nobody Knows My Name. New York: Dial Press, 1961.

Another Country. New York: Dial Press, 1962.

The Fire Next Time. New York: Dial Press, 1963.

Blues for Mister Charlie. New York: Dial Press, 1964.

Going To Meet The Man. New York: Dial Press, 1965.

Tell Me How Long The Train's Been Gone. New York: Dial Press, 1968.

ARNA BONTEMPS

God Sends Sunday. New York: Harcourt, Brace & Co., 1931.

Black Thunder. New York: The Macmillan Co., 1936.

Sad Faced Boy. Boston: Houghton Mifflin Co., 1937.

Drums at Dusk. New York: The Macmillan Co., 1939.

We Have Tomorrow. Boston: Houghton Mifflin Co., 1945.

Chariot in the Sky. Chicago: John C. Winston Co., 1951.

Story of the Negro. New York: Alfred A. Knopf, Inc., 1958.

One Hundred Years of Negro Freedom. New York: Dodd, Mead and Co., 1961.

Personals. London: Paul Breman, Ltd., 1963.

CHARLES WADDELL CHESNUTT

The Conjure Woman. Boston: Houghton, Mifflin and Co., 1899.

The Wife of His Youth and Other Stories of the Color Line. Boston: Houghton, Mifflin and Co., 1899.

The House Behind the Cedars. Boston: Houghton, Mifflin and Co., 1900.

The Marrow of Tradition. Boston: Houghton, Mifflin and Co., 1901.

The Colonel's Dream. New York: Doubleday, Page and Co., 1905.

W. E. B. DuBois

The Philadelphia Negro: A Social Study. Philadelphia: University of Pennsylvania Press, 1899.

The Souls of Black Folk: Essays and Sketches. Chicago: A. C. McClurg & Co., 1903.

The Quest of the Silver Fleece. Chicago: A. C. McClurg & Co., 1911.

Dark Princess. New York: Harcourt, Brace & Co., 1928.

Black Reconstruction in America, 1860-1880. New York: Harcourt, Brace & Co., 1935.

Black Folk, Then and Now: An Essay in the History and Sociology of the Negro Race. New York: Henry Holt and Co., 1939.

Dusk of Dawn: An Essay Toward an Autobiography of a Race Concept. New York: Harcourt, Brace & Co., 1940.

The Ordeal of Mansart. New York: Mainstream Publishers, 1957. (Volume one of the trilogy, *Black Flame*).

Mansart Builds a School. New York: Mainstream Publishers, 1959. (Volume two of the trilogy, *Black Flame*).

Worlds of Color. New York: Mainstream Publishers, 1961. (Volume three of the trilogy, *Black Flame*).

The Autobiography of W. E. B. DuBois: A Soliloquy on Viewing My Life From the Last Decade of its First Century. ed. Herbert Aptheker. New York: International Publishers Co., 1968.

PAUL LAURENCE DUNBAR

Folks From Dixie. New York: Dodd, Mead and Co., 1898.

The Uncalled. New York: Dodd, Mead and Co., 1898.

The Love of Landry. New York: Dodd, Mead and Co., 1900.

The Strength of Gideon and Other Stories. New York: Dodd, Mead and Co., 1900.

The Fanatics. New York: Dodd, Mead and Co., 1901.

The Sport of the Gods. New York: Dodd, Mead and Co., 1902.

In Old Plantation Days. New York: Dodd, Mead and Co., 1903.

The Heart of Happy Hollow. New York: Dodd, Mead and Co., 1904.

The Complete Poems of Paul Laurence Dunbar. New York: Dodd, Mead and Co., 1940.

RALPH ELLISON

"Slick Gonna Learn," *Direction* (September 1939), pp. 10-16.

"Mister Toussan," *The New Masses,* XLI (November 4, 1941), 19, 20.

"That I Had the Wings," *Common Ground,* III (Summer 1943), 30-37.

"Flying Home," *Cross Section,* ed. Edwin Seaver. New York: L. B. Fischer, 1944, pp. 469-85.

"In a Strange Country," *Tomorrow,* III (July 1944), 41-44.

"King of the Bingo Game," *Tomorrow,* IV (November 1944), 29-33.

Invisible Man. New York: Random House, 1952.

"Did You Ever Dream Lucky?" *New World Writing No. 5.* New York: The New American Library of World Literature, Inc., 1954, pp. 134-45.

"A Coupla Scalped Indians," *New World Writing No. 9.* New York: The New American Library of World Literature, Inc., 1956, pp. 225-36.

"The World and The Jug: A Reply to Irving Howe," *The New Leader,* XLVI (December 9, 1963), 22-26.

"The Writer and the Critic—An Exchange: A Reply to Ralph Ellison [by Irving Howe]; A Rejoinder [by Ralph Ellison]," *The New Leader,* XLVII (February 3, 1964), 12-22.

Shadow and Act. New York: Random House, 1964.

JESSIE FAUSET

There Is Confusion. New York: Boni and Liveright, 1924.

Plum Bun. New York: Frederick A. Stokes Co., 1929.

The Chinaberry Tree. New York: Frederick A. Stokes Co., 1933.

Comedy American Style. New York: Frederick A. Stokes Co., 1933.

SUTTON E. GRIGGS

Imperium In Imperio. Cincinnati, Ohio: The Editor Publishing Co., 1899.

Overshadowed. Nashville, Tennessee: The Orion Publishing Co., 1901.

Unfettered. Nashville, Tennessee: The Orion Publishing Co., 1902.

The Hindered Hand, or the Reign of the Repressionist. Nashville, Tennessee: The Orion Publishing Co., 1905.

Pointing The Way. Nashville, Tennessee: The Orion Publishing Co., 1908.

ZORA NEALE HURSTON

Jonah's Gourd Vine. Philadelphia: J. B. Lippincott, 1934.

Mules and Men. Philadelphia: J. B. Lippincott, 1935.

Their Eyes Were Watching God. Philadelphia: J. B. Lippincott, 1937.

Tell My Horse. Philadelphia: J. B. Lippincott, 1938.

Moses Man of the Mountain. Philadelphia: J. B. Lippincott, 1939.

Dust Tracks On A Road. Philadelphia: J. B. Lippincott, 1942.

Seraph on the Suwanee. New York: Charles Scribners Sons, 1948.

CLAUDE McKAY

Home To Harlem. New York: Harper & Bros., 1928.

Banjo. New York: Harper & Bros., 1929.

Gingertown. New York: Harper & Bros., 1932.

Banana Bottom. New York: Harper & Bros., 1933.

A Long Way From Home. New York: Lee Furman, Inc., 1937.

Selected Poems of Claude McKay. New York: Bookman Associates, Inc., 1953.

WILLIAM GARDNER SMITH

Last of the Conquerors. New York: Farrar, Straus and Co., 1948.

Anger at Innocence. New York: Farrar, Straus and Cudahy, Inc., 1950.

South Street. New York: Farrar, Straus and Young, Inc., 1954.

The Stone Face. New York: Farrar, Straus and Co., 1963.

JEAN TOOMER

Cane. New York: Boni and Liveright, 1923.

"Winter on Earth," *The Second American Caravan, A Yearbook of American Literature,* ed. Alfred Kreymborg *et al.* New York: Macaulay, 1928, pp. 694-715.

"Race Problems and Modern Society," *Problems of Civilization.* New York: D. Van Nostrand, 1929.

"York Beach," *The New American Caravan,* ed. Alfred Kreymborg *et al.* New York: Macaulay, 1929, pp. 12-83.

Essentials. Definitions and Aphorisms. Private edition. Chicago: Lakeside Press, 1931.

The Flavor of Man. Philadelphia: Young Friends Movement of the Philadelphia Yearly meetings, 1949.

JOHN A. WILLIAMS

The Angry Ones. New York: Ace Books, 1960.

Night Song. New York: Farrar, Straus and Cudahy, 1961.

Africa, Her History, Land and People. New York: Cooper Square Publishers, 1962.

Sissie. New York: Farrar, Straus and Cudahy, 1963.

This Is My Country Too. New York: New American Library, 1965.

Beyond The Angry Black. New York: Cooper Square Publishers, 1966.

The Man Who Cried I Am. Boston: Little, Brown & Co., 1967.

Sons of Darkness, Sons of Light. Boston: Little, Brown & Co., 1969.

RICHARD WRIGHT

Uncle Tom's Children: Four Novellas. New York: Harper & Bros., 1938.

Native Son. New York: Harper & Bros., 1940.

Uncle Tom's Children: Five Long Stories. New York: Harper & Bros., 1940.

12 Million Black Voices: A Folk History of the Negro in the United States. New York: The Viking Press, 1941.

Native Son, the Biography of a Young American. A Play in Ten Scenes. By Paul Green and Richard Wright. New York: Harper & Bros., 1941.

Black Boy; a Record of Childhood and Youth. New York: Harper & Bros., 1945.

The Outsider. New York: Harper & Bros., 1953.

Savage Holiday. New York: Avon, 1954.

Black Power. New York: Harper & Bros., 1954.

The Color Curtain; a Report on the Bandung Conference. Cleveland and New York: Bobson Books, Ltd., 1956.

White Man, Listen! Garden City, New York: Doubleday, 1957.

Pagan Spain. New York: Harper & Bros., 1957.

The Long Dream. Garden City, New York: Doubleday, 1958.

Eight Men. Cleveland and New York: Avon, 1961.

Lawd Today. New York: Walker and Co., 1963.

FRANK YERBY

The Foxes of Harrow. New York: Dial Press, 1946.

The Vixens. New York: Dial Press, 1947.

The Golden Hawk. New York: Dial Press, 1948.

Pride's Castle. New York: Dial Press, 1949.

Floodtide. New York: Dial Press, 1950.

The Saracen Blade. New York: Dial Press, 1952.

Captain Rebel. New York: Dial Press, 1956.

The Serpent and The Staff. New York: Dial Press, 1958.

The Garfield Honor. New York: Dial Press, 1961.

Griffin's Way. New York: Dial Press, 1962.

An Odor of Sanctity. New York: Dial Press, 1965.

Judas My Brother. New York: Dial Press, 1968.

Secondary Studies

The American Negro Writer and His Roots. Selected Papers from The First Conference of Negro Writers. New York: American Society of African Culture, 1960.

Ames, Russell. "Social Realism in Charles Chesnutt," *Phylon*, XIV (June 1953), 199-206.

Aptheker, Herbert. "Some Unpublished Writings of W. E. B. DuBois," *Freedomways*, V (First Quarter 1965), 103-28.

Baumbach, Jonathan. "Nightmare of a Native Son: Ellison's *Invisible Man*," *Criticism*, VI (1963), 48-65.

"Black Writers' Views on Literary Lions and Values," Symposium in *Negro Digest*, XVII, No. 3 (January 1968), 10-48, 81-89.

Bone, Robert. "The Novels of James Baldwin," *Tri-Quarterly*, No. 2 (Winter 1965), 3-20.

––––––. "Ralph Ellison and the Uses of Imagination," *Tri-Quarterly*, No. 6 (1966), 39-54.

––––––. *The Negro Novel in America*. New Haven: Yale University Press, 1958, 1965.

Braithwaite, William Stanley. "The Novels of Jessie Fauset," *Opportunity*, XII (January 1934), 24-28.

Brawley, Benjamin. *Paul Laurence Dunbar: Poet of His People*. Chapel Hill: University of North Carolina Press, 1936.

––––––. "The Negro Literary Renaissance," *Southern Workman*, LVI (April 1927), 177-84.

Broderick, Francis L. *W. E. B. DuBois, Negro Leader in a Time of Crisis.* Stanford: Stanford University Press, 1959.

Bronz, Stephen H. *Roots of Negro Racial Consciousness. The 1920's: Three Harlem Renaissance Authors.* New York: Libra Publishers, Inc., 1964.

Brown, Sterling. "The Negro Author and His Publisher," *The Quarterly Review of Higher Education Among Negroes,* IX (July 1941), 140-46.

————. *The Negro in American Fiction.* Washington, D.C.: The Associates in Negro Folk Education, 1937.

Bryer, Jackson. "Richard Wright: A Selected Checklist of Criticism," *Wisconsin Studies in Contemporary Literature,* I (Fall 1960), 22-33.

Burgum, Edwin Berry. "The Promise of Democracy in Richard Wright's *Native Son," The Novel and the World's Dilemma.* New York: Oxford University Press, 1947.

Butcher, Margaret Just. *The Negro in American Culture* (based on materials left by Alain Locke). New York: Alfred A. Knopf, Inc., 1956.

Chamberlain, John. "The Negro as a Writer," *Bookman,* LXX (February 1930), 603-11.

Charney, Maurice. "James Baldwin's Quarrel with Richard Wright," *American Quarterly,* XV (1963), 65-76.

Chesnutt, Helen M. *Charles Waddell Chesnutt; Pioneer of the Color Line.* Chapel Hill: University of North Carolina Press, 1952.

Cohn, David L. "The Negro Novel: Richard Wright," *Atlantic Monthly,* CLXV (May 1940), 659-61.

Coles, Robert. "Baldwin's Burden," *Partisan Review,* XXXI (Summer 1964), 409-16.

Cory, E. L. "Fiction by Negro Writers," *Book Buyer,* XXIII (1901), 26.

Cunningham, Virginia. *Paul Laurence Dunbar and His Song.* New York: Dodd, Mead and Co., 1947.

Davis, Arthur P. "*The Outsider* as a Novel of Race," *Midwest Journal,* VII (1955-56), 320-26.

Dreer, Herman. *American Literature by Negro Authors.* New York: The Macmillan Co., 1950.

Fabre, Michel and Margolies, Edward. "Richard Wright (1908-1960)," *Bulletin of Bibliography*, XXIV (1965), 131-33, 37.

Farrison, William Edward. "William Wells Brown," *Phylon* (First Quarter 1948), 13-23.

Finkelstein, Sidney. "W. E. B. DuBois' Trilogy: A Literary Triumph," *Mainstream*, XIV (1961), 6-17.

Finn, James. "The Identity of James Baldwin," *Commonweal*, LXXVII (October 26, 1962), 113-16.

Ford, Nick Aaron. "Four Popular Negro Novelists," *Phylon*, XV (First Quarter 1954), 29-39.

————. *The Contemporary Negro Novel*. Boston: Meador Publishing Co., 1936.

————. "The Negro Novel as a Vehicle of Propaganda," *Quarterly Review of Higher Education Among Negroes*, IX (July 1941), 135-39.

Glicksberg, Charles. "Existentialism in *The Outsider*," *Four Quarters*, VII (January 1958), 17-26.

————. "Negro Fiction in America," *South Atlantic Quarterly*, XLV (October 1946), 477-88.

————. "The Furies in Negro Fiction," *Western Review*, XII (Winter 1949), 107-14.

Gloster, Hugh M. "Charles W. Chesnutt: Pioneer in the Fiction of Negro Life," *Phylon*, II (First Quarter 1941), 57-66.

————. *Negro Voices in American Fiction*. Chapel Hill: University of North Carolina Press, 1948.

————. "Richard Wright: Interpreter of Racial and Economic Maladjustments," *Opportunity*, XIX (December 1941), 361-65.

————. "Sutton E. Griggs," *Phylon*, IV (Fourth Quarter 1943), 335-45.

————. "The Van Vechten Vogue," *Phylon*, VI (Fourth Quarter 1945), 310-14.

Gross, Theodore L. "The World of James Baldwin," *Critique*, VII (Winter 1964-65), 139-49.

Hagopian, John V. "James Baldwin: The Black and the Red-White-and-Blue," *CLA Journal*, VII (1963), 133-40.

Hill, Herbert, ed. *Anger, and Beyond: The Negro Writer in the United States.* New York: Harper & Row, 1966.

————. "The Negro Writer and the Creative Imagination," *Arts in Society,* V (1968), 245-55.

Holmes, Eugene. "Jean Toomer, Apostle of Beauty," *Opportunity,* III (August 1925), 252-54, 260.

Horowitz, Floyd Ross. "Ralph Ellison's Modern Version of Brer Bear and Brer Rabbit in *Invisible Man,*" *Midcontinent American Studies Journal,* IV, ii (1963), 21-27.

————. "The Enigma of Ellison's Intellectual Man," *CLA Journal,* VII (December 1963), 126-32.

Howe, Irving. "James Baldwin: At Ease in Apocalypse," *Harper's,* CCXXXVII (September 1968), 92-100.

————. "Black Boys and Native Sons," *Dissent,* X (Fall 1963), 353-69.

Howells, William Dean. "Charles W. Chesnutt's Stories," *The Atlantic Monthly,* LXXV (May 1900), 699-700.

Hughes, Carl Milton. *The Negro Novelist.* New York: Citadel Press, 1953.

Hughes, Langston. "Harlem Literati in the 20's," *Saturday Review Gallery,* ed. J. Beatty. New York: Simon & Schuster, 1959, 207-12.

Jacobson, Dan. "James Baldwin as Spokesman," *Commentary,* XXXII (December 1961), 497-502.

Johnson, James Weldon. "Race Prejudice and the Negro Artist," *Harper's,* CLVII (November 1928), 769-76.

————. "The Dilemma of the Negro Author," *The American Mercury,* XV (December 1928), 477-81.

Kaiser, Ernest. "A Selected Bibliography of the Published Writings of W. E. B. DuBois," *Freedomways Memorial Issue,* V, No. 1 (Winter 1965), 207-13.

Kent, George. "Baldwin and the Problem of Being," *CLA Journal,* VII (March 1964), 202-14.

Klein, Marcus. *After Alienation: American Novels in Mid-Century.* New York: The World Publishing Company, 1962.

Knox, George. "The Negro Novelist's Sensibility and The Outsider Theme," *Western Humanities Review,* XI (Spring 1957), 137-48.

Kostelanetz, Richard. "Fiction of a Negro Politics: The Neglected Novels of W. E. B. DuBois," *Xavier University Studies*, VII, ii (1968), 5-39.

Lash, John S. "Baldwin Beside Himself: A Study in Modern Phallicism," *CLA Journal*, VII (December 1964), 132-40.

Lawson, Victor. *Dunbar Critically Examined.* Washington, D.C.: Associated Publishing, Inc., 1941.

Littlejohn, David. *Black on White: A Critical Survey of Writing by American Negroes.* New York: Grossman Publishers, 1966.

Locke, Alain. *The New Negro; An Interpretation.* New York: A & C Boni, 1925.

————. "The Saving Grace of Realism," *Opportunity*, XIII (January 1934), 8-11, 30.

Loggins, Vernon. *The Negro Author: His Development in America.* New York: Columbia University Press, 1931.

Mac Innes, Colin. "Dark Angel: The Writings of James Baldwin," *Encounter*, XXI, ii (August 1963), 22-33.

Marcus, Steven. "The American Negro in Search of Identity," *Commentary*, CXVI (November 1953), 456-63.

Margolies, Edward. *Native Sons.* New York: J. B. Lippincott, 1968.

————. *Richard Wright.* Carbondale, Illinois: Southern Illinois University Press, 1969.

Masare, Julian D., Jr. "Charles W. Chesnutt as Southern Author," *Mississippi Quarterly*, XX (Spring 1967), 77-89.

Maund, Alfred. "The Negro Novelist and the Contemporary Scene," *Chicago Jewish Forum*, XII (Fall 1954), 28-34.

Morris, Lloyd. "The Negro 'Renaissance'," *Southern Workman*, LIX (February 1930), 82-86.

Munson, Gorham. "The Significance of Jean Toomer," *Opportunity*, III (September 1925), 262-63.

Nelson, John H. *The Negro Character in American Literature.* Lawrence, Kansas: University of Kansas Journalism Press, 1926.

O'Daniel, Therman B. "James Baldwin: An Interpretive Study," *CLA Journal*, VII (September 1963), 37-47.

Podhoretz, Norman. "In Defense of James Baldwin," *Doings and Undoings*. New York: Farrar, Straus, and Co., 1964, pp. 244-50.

Rascoe, Burton. "Negro Novel and White Reviewers: Richard Wright's *Native Son*," *American Mercury*, L (May 1940), 113-17.

Redding, Saunders, "Since Richard Wright," *African Forum*, I (1966), 21-31.

Rosenfeld, Paul. "Jean Toomer," *Men Seen*. New York: Dial Press, 1925.

Rovit, Earl. "Ralph Ellison and the American Comic Tradition," *Wisconsin Studies in Contemporary Literature*, I (Fall 1960), 34-42.

Schafer, William J. "Ralph Ellison and the Birth of the Anti-Hero," *Critique*, X (1968), 81-93.

Scott, Nathan A., Jr. "Judgment Marked by a Cellar: The American Negro Writer and the Dialectic of Despair," *University of Denver Quarterly*, II (1967), 5-35.

————. "Search for Beliefs: The Fiction of Richard Wright," *University of Kansas City Review*, XXIII (1956), 19-24, 131-38.

————. "The Dark and Haunted Tower of Richard Wright," *Black Expression*, ed. Addison Gayle, Jr. New York: Weybright and Talley, 1968.

Shipman, Carolyn. "The Author of *The Conjure Woman*, Charles W. Chesnutt," *Critic*, XXXLI (July 1899), 632-34.

Sillen, Samuel. "Charles W. Chesnutt: A Pioneer Negro Novelist," *Masses and Mainstream*, VI (February 1953), 8-14.

————. "The Meaning of Bigger Thomas," *New Masses*, XXXV (April 1940), 26-28.

Smith, William Gardner. "The Negro Writer: Pitfalls and Compensations," *Phylon*, XI (Fourth Quarter 1950), 297-303.

Spender, Stephen. "James Baldwin: Voice of a Revolution," *Partisan Review*, XXX (Summer 1963), 256-60.

Standby, Fred. "James Baldwin: A Checklist, 1963-67," *Bulletin of Bibliography*, XXV (1968), 135-37, 160.

Starkey, Marion L. "Jessie Fauset," *Southern Workman*, LXI (May 1932), 217-20.

Thomas, Will. "Negro Writers of Pulp Fiction," *Negro Digest*, VIII (July 1950), 81-84.

Turner, Darwin T. "Frank Yerby as Debunker," *Massachusetts Review,* IX (1968), 569-77.

―――――. "Paul Laurence Dunbar: The Rejected Symbol," *Journal of Negro History,* LII (January 1967), 1-13.

Turpin, Waters E. "Four Short Fiction Writers of the Harlem Renaissance: Their Legacy of Achievement," *CLA Journal,* XI (1967), 59-72.

Webb, Constance. *Richard Wright, A Biography.* New York: G. P. Putnam's Sons, 1968.

Whiteman, Maxwell. *A Century of Fiction by American Negroes, 1853-1952.* Philadelphia: Saifer, 1955.

Wiggins, Lida Keck. *The Life and Works of Paul Laurence Dunbar.* Napierville, Illinois: J. L. Nichols & Co., 1907.

Widmer, Kingsley. "The Existential Darkness: Richard Wright's *The Outsider,*" *Wisconsin Studies in Contemporary Literature,* I (Fall 1960), 13-21.

Williams, John A. "The Literary Ghetto," *Saturday Review,* XLVI (April 20, 1963), 21, 40.